The Rhodesian
Air Force in Zimbabwe's
War of Liberation,
1966–1980

The Rhodesian Air Force in Zimbabwe's War of Liberation, 1966–1980

DARLINGTON MUTANDA

McFarland & Company, Inc., Publishers
Jefferson, North Carolina

LIBRARY OF CONGRESS CATALOGUING-IN-PUBLICATION DATA

Names: Mutanda, Darlington, 1985– author.
Title: The Rhodesian Air Force in Zimbabwe's war of liberation, 1966–1980 / Darlington Mutanda.
Description: Jefferson, North Carolina : McFarland & Company, Inc., Publishers, 2017. | Includes bibliographical references and index.
Identifiers: LCCN 2016046440 | ISBN 9781476666204 (softcover : acid free paper) ∞
Subjects: LCSH: Zimbabwe—History—Chimurenga War, 1966–1980—Aerial operations. | Southern Rhodesia. Rhodesian Air Force—History. | Zimbabwe—History—Chimurenga War, 1966–1980. | Zimbabwe—History, Military—1965–1980.
Classification: LCC DT2988 .M88 2016 | DDC 968.9104—dc23
LC record available at https://lccn.loc.gov/2016046440

BRITISH LIBRARY CATALOGUING DATA ARE AVAILABLE

ISBN (print) 978-1-4766-6620-4
ISBN (ebook) 978-1-4766-2577-5

© 2017 Darlington Mutanda. All rights reserved

No part of this book may be reproduced or transmitted in any form or by any means, electronic or mechanical, including photocopying or recording, or by any information storage and retrieval system, without permission in writing from the publisher.

Front cover images © 2017 jacobeukman/iStock

Printed in the United States of America

McFarland & Company, Inc., Publishers
  Box 611, Jefferson, North Carolina 28640
  www.mcfarlandpub.com

My daughters, Miriro Gracious and Milada-"Mamoyo Specials,"
welcome to the world. It needs you and you need it,
but glory belongs to the Most High Jehovah.
Remember, no man is an island!

To all the guerrillas and civilians who lived through
the horrors of the Second Chimurenga/Umvukela
in defense of the motherland. We will forever
cherish your sacrifice. For this reason, we will
never stop writing about these matters!

Acknowledgments

I would like to start by thanking the University of Zimbabwe History Department staff (2011–2014) for standing by me through thick and thin. Special and dearest mention goes to my super mentor, Dr. Mediel "Fish" Hove, and my MPhil supervisor, Dr. K.D. Manungo, for all their assistance, unfailing faith and never-ending support.

My heartfelt gratitude goes to my parents Grey "Moyo" and Nyaradzo "VaMangoyi," my wife Eliza, and my other relatives and friends for being pillars of strength and sources of encouragement. *Namatai Mwari Mupenyu* (Worship the Living God). We say Ebenezer! (1 Samuel 7:12).

More special thanks go to Uncle Obed "Hunzvi" Mutanda for being a role model, the definition of how to be successful through hard work and humility. In addition, I salute big brother Bronson "Bronso" Mutanda for being a comrade-in-arms from 2005 to the present. We shared a lot in common, man. It is time to enjoy the fruits of hard work, perseverance and belief!

Lastly, I would like to extend many thanks to my younger brother, Treasure Mutanda, for being so supportive in this exciting but difficult journey. *Vana Gono vose munokosha*!

Table of Contents

Acknowledgments	vi
Preface	1
Introduction	3
Abbreviations and Acronyms	9
1 Background to the Liberation War in Zimbabwe	13
2 Conceptualizing the Development of Air Power as a War Asset	31
3 The Establishment of the Rhodesian Air Force	47
4 The Development of the Air Force During the Interwar Period	71
5 The Impact of the Rhodesian Air Force During the Second Chimurenga	95
6 Guerrilla Counterstrategies to RhAF Operations	112
7 Challenges Faced by the Rhodesian Air Force During the Second Chimurenga	122
8 Challenging "Air Supremacy" from Outside: Analyzing the Feasibility of ZPRA's Conventional Plan	143
9 The Effects of Civilian Bombing on Guerrilla Strategy	158
10 The Significance of Air Power in Guerrilla Warfare: An Analysis	170
Conclusion	186
Chapter Notes	193
Bibliography	217
Index	229

Preface

This book analyzes the tactical impact of the Rhodesian Air Force in the conduct of Zimbabwe's liberation war. The war provides useful insights into the role of air power fighting guerrilla forces in modern warfare. Zimbabwe's liberation war reveals the ineffectiveness of conventional forces when confronted by resolute irregular bands.

The effectiveness or ineffectiveness of the air force in modern warfare is a subject of increased debate in light of the growing reliance by governments on air power rather than ground forces in military encounters. The study argues that although air power is not a panacea to guerrilla warfare, it still remains significant at tactical level, as revealed by Zimbabwe's war of liberation. The tactical use of air power was more important than strategic bombing, as revealed by the Rhodesian twin concepts of fireforce and hot pursuit, in which planes were used in conjunction with ground forces for counterinsurgency. These tactical advantages, however, lacked an adequate ground force to consolidate the gains made by airmen.

Air power was essential to the Rhodesian armed forces, but failed to be effective because it was used as a war-winning weapon, instead of playing complementary roles, due to the shortage of manpower. Its utility was significantly hampered by the shortage of material and recruits, whereas the guerrilla forces poured out in huge numbers. Evidence emanating from this work demonstrates that although the RhAF failed to annihilate guerrilla forces, the effects were deeply felt. The operations of the air force strained guerrilla recruitment and tactics and shattered morale. On the other hand, the Rhodesian Security Forces enjoyed the tactical advantages of air power such as tactical mobility and deployment, air strikes, air searches, air reconnaissance, and casualty evacuation, to name a few. This sharply contrasted with the dire situation of the guerrilla forces, who lacked superior mobility, firepower and supplies.

Despite its notable achievements, the RhAF had explicit weaknesses which worked to the benefit of the guerrilla forces. The war thus resulted in a political victory for ZANU. The study therefore concludes that while air power is an indispensable weapon of warfare, its use should not be blanketed. Rather, a case-specific approach should be taken depending on the objectives of the war and enemy strategy. It is foolhardy to think that guerrilla fighters enjoying the benefits of hit-and-run tactics and popular support could easily be wiped out by bombardments from the air.

Introduction

"I think it is well also for the man in the street to realise that there is no power on earth that can protect him from being bombed, whatever people may tell him. The bomber will always get through. The only defence is in offence, which means that you have got to kill more women and children more quickly than the enemy if you want to save yourselves. I mention that so that people may realize what is waiting for them when the next war comes."—*Stanley Baldwin (former British Prime Minister)*[1]

It is imperative for readers to take note of the reality that the task of documenting Zimbabwe's military history demands a lot of commitment. This emanates from the fact that a lot of Rhodesian documents were smuggled out of the country before and just after independence in 1980. The unavailability of these pertinent documents poses some tricky problems for researchers on the subject. The Rhodesian Army Association archives have been catalogued but are currently inaccessible. The archives contain emotional photographs of soldiers on both sides of the war for independence, intelligence reports, operational instructions, and policy debates exposing the strengths and weaknesses of a doomed but desperate government.[2] ZAPU/ZPRA files did not survive the transfer to Zimbabwe after independence. The ZANU PF archive in Harare is in a shambles. Where important official documents are expected to be in order, such as at the University of Zimbabwe Main Library Government Publications section, the material is usually haphazard. It takes a great deal of effort, luck and commitment to locate whatever one wants to use. These organizations should, however, be commended for providing important reading material.

In addition, interviews are difficult to arrange as a result of political violence especially during election time. People are normally afraid to express their thoughts. It therefore calls for unlimited creativity and energy to come up with an acceptable piece of work on the country's military history as espoused by Zimbabwean historian McLaughlin: "The prospects for the researcher in the field of recent Rhodesian military history are depressing. Official archives are closed to all but those who will make poor history from them. Although a picture of sorts can be made out for the past three decades of Rhodesian military experience, it is likely that the military history of the post–Second World War era will remain forever in some historical twilight zone."[3]

While it is true that a number of scholars are not privileged to access the Rhodesian war documents, there are documents which are still handy and can be effectively used to tell the story of the liberation war in Zimbabwe. A huge corpus of annual reports produced by the military, legislative and senate debates (from the pre–Federal era) and other documents housed in libraries and archives around the country were useful in investigating the operations, successes and/or challenges faced by the Rhodesian and African soldiers. Of course, there are some units of the RSF such as the Rhodesian Intelligence Corps whose information is hardly accessible except to a few privileged scholars.

Motivation for the Study

This book was inspired by the lack of air power studies in the military history of Zimbabwe from an African perspective. It was imperative from the standpoint of the author to write a story of the Rhodesian Air Force (RhAF) that fills the knowledge gaps that exist in the available literature. This is actually a contribution to both military history and military science. Quite a lot has been written about the ground war, whereas the impact of the "flying birds" has been largely if not wholly portrayed from the viewpoint of the white authors, especially journalists and the combatants themselves.[4] The overall impact is that little has been recorded on the impact of the Rhodesian Air Force during the Second Chimurenga (Shona term for revolutionary struggle) from an African perspective.[5] Accordingly, this study investigates the impact of the RhAF on the operations of the guerrillas, thereby providing a comprehensive analysis on the impact of air power during Zimbabwe's war of liberation. There is undoubtedly limited documentary evidence on the military history of the Second Chimurenga, particularly the weaknesses and impact of the RhAF during the prosecution of this campaign. Literature is plentiful on the war detailing the causes of the war, the formation of nationalist parties, the lack of discipline among guerrilla fighters, guerrilla mobilization and fighting tactics, the role of spirit mediums and peasants, and the numerous atrocities committed by the guerrilla movements and Rhodesian Security Forces (RSF).[6]

There was also a deliberate neglect by previous writers of air power studies to explicate the fundamental reasons that led the RhAF to lose the war despite claiming to be an extremely competent force.[7] The impression created by authors such as Cowderoy and Nesbit, Petter-Bowyer and Beverly was that of an air force that managed to defy all the odds. Benefiting from a wide range of sources such as interviewing veterans of the war and civilians, as well as carrying out an extensive survey of the archives and making use of "gray" sources such as magazines and newspapers, this study concurs with previous studies on the point that the RhAF provided numerous tactical puzzles to the guerrilla armies, but takes a bold stance in portraying that they were fighting a war beyond their resources and strategic doctrine. The RhAF was burdened by technical challenges caused by aging aircraft and the shortage of manpower, to name but a few. Prominent authors of Zimbabwean history such as Ngwabi Bhebe and Terence Ranger observed that the white Rhodesian side of the war is marked by general accounts of the war, boasts of the triumphs of the Rhodesian intelligence services, glorifications of the "Special Forces," picture books, or white autobiographies. The observation compelled the historians to conclude that the "Rhodesian side of the struggle needs to be made into history rather than myth."[8] In the case of the Rhodesian Air Force, this could be achieved by examining the impact of its operations during the war of liberation. Although this study is certainly not pioneering, it brings out a fresh and enlightening dimension to the story of the Rhodesian Air Force.

The Rhodesian Security Forces (RSF) comprised numerous units. These included the colored-dominated Rhodesian Defence Regiment (RDR), the Central Intelligence Organisation (CIO), the Rhodesian African Rifles (RAR) dominated by Africans, the cavalry unit Grey's Scouts, the all-white Rhodesian Light Infantry (RLI), and the British South Africa Police (BSAP), to name but a few. The RhAF is getting special attention in this study because of the strategic and tactical role of air power in modern warfare.[9] Zeroing in on the Second Chimurenga, it is apparent that air power played a decisive role in enabling the RSF to sustain their war effort. The significance of air power in warfare cannot be overemphasized. The strategic and tactical impact of air power prompted the People's Republic of China (PRC) to ditch technology restrictions from Western Europe and the United States to Israel and Russia for assistance.[10] During a September 2012 visit to Brussels, then Chinese Prime Minister Wen Jiabao reiterated China's unhappiness that the arms embargo remained in place.[11] The study basically argues that air power is not the final word in military campaigns, especially not in guerrilla warfare. While it is practical to launch incessant air raids capable of decimating the whole population and infrastructure in a given area, that alone does not guarantee military victory in guerrilla campaigns. The bombing of the Chimoio "military base" in 1977, code named Operation Dingo, along with a large number of other internal and external guerrilla bases, is a testimony to that. The attacks carried out by the RhAF did not, per se, contribute much in facilitating the cause of the Smith regime, especially in curbing guerrilla infiltration. However, a well-coordinated mobilization of military assets is a recipe for victory. Adolf Hitler's experiences in the opening phase of the Second World War proved the effectiveness of combined operations.

Air power theorists Giulio Douhet and Arthur "Bomber" Harris, for example, argued that the heart of an enemy's resistance was its population. This then provides the rationale for the intense bombardment of the civilian population in both regular and irregular wars.[12] Since the emergence of air power as a military weapon, the theory of the bombing of civilian centers of population has been religiously implemented by the belligerents as they seek to fulfill their political objectives. War kills indiscriminately. However, the targeting of civilians (area bombing) in modern warfare is not accidental, but a calculated move to compel the enemy to surrender. Douhet argued that the civilians should be targeted as part of the broader strategy to compel their government to go to the negotiating table. Although the RhAF did not bomb civilians in the spirit of the theory of civilian bombing, civilians were indeed targets in Zimbabwe's liberation war. The attacks were not, however, carried out as a war-winning strategy, but targeted especially those civilians who were said to be breaking curfew laws, spotted delivering supplies to the guerrillas, suspected of giving support to the guerrillas, or intermingled with combatants in refugee camps. It is thus imperative to evaluate the challenges faced by civilians as a result of the operations of the RhAF, but not within the context of the theory of bombing civilian populations in cities.

Book Structure

Each of this book's ten chapters contains a unique theme that enriches the study. The chapters are, however, interrelated, so they must not be read in isolation. Chapter 1 provides the background to Zimbabwe's war of liberation. The second chapter focuses on the conceptualization of air power as an instrument of war. This entails espousing the major brains behind the development of military aviation. The chapter utilizes works which document the evolution and role of air power from the earliest times up to the end of the Second World War in 1945. This was important in comprehending the evolution and transformation of air power roles in military history. The third chapter investigates the establishment of the Rhodesian Air Force as a weapon of war and explicitly asserts that the growth of civil aviation in Southern Rhodesia emerged as an important factor in stimulating the establishment and expansion of the RhAF. The government of Southern Rhodesia played a prominent role in promoting aeronautical activities in the colony prior to the establishment of the Rhodesia Air Training Group (RATG).[13] This was strategically done on the premise that the trained airmen would play important roles in case of emergency. However, aircraft roles were limited to reconnaissance since the airplanes were not designed to perform any meaningful military duties.

Chapter 4 examines the transformation of the Rhodesian Air Force during the interwar period (1946–1965).[14] At the end of World War II, the British Air Ministry expressed little interest in continuing air training in Southern Rhodesia. The Air Ministry sought to reduce the costs of air training by halting similar exercises in the colonies. Air training became practically dormant in Southern Rhodesia starting in November 1946 but was resuscitated in April 1947. Henceforth, it is important to find out why the Rhodesian military and British Air Ministry revived the nearly dead air training project. The chapter also analyzes the impact of the Central African Federation on the development of the RhAF as an instrument of war.

The fifth chapter assesses the impact of the RhAF operations on the conduct of the Second Chimurenga. This has been achieved through the use of case studies which display how the RhAF attacked guerrilla bases or centres of training. Put differently, it evaluates the challenges faced by the guerrillas as a result of the operations of the RhAF. The effects of the RhAF operations on guerrilla strategy were measured by yardsticks such as the air strikes launched, the impact of troop transportation, and casualty evacuation provided by the RhAF. As maintained throughout the study, air power proved useful at tactical level. Chapter 6 analyzes the survival strategies which were devised by guerrillas to overcome the obstacles posed by air power.

The seventh chapter scrutinizes the efficiency of the RhAF as a weapon of war. This was done in two ways: analyzing the impact of guerrilla tactics on the operations of the RhAF and assessing the weaknesses of the RhAF. On the first part, attention was precisely given to aspects such as the role of Frontline states, the effects of selected guerrilla tactics, and the impact of terrain in the outcome of the war. The second part dwells on the inherent weaknesses of the RhAF. Overall, the section investigates the effectiveness of the RhAF through a scrutiny of the challenges experienced by the air force.

Although the Rhodesian Air Force was not as effective as previous white writers have made us believe, its impact cannot be understated. The air force was a failure insofar as bringing about the defeat of the insurgents was concerned. However, the same cannot be said if a conventional war had been fought. The Zimbabwe People's Revolutionary Army planned to use conventional methods of war including an air force. Accordingly, the eighth chapter evaluates the perils that could have befallen the ZPRA forces if they had decided to adopt a conventional war strategy. This emanates from the fact that the RhAF was a seasoned force capable of launching external raids which ZPRA and/or the host countries could do nothing to resist.

The key proponents of the air power doctrine, Giulio Douhet and Hugh Trenchard, advocated for the bombardment of the civilian population as a strategy to destroy enemy morale. Although the theory was not applied by the RhAF, Chapter 9 evaluates the various ways through which the RhAF alternatively sought to deter the civilians from supporting guerrilla armies during the Second Chimurenga. Added to that, the chapter briefly examines the causes of the Second Chimurenga in order to amplify the reasons that led the civilians to support the war in favor of the guerrillas. The discussion helps us understand the rationale behind the brutalization of the African peasantry by the RhAF and other branches of the RSF during the liberation war. It is thus vital to investigate the effects of the air strikes on the civilians and how this influenced the conduct and outcome of the guerrilla war. The role of air power in the country's war of liberation deserves more attention than it currently enjoys.

The aim of the tenth chapter is to evaluate the future of air power in guerrilla warfare or vice-versa. The chapter is supported by facts from Zimbabwe's war of liberation and other guerrilla wars fought over the years. The outcome of these wars shed light into the role and limitations of an air force fighting guerrilla forces. An in-depth analysis of guerrilla warfare helps to examine the ingredients of guerrilla warfare and how this strategic doctrine has tremendously benefitted from military technology. Case studies involving guerrilla warfare were essential in analyzing the potentialities of guerrilla armies in frustrating well-equipped regular soldiers. A Conclusion wraps up the book.

Abbreviations and Acronyms

AEF	American Expeditionary Forces
ANC	African National Congress (South Africa)
AOC	Air Officer Commanding
AVM	Air Vice-Marshal
Brig.	Brigadier
BSAC	British South African Company
BSAP	British South Africa Police
CAA	Central African Airways
Capt.	Captain
CIA	Central Intelligence Agency
CIO	Central Intelligence Organisation
COIN	Counterinsurgency
Col.	Colonel
COMOPS	Combined Operations
DAI	Director of Air Intelligence
DoD	Department of Defense (U.S.)
EATS	Empire Air Training Scheme
EFTS	Elementary Flying Training Schools
FFU	Field Force Units
FLS	Frontline states
Flt.	Flight
FRELIMO	Front for the Liberation of Mozambique
ISAF	International Security Assistance Force
JAPCC	Joint Air Power Competence Centre
JOC	Joint Operations Command
LMG	Light Machine Gun
Lt.	Lieutenant
Ltd.	Limited
MO	Medical Officer

MPLA	Popular Movement for the Liberation of Angola
NATO	North Atlantic Treaty Organization
NCO	Noncommissioned Officer
NDP	National Democratic Party
OAU	Organisation of African Unity
PATU	Police Anti-Terrorist Unit
PCC	People's Caretaker Council
PLA	People's Liberation Army
PM	Prime Minister
PSYOPs	Psychological operations
PVs	Protected Villages
PWD	Public Works Department
RAAC	Rhodesia Air Askari Corps
RAF	Royal Air Force
RANA	Rhodesian and Nyasaland Airways
RAP	Rhodesian Action Party
RAR	Rhodesian African Regiment
RAR	Rhodesian African Rifles
RATG	Rhodesia Air Training Group
RCAF	Royal Canadian Air Force
RDR	Rhodesian Defence Regiment
RF	Rhodesia Front
RFC	Royal Flying Corps
RhAF	Rhodesian Air Force
RLI	Rhodesian Light Infantry
RRAF	Royal Rhodesian Air Force
RSAS	Rhodesia Special Air Service
RSB	Rhodesian Special Branch
RSF	Rhodesian Security Forces
SAAF	South African Air Force
SAS	Special Air Service
Sgt.	Sergeant
Sqdn.	Squadron
SRAAF	Southern Rhodesia Auxiliary Air Force
SRAF	Southern Rhodesian Air Force
SS	Selous Scouts
SSU	Short Service Unit
Terrs	Terrorist
TNSD	Total National Strategy Document
TTLs	Tribal Trust Lands

UAV	Unmanned Aerial Vehicle
UDI	Unilateral Declaration of Independence
UK	United Kingdom
UNHCR	United Nations High Commission for Refugees
UNITA	National Union for the Total Independence of Angola
U.S.	United States
VHF	Very High Frequency
WCC	World Council of Churches
WHAMP	Win the hearts and minds of the people
WMD	Weapons of Mass Destruction
ZAF	Zambian Air Force
ZANLA	Zimbabwe African National Liberation Army
ZANU	Zimbabwe African National Union
ZAPU	Zimbabwe African People's Union
ZIPA	Zimbabwe People's Army
ZPRA	Zimbabwe People's Revolutionary Army

1
Background to the Liberation War in Zimbabwe

Introduction

This chapter provides a background to the liberation war in Zimbabwe. It is structured in such a way that readers who are not familiar with the history of Zimbabwe can come to understand the major watersheds from 1890 when the country was colonized, up to 1980 when independence was attained.

The Invading Team

Zimbabwe was colonized by Cecil John Rhodes and his British South Africa Company (BSAC) in 1890. The myth of the Second Rand, which was linked directly to the discovery of rich gold deposits in the Witwatersrand in 1886, facilitated the stampede for Lobengula's signature.[1] The British wrongly assumed that Lobengula was the paramount ruler of the present-day country called Zimbabwe. Rhodes believed that, as in South Africa, riches of gold and diamonds lay untapped north of the Limpopo.[2] The hopes of striking mineral riches drove Transvaal President Paul Kruger to send an emissary, Piet Grobler, to sign a "treaty of friendship" with the Ndebele king. The agreement, known as the Grobler Treaty, was signed in 1887. Lobengula was required to provide troops or other assistance whenever called upon by the Transvaal. Moreover, it was incumbent for him to recognize and assist any Transvaal consul, providing any and all Transvaalers with passes to hunt or trade, just to name a few. Upon hearing news of the Grobler Treaty, Rhodes hastened to send John Smith Moffat to persuade the king to cancel the treaty and enter into a new agreement with Rhodes's agents. Because their fathers (Robert Moffat and Mzilikazi) were good friends, it was therefore easy for Moffat to obtain the King's signature. The Ndebele people remembered Robert Moffat as a renowned missionary, a good man of God. Little did Lobengula know that John Moffat had become an agent of European imperialism. Added to that, Lobengula believed the treaty to be a renewal of a limited treaty signed by his father, Mzilikazi. The Moffat Treaty placed Matabeleland directly in the sphere of British influence. The treaty signed in 1888 compelled Lobengula not to enter into any treaty with other concession seekers without the knowledge and sanction of Her Majesty's High Commissioner for South Africa.

Again in 1888, Rhodes sent Charles Dunell Rudd of Kimberley; Rochfort Maguire of London; and Francis Robert Thompson of Kimberley to enter into another agreement with the Ndebele king. But the emissaries had to wait for six weeks because the king was now impatient with the growing white community at his court. The Rudd concession promised to reward Lobengula with a thousand Martini-Henry breech-loading rifles, 100,000 rounds of ammunition, the sum of one hundred pounds sterling, British currency, on the first day of every lunar month, and to deliver on the Zambezi River a steamboat with guns suitable for defensive purposes upon the said river. Apart from these terms, there were also verbal agreements that were never contained in the signed treaty. The British community promised Lobengula that no more than ten men would be allowed to mine on Ndebele lands at any one time. The miners were required to surrender their ammunition to the king and abide by the laws of the land. Scholars and commentators alike agree that Lobengula signed these treaties in order to play his enemies off against each other, thus delaying the conquest of his kingdom, already under siege. After all, the conquest of his kingdom was now inevitable. Moreover, like the Ngwato chief called Khama, Lobengula wanted British protection. When Lobengula later discovered what the concession really meant, he tried to renounce it, but it was "too late." In October 1889, the British government granted Cecil John Rhodes a royal charter to exploit the concession on the grounds that a business company administering the new territory would relieve Her Majesty's government of diplomatic difficulties and heavy expenditure. After the granting of the charter, events moved swiftly. The Pioneer Column was assembled and the British marched into Zimbabwe.

The invading team avoided Matabeleland because of its strong military tradition. They concentrated themselves in eastern Zimbabwe. A myth was created that the Shona were grateful to the Europeans for their "protection." On the other hand, the Ndebele were portrayed as bloodthirsty warmongers. The whites thus impatiently waited for an opportunity to pounce on Matabeleland. The opportunity presented itself on a silver platter in 1893 in what is widely referred to as the Victoria Incident. Lobengula was angry with the Shona people in Fort Victoria (Masvingo), who were in the habit of stealing and using his cattle for their personal use, yet they were supposed to use them for draught power, manure and milk under an African tradition called *kuronzera/ukulagisa*. Lobengula then decided to impart a valuable lesson to the Shona people in Victoria. The *amajaha* (Ndebele soldiers) were deployed under the command of Manyao and Mgandani. Upon arrival, they burnt homes and killed men. Women and cattle were also seized. The victims ran away to the mountains for safety. Even though Lobengula had assured the whites that they were not supposed to panic because they were not targets, they were angered by the fact that their laborers had deserted the farms and mines. Although the whites had in the past quarreled with Lobengula over border issues and his attitude towards the Shona, the Victoria Incident was all what the whites needed to demolish the Ndebele State, which had remained intact three years after conquest. Eventually, the Victoria Incident culminated in the Anglo-Ndebele War (1893), also known as the Matabele War, which saw the capitulation of the brave Ndebele warriors to white authority. As was the trend throughout the African continent, the colony was established through violence.

In 1896, the Shona and Ndebele again took up arms against the settlers. Numerous grievances led to the First Chimurenga/Imfazwe (war of liberation). The Ndebele people were frustrated with the land seizures that happened after the Anglo-Ndebele War. They were driven to the tsetse-infested and infertile Gwaai and Shangani Reserves, created in 1894, and seen as equivalent to graves. Also, the use of Shona policemen in their areas, assigned by the white settlers, amplified their humiliation. The Africans also resented taxation in their motherland because they were more familiar with annual tributes. The punishments meted out to the defaulters caused great irritation amongst the Africans. Moreover, both the Shona and Ndebele interpreted the outbreak of rinderpest, which killed thousands of cattle, and the emergence of swarms of locusts as a sign of God's anger. As would be the case in the 1905–7 Maji Maji Uprising in German East Africa (Tanzania), the spirit mediums rallied people to eject the whites, who were blamed for the ills which were ravaging the country. In both contests (Anglo-Ndebele War and First Chimurenga/Imfazwe), the white settlers emerged victorious mainly because of their possession of superior weaponry and the divisions among the African armies. In the case of German East Africa, a spirit medium by the name Kinjikitile Ngwale claimed to be possessed by a snake spirit called Hongo. Ngwale began calling himself Bokero and developed a belief that the people of German East Africa had been called upon to eliminate the Germans. Accordingly, he gave his followers war medicine that he said would turn German bullets into water. This "war medicine" was in fact water (maji in Swahili) mixed with castor oil and millet seeds. Empowered with this new liquid, Bokero's followers began what would become known as the Maji Maji Rebellion.[3]

The British South Africa Company administered the territory until 1923, when the referendum of the white settlers determined that it should be governed by them in what was called Responsible Self-Government rather than join the Union of South Africa.[4] The Africans lived under oppressive British rule where one's destiny was determined by the color of his skin. The Africans clearly realized that white rule had come to ruin their dignity and sources of livelihood. They were not allowed to compete with the whites, and it therefore became a deliberate policy to separate blacks and whites along racial lines through the policy of separate development. The Africans were not fairly accommodated in the political, military, economic and social spheres of life in Rhodesia.

A Day in the Life of a "Native" in Rhodesia

Racism played a dominant role in defining the place of Africans in Rhodesia. It was the pillar of successive white settler regimes. Competition across the color line was anathema to the philosophy of white superiority; hence the gap between white and black had to be maintained in all economic spheres.[5] Consequently, the African middle class built their political base on the grievances of the masses, thereby assured of massive popular support. This explains why the peasants were attacked by the various units of the Rhodesian Security Forces during the liberation war. It was mainly the policy of separate development which compelled Africans to take up arms with the knowledge that their fate was already sealed. Ironically, some sectors of the white population still believed that Africans had nothing to fight for, as exemplified by the utterance of a Shamva farmer, Val Ross: "We are fighting for our country, for a beloved country. The terrorists? I don't really know what they were fighting for."[6] The reasons why Africans took up arms can be summed up by the words of one Senator Whaley, who said: "The truth of the matter is that Rhodesia has never been committed to a policy of black majority rule, whether in the short or in the long term. As regard the short term, our constitutional forms speak for themselves.... There is not a set long term plan for the Government to pass into the hands of a black majority."[7]

The myth about the need to civilize Africans was firmly rooted in the minds of the white population. Federal Prime Minister Welensky argued in 1962 that disease, ignorance, poverty and superstition were the problems to be overcome in Africa.[8] Delivering an address at the first Informal Wartime Meeting of the Royal African Society, held as a sherry party at the India Hall of the Overseas League, St. James's Street, London on May 1, 1940, the Hon.

S.M. Lanigan O'Keeffe, C.M.G., High Commissioner in London for Southern Rhodesia, described Africans as very uncivilized: "It is true that fifty years ago the Pioneers took possession of a very savage country without a house even of tin, or a road in it, to say nothing of mines or farms."[9] The truth is that Africans were described as backward for the sole reason that Europeans wanted to exploit them in the name of civilization.[10] The Rhodesians were well aware of the demands of the Africans but they were not ready to give in. They could even argue: "This is, as is well known, not a race war but a war that is endeavouring to avoid Marxist domination of this country."[11] A plethora of reasons were thus influential in leading to the armed struggle that ultimately saw the liberation of Zimbabwe in 1980.

In his speech in 1977, President John Wrathall revealed the rate at which the Rhodesians were plundering the mineral resources of the country: "In the field of mining my Government will continue its policy of encouraging the maximum exploitation of our mineral resources and it is hoped that mining production figures will achieve further record level in 1977."[12] Still, these benefits did not trickle down to the masses. Additionally, the Rhodesians had little respect for African values. The disregard of local culture, which was castigated as backward, was a clear violation of the fundamental values which shaped the lives of Africans. To add insult to injury, African men were called boys. White settlements were therefore serviced by "cook boys" and "garden boys", regardless of their age. Likewise, African nannies were called girls.[13] Despite attaining independence, colonial hangover still exists in Zimbabwe and many other African countries. It is intriguing to note that the terms "garden boy and house girl" continue to be proudly used. Overall, the Africans were determined to fight for their dignity that the Rhodesians had deliberately eroded. Undoubtedly, it was this dignity that defined how the Africans felt and thought.

Unilateral Declaration of Independence and the Imposition of Sanctions

In 1953, Southern Rhodesia joined the Federation of Rhodesia and Nyasaland. The Federation of Rhodesia and Nyasaland was established by Order in Council S.I. 1953, No. 1199, dated August 1, 1953.[14] The provisions of the Constitution were brought into force on September 3, 1953. The federal legislature held its first session on February 2, 1954.[15] The Central African Federation was established by the British conservative government on the premise that there was strength in unity. The British government finally sent a commission to Africa to dismantle the Federation in 1963 after succumbing to pressure from the nationalists.[16] Although the Federation was hatched in 1953, the idea had long been cherished by whites in the three territories that finally amalgamated. The MP for Ndola Electoral Area, K.E.W. Harris, highlighted in 1930 that countries were like industries and the tendency was to amalgamate. The advantages were that it enabled sound administration and helped cut down government expenses.[17] Harris made his intentions clear when he argued that he believed in the union of the two Rhodesias and in the making of one greater Rhodesia when the time was ripe.[18]

Southern Rhodesia dominated the Federation from the outset because of its more powerful economy and larger white population. The European population in Southern Rhodesia, Northern Rhodesia and Nyasaland numbered 211,000, 72,000 and 8,600 respectively in 1959.[19] A lot of infrastructural development took place in Southern Rhodesia at the expense of the northern territories, and this seriously cracked the Federation. Consequently, it was a matter of time before the merger was dissolved. Other partners did not significantly benefit. The government of Northern Rhodesia was offered a grant-in-aid of £200,000 in 1953.[20] The Federation was oddly shaped from the start. The colony was induced to join it by the promise of markets in Northern Rhodesia and Nyasaland and of flows of labor and raw materials from them. The Federation provided a huge boost to Southern Rhodesian industry, as evidenced by the booming of Salisbury as well as Bulawayo. Admittedly, there were remarkable infrastructural developments in Southern Rhodesia, mainly because it was home to the headquarters of the Federation. The colony was the home of the Federal University College, the Federal Art Gallery and the Federal Archives.[21] The Kariba Dam was another product of the Federation. There were also important military developments which took place in Southern Rhodesia. The Federation "gifted" Southern Rhodesia with a formidable air unit, which proved pivotal in the Second Chimurenga. The responsibility for African affairs in the Federation was retained by the territorial governments. This meant that the position of Africans was not bettered by the Federation. On the other hand, the federal government was responsible for European agriculture, education, health, and the provision of infrastructure like roads, railways and power supplies, to name but a few. Discrimination was therefore built into the whole federal system from the beginning. In Northern Rhodesia and Nyasaland, African affairs remained the responsibility of colonial office governors. In Southern Rhodesia, the Native Affairs Department was the key organ of the state. The native commissioners controlled Africans in the reserves, while white farmers, who possessed much more and much better land, enjoyed federal subsidies and scientific support.[22]

The Suez crisis in 1956 led the British government to speed up the granting of independence to its other African colonies. Black nationalists in the Federation's three territories (Southern Rhodesia, Northern Rhodesia and Nyasaland) began to accelerate their own demands for an end to colonialism. As Britain had done in its other African colonies, she granted independence to the two northern territories of the Federation only after assuring, through constitutional legislation, that political power would revert to the black majorities. Northern Rhodesia (Zambia) and Nyasaland (Malawi) attained independence in 1964 and 1963 respectively. Southern Rhodesia (Zimbabwe) was renamed Rhodesia after the two northern colonies became independent. Britain was tied up to take similar steps in Rhodesia because of that colony's tradition of self-rule. Even if Rhodesia was a British crown colony prior to 1965, its constitution, unlike those of the neighboring British colonies, afforded it control over domestic affairs, with Great Britain retaining only the right to intervene in matters involving foreign governments. The British government refused to grant Rhodesia independence until the white-minority government formally began to transfer power to the country's black majority.[23] The moderate Rhodesian United Federal Party (UFP) attempted to ease pressures with both Britain and domestic black nationalists by agreeing to a new constitution that reserved 15 parliamentary seats for blacks. However, the demands were denied by the nationalists, who wanted majority rule to be unconditionally granted. The events in Southern Rhodesia led the whites to replace the UFP in the 1962 general election. By 1965, talks between Rhodesia and Britain on majority rule and the related constitutional issue had stalled. This subsequently led Rhodesia to declare that the country was now independent. The action is popularly referred to as the Unilateral Declaration of Independence (UDI). Britain responded by instantly imposing trade sanctions against Rhodesia, including an oil embargo, that were subsequently embraced by much of the international community.[24]

Rhodesia came up with a number of sanction-absorbing measures. In the military, Minister of Defense Howmann assured the RSF in 1969 and the public that the efficiency of the army was unimpeded and unaffected. Principally, he argued that the army did not suffer as a result of UDI.[25] Of course, that was plain propaganda. Before UDI, aircraft spares were obtained from Britain, but under the new British government regulations, they were supposed to be completely cut off.[26] However, spares continued to be smuggled in, and the suspected "leak" route was Switzerland, after the parts had been exported by a British firm. Besides, Canberra and Hunters were still flown by about 20 air forces all over the world. Therefore, it was hard to locate the original source of the leaks.[27] Before November 1965, jet engines were sent overseas for reconditioning, but this became impossible once the sanctions were imposed.[28] According to Wing Commander Haddon, OC Technical Wing at New Sarum, 95 percent of the tools used in the engine repair section were homemade and "perfect" for their various purposes.[29] Various strategies and tactics to counter the effects of sanctions were devised, as underscored by Minister of Law and Order Lardner-Burke: "Rhodesia has, I am glad to say, more than held her own, but we cannot afford to relax our efforts or our vigilance in any respect in our successful fight against sanctions."[30]

The War Begins

Different dates have been used to mark the beginning of the Second Chimurenga. The attack in Chipinge in 1964 by the "Crocodile Group" led by a veteran ZANLA leader, William Ndangana, is heralded by scholars such as Fay Chung as the beginning of the armed struggle.[31] Ndangana was one of the first freedom fighters who joined in the liberation struggle at a time when it was literally suicidal to challenge the Smith regime.[32] The Crocodile Gang was a special sabotage unit. As part of their mission, they blew up trains and also killed a white farmer. Members of this group were executed, but Emmerson Mnangagwa, later Zimbabwe's vice-president, was spared because he was under 21. Instead, he went to jail and shared a cell with Mugabe, where they bonded.[33] Nonetheless, he was severely tortured and received beatings which affected the hearing in his left ear. The treatment he received may also explain why he later became indifferent to critics.[34] ZANU PF's version is that the party ignited the Second Chimurenga in Chinhoyi in 1966. However, this has been disputed by former ZPRA intelligence supremo Dumiso Dabengwa and many of his former ZAPU colleagues. ZAPU argues that armed conflict using modern weapons started in September 1962 with the attack on Sidube ranch.[35] In view of the divergent dates as to when the Second Chimurenga campaign began, this study begins in 1966, the year when the Sinoia (Chinhoyi) battle took place. The first officially acknowledged military engagement following UDI occurred at the end of April 1966, when seven Zimbabwe African National Liberation Army members were killed in Chinhoyi.[36] Prior to 1966, there were various acts of sabotage against the Smith regime, but these did not actually constitute a sustained campaign for the liberation of the country.

Without exhausting much thought into the "actual" date, the Chinhoyi Battle is of particular interest to this study because that was when the RhAF was deployed in the colony for the first time to undertake military duties. The Battle of Chinhoyi (Sinoia) was the first organized act of armed insurrection since the ZANLA guerrillas died in a shoot-out.[37] It was at this battle that the RhAF supported the police and had a successful operation which led to the death of allegedly seven ZANLA guerrillas. The band was on a mission to perform acts of sabotage. They were, however, detected by Rhodesian forces, who reacted in full force.[38] The RhAF (then called the Royal Rhodesian Air Force, or RRAF) therefore first saw action in Rhodesia on April 27, 1966, when seven ZANU insurgents entered Rhodesia to undertake sabotage and attack white farmers and police.[39] The police commissioner called the RRAF to assist and four helicopters of No. 7 Squadron inflicted their first casualties.[40] Although the battle signified the beginning of the Second Chimurenga, it also exposed the inadequacies of the tactics used by the nationalists. ZAPU's efforts were even less threatening.[41] Groups of 80 to 100 ZAPU guerrillas and members of the South African National Congress (ANC) crossed into Rhodesia in order to fight but were defeated, without seriously challenging white rule. This occurred three times, from 1967 to 1968, in battles known as Wankie and Sipolilo.[42] In mid–1967, a large combined force of ZAPU and the South African ANC crossed the Zambezi River from Victoria Falls. In a series of engagements with security forces, both sides sustained heavier casualties than before.[43] Moreover, up until the late sixties and early seventies (1969–70), guerrilla incursions into Rhodesia were not successful. They were inhibited by the natural barriers such as the Zambezi River and Lake Kariba.[44]

The Battle of Chinhoyi undoubtedly exhibited the need for teamwork among the various branches of the security forces. Teamwork among the air force, army, and police was formally institutionalized following the engagement. Joint Operations Centres established throughout the country were effective in integrating all five entities responsible for Rhodesian defense: the police, the Special Branch, the army (and its special forces), the air force, and the Internal Affairs Department.[45] In addition, the Battle of Chinhoyi highlights the inaccuracies contained in the liberation war history. The then Prime Minister Robert Mugabe mentioned eight, contrary to the generally accepted figure of seven, as the number of people who died at the Chinhoyi battle.[46] In December 2014, it was revealed to us that then Vice-President Joice Mujuru never downed an airplane, as previously claimed. The state-owned newspaper, the *Herald*, stated that Mujuru was nowhere near Murehwa when the incident happened. Former War veteran Christopher Mutsvangwa, the Minister of Welfare Services for War Veterans, War Collaborators, Former Detainees and Restrictees, said it was propaganda peddled by political commissar Webster Shamu meant to prop up Joice Mujuru.[47] Therefore, it is notable to ask: if that was actually true, why were they peddling falsehoods all these years, and how many lies were told since independence in 1980? People were also informed that Emmerson Mnangagwa never belonged to the Crocodile Group.[48] We also learned that real fighters wallowed in abject poverty while opportunists enjoyed the riches of the land. Nonetheless, by commencing in 1966, this study manages to critically examine the impact of the operations of the Rhodesian Air Force up to the period when the air unit was disbanded, thereby paving way for the formation of the Air Force of Zimbabwe (AFZ) in 1980. The Rhodesian fascination with air power was inherited and continued by the Mugabe regime after Zimbabwe's independence. The post-independence government attempted to maintain a "First World"–standard air force despite the lack of economic and technical resources.

Memories of conquest in 1893, the crushing of the 1896–7 uprisings, and the land-grabbing and looting of livestock, provided a combination of factors which sowed the seeds of a nationalist movement for independence.[49] In 1966, the liberation war commenced as the nationalists sought to free the country from oppression. The belligerents were the Rhodesian Security Forces (RSF), the Zimbabwe African People's Union (ZAPU) and its military wing the Zimbabwe People's Revolutionary Army (ZPRA), and the Zimbabwe African National Union (ZANU) and its military wing the Zimbabwe African National Liberation Army (ZANLA). Addressing the ZANU PF Youth League at the National Sports Centre in Harare on July 16, 1983, Prime Minister Mugabe highlighted that the ZANU 1964 May Congress explicitly gave a full mandate to the newly elected Central Committee to organize a nationalist struggle for the liberation of Zimbabwe. This was the first party congress since the split from ZAPU in 1963. Ndabaningi Sithole, Henry Hamadziripi, Mukudzei Midzi, Herbert Chitepo, Edgar Tekere and Leopold Takawira decided to split from ZAPU at the house of Enos Nkala in Highfield in 1963. It was at the 1964 congress that the party adopted the raised fist as its revolutionary sign to mark a departure from the passive form of the struggle they had hitherto adopted. The leadership elected at the congress was as follows:

1. President: Ndabaningi Sithole, who later turned renegade.
2. Vice-President: Leopold Takawira, who died in June 1970 in Harare Prison.
3. Secretary General: Robert Mugabe.
4. Deputy Secretary General: Eddison Zvobgo.
5. Treasurer General: Enos Nkala.
6. National Chairman: Herbert Chitepo, who died in Lusaka in 1975 because of a bomb planted in his car by the enemy. The bomb exploded, killing him and one of his bodyguards.
7. National Organising Secretary: Michael Mawema, who turned renegade. He was deputized by Simon V. Muzenda.
8. Secretary for External Affairs: Simpson Mutambanengwe, who turned renegade. His deputy was Henry Hamadziripi, who also turned renegade.
9. Secretary for Public Affairs (really for organizing military training and

acts of sabotage): Noel Mukono, who also turned renegade, and whose deputy was Maurice Nyagumbo.
10. Secretary for Publicity and Information: Edison Sithole, who was kidnapped by enemy and never found.
11. Secretary for Women's Affairs: Mrs. Chakonda, who later resigned.
12. Secretary for Legal Defence and Welfare: Dr. Mutasa.
13. Secretary for Youth and Culture: Morton Malianga, assisted by Edgar Tekere.[50]

While in restriction at Sikombela from 1964, ZANU leaders held a meeting in the period August–October 1965. They drew up a brief document (Sikombela declaration) in which they spelled out the form of struggle that should be carried out. They then mandated those members of the Central Committee in exile to constitute, under the leadership and chairmanship of Herbert Chitepo, a Revolutionary Council or Dare reChimurenga, to organize and train a guerrilla force for the prosecution of the struggle, which congress had tasked the leaders to prosecute. Some military training of cadres had already begun with a small group that had gone to China in 1963 and a larger group of 50 which had gone to Ghana.[51] ZANU sent its first contingent of five men led by Emmerson Mnangagwa to the People's Republic of China for military training in September 1963. They formed the nucleus of ZANU's armed wing, the Zimbabwe African National Liberation Army.[52]

More training programs, were, however, affected by Dare reChimurenga, when it was eventually established in 1966. Training camps sprang up in successive stages in Tanzania. China was also offering training facilities in its country in addition to providing instructors for the training in Tanzania.[53] Members of the Central Committee in detention were finally released in December 1974. They conferred in Lusaka with members of Dare reChimurenga, before the death of Chitepo, to deliberate on the continuance of the struggle. Recruitment began immediately upon release, with Maurice Nyagumbo as the chief recruitment officer. Home-based members of the Central Committee agreed that its secretary general, Robert Mugabe, accompanied by Edgar Tekere, should leave the country to reorganize the party and the armed struggle. As the struggle once again started unfolding from January 1976, and Zambia released members of Dare and others, including members of the general staff, an opportune moment came in 1977, to restructure the party by reconstituting its Central Committee and the ZANLA High Command as well. Some members of the High Command were now made members of the Central Committee so that the High Command would participate in the policy-making function of the party. The Central Committee directed the struggle.[54] The political-military axis between Mugabe and Tongogara, coupled with Frontline states support, enabled them to have the entire ZIPA leadership arrested and imprisoned in early 1977, with the exception of Nhongo, who defected to Mugabe. At a nine-day meeting of the ZANU Central Committee held at Chimoio which started on August 31, 1977, Mugabe was dictatorially pronounced head of both the party and the army.[55] War veteran Benard Manyadza revealed that Rugare Gumbo and the late ZANLA commander, General Josiah "Magama" Tongogara, propped up Robert Mugabe by marketing him to both guerrilla leaders and the Frontline states (Zambia, Angola, Tanzania, Mozambique and Botswana). After the arrest of members of Dare reChimurenga such as Tongogara, Gumbo, Henry Hamadziripi, and Cletus Chigove in 1975 at Mpima Prison in Kabwe on allegations of assassinating ZANU chairperson Herbert Chitepo, the incarcerated Gumbo played a huge role in convincing the war combatants to endorse Mugabe.[56] In addition, Mugabe decampaigned the Rev. Ndabaningi Sithole by portraying himself as a better leader than Sithole, the founder of ZANU. Comrades in Zambia were led by the late Simon Muzenda to believe that Mugabe was a Karanga from Masvingo. The Karanga dominated ZANU. Muzenda played off the fact that in Masvingo there was a chief by the name Mugabe who lived near Great Zimbabwe, although there was no blood relationship at all.[57]

The Dynamics of the War

At a time when the guerrilla forces received advisory and material support from Communist bloc countries, Rhodesia functioned under international trade sanctions. In addition to civilian support, the assistance rendered by the Frontline states (FLS), the Organisation of African Unity and its Liberation Committee headed by Executive Secretary Hashim Mbita, was invaluable. In Tanzania, the guerrillas trained at Chunya, Itumbi, Mgagao, Morogoro and Nachingwea.[58] On the other hand, the Rhodesian Security Forces suffered from manpower shortage while the guerrilla forces poured out in huge numbers. In fact, a combination of factors facilitated guerrilla victory. Nonetheless, numerous hurdles were faced along the way. Guerrilla actions were initially limited to ambushes and attacks on isolated farms. Reaction by Rhodesian forces was usually swift. By 1968, the guerrilla campaign had come to a standstill. In 1969, the security forces felt they had defeated the guerrilla threat and, as a result, they were reluctant to accept the evidence of increased and more sophisticated insurgent activity. On their part, the guerrilla forces spent the year under the guidance of their Soviet, Chinese, and Cuban advisors. The guerrillas entered 1970 better trained and organized. There were two major clashes in 1970: a partially successful attack on a police garrison in Chisuma, and an unsuccessful attempt to cut the railway line running from the northern frontier to Salisbury. However, from 1971 to 1973 the complexion of the war began to change. Insurgent activity developed to a point that demanded the total commitment of the security forces, including the RhAF. Initially, the army was able to isolate the war to the northern border region with Zambia. As the Portuguese failures in Mozambique became more apparent, the basis for support and operations of the nationalists began to expand into Mozambique. This extension, when linked to a larger and better-trained insurgent element, resulted in several guerrilla military successes throughout 1973. The insurgents began to effectively utilize landmines, small rocket launchers, grenades, and automatic weapons, including light machine guns. Their tactics became more sophisticated. These tactics resulted in few white casualties, however. The ZIPA period and Nhari rebellion attests to this fact. The primary victims were local blacks who supported European interests such as farms.

The friendship between Zimbabwe and Mozambique deepened in the northeastern offensive in 1972–73. ZANU was able to launch attacks from the liberated areas of Mozambique.[59] From 1973 to 1975, both sides of the conflict began to learn the lessons of unconventional warfare. The guerrillas received a higher degree of training and demonstrated the discipline required to wage an effective campaign. The Rhodesian Security Forces developed counter-guerrilla tactics involving air and ground and special operations forces that would bring it so much recognition in the following years. The withdrawal of the Portuguese from Mozambique in 1975 allowed the Frontline nations to form a confederation in order to direct their support and some limited resources to the overthrow of the white minority government in Salisbury. Rhodesia's position worsened when South Africa withdrew its auxiliary forces from combat and eventually from Rhodesia altogether over differing national policies on relations with the Frontline states. At the same time, as a result of greater Chinese and Soviet support, the numbers of insurgents began to increase, and units in excess of 100 men moved through the northern and eastern border regions. The Rhodesian Security Forces—even with such novel employment of aviation such as the "fireforce" and "hot pursuit" concepts—simply could not cope. By 1976, the pressure on the Rhodesian military began to intensify. Insurgent attacks were initiated from Botswana. The addition of Botswana as a sanctuary had a noticeable impact on white Rhodesia. The main railway from Rhodesia to South Africa passed through Botswana. Thus, Salisbury could no longer depend upon a secure line of communications with its only ally. This resulted in the construction of the Beitbridge-Rutenga railway line. Throughout the war, this route served as Rhodesia's only direct link with the international community.

The immediate result of this intensification of guerrilla effort was that the Rhodesian Security Forces lost control of the civilian population in the northeast and most of the rural areas of the country. As with the United States' experience in the Republic of Vietnam, the security forces controlled the rural areas by day but the guerrillas held sway at night. This increase in strength and the capabilities of the nationalist liberation movement resulted in an increased measure of popular support from the indigenous black population. This ensured the insurgents of a local source of food, shelter and information, and more importantly, indigenous recruits. In the face of these realities and with only a relatively small force and obsolete and elderly equipment (especially aircraft), General Peter Walls, first as Army Commander in 1972, and later as Commander Combined Operations in 1977, deserves credit for waging a losing campaign of professional competence. The war effort of the RSF in the face of multiple challenges is ascribable to his military aptitude, and to his generalship.

The liberation struggle was derailed by problems at the rear bases. In the wake of the death of Chitepo in 1975, Zambia arrested all the cadres in the country plus all members of the Dare. It is alleged that Chitepo wanted Nhari to be given a fair hearing, but Nhari and company were killed for rebelling against the leadership of the party and high command. War veteran and author Fay Chung noted that towards 1974 there was a huge influx of guerrilla fighters. These had mixed backgrounds, ranging from illiterate peasants to university students. These new recruits faced a severe shortage of food. There was also a short supply of plates, which meant recruits had to receive the little food available on leaves or in their bare hands.[60] These challenges were compounded by a serious shortage of guns and ammunition, making it difficult to exploit the many military opportunities. Thousands of young men had to cope without any food and armaments, and under these circumstances, disillusionment set in quickly. Junior commanders were also angry with the abuse of women by their superiors. An example was a junior officer called Dakarai Badza, who lost his wife to his senior commander, who had sent him on a dangerous mission at the front. Badza retaliated by joining in a rebellion against the ZANLA leadership.[61] The disgruntled young officers created what was later known as the Nhari group, named after their leader, Thomas Nhari. Together with Badza, Nhari led the young officers from the front into an attack on the ZANU and ZANLA leadership in Lusaka. Both the ZANU and ZANLA leaders were taken completely by surprise. This led to the growth of misunderstanding and distrust in the organization. Some ZANU leaders, mainly Chitepo, chairman of ZANU and head of its external wing, and John Mataure, the political commissar, believed that they should listen to the young officers. Tongogara, on the other hand, who was the main focus of the young officers' criticism, believed that giving an audience to these officers was tantamount to treason and encouragement of rebellion. Rhodesian intelligence is said to have fomented the disgruntlement. The captured leaders, including Josiah Tungamirai and Charles Dauramanzi, were taken to Chifombo, a ZANLA transit camp in eastern Zambia. Some 70 colleagues who had refused to take part in the rebellion were executed in military style. This led to defections. With the help of these defectors, Tongogara was able to recapture Chifombo in an astute military maneuver involving 300 guerrillas who had been brought from Mgagao training camp in Tanzania.[62]

ZANU is blamed for the death of Chitepo because he had previously agreed to have an informal meeting with the rebels, and this made some of the veterans, especially Tongogara, suspect that he secretly supported them. Chitepo condemned the rebels and their activities, particularly the killing of their comrades-in-arms. The rebels were given a number of punishments, mainly demotions in military rank. Chitepo further ordered that the rebels be handed over to the Zambian authorities for further punishment. While satisfied with the conduct of the trials, the military leaders under Tongogara were not pleased with the punishments meted out. There was a belief that Chitepo had revealed great kindness, bearing in mind that the rebels had actually disturbed the armed struggle and killed some of their own colleagues. Soon after the trial, the military leaders executed the rebels secretly, without the consent of the political leadership. These extra-judicial executions were to cause further internal conflict within ZANU, with the political leaders dividing against the military leaders.[63] Cletus Chigove, the chief of intelligence, Josiah Tongogara and others hunted down members of the Dare who were from Manicaland (the Manyikas). They wanted to kill them in revenge for the kidnapping of Tongogara's wife and children by the Nhari group.[64] In the tense, troubled phase of ZANU infighting that characterized the months before his death in Lusaka, Chitepo confided to war veteran Cornelius Sanyanga about his thoughts and fears.[65] The Manyika such as Noel Mukono, Simpson Mutambanengwe, Washington Malianga, Felix Mpunga and others did not attend Chitepo's funeral for fear of being killed. ZANU district council member Dr. Edgar Madekurozwa was abducted, killed and buried in a shallow grave. Investigations proved that Dr. Madekurozwa was abducted by Chigove and his group.[66] The Chitepo assassination reveals two important things about the liberation war in Zimbabwe: the role of Rhodesian intelligence in creating divisions in the guerrilla movements, and the purges that took place within the liberation parties. Nonetheless, internal strife, mainly motivated by tribal tendencies, claimed the lives of many fighters.

The assassination of Chitepo made it impossible for ZANLA to secure more external support. This incident provoked the fury of Zambian President

Kenneth Kaunda who had allowed the nationalist organizations to operate in his country only on the condition that there was no internecine violence. When Kaunda discovered that dissident ZANLA elements were suspected in Chitepo's murder, he ordered the arrest of all senior ZANLA officials (including military commander Josiah Tongogara), the expulsion of the organization's fighters, and the suspension of all ZANLA activities in Zambia. The fortunate part for ZANU was that the Mgagao camp remained solid and was used to rekindle the struggle. The arrested officials were brutally interrogated until they falsely confessed to involvement in Chitepo's murder, while other alleged conspirators were shot.[67] The Frontline states persuaded Zambia to put the larger goal of liberating Zimbabwe ahead of the criminal matter of who killed Chitepo.[68] By and large, the incident was a severe setback for ZANLA operations.

According to Ken Flower, the arrests cost ZANLA an estimated two years in its war against Rhodesia.[69] For most of 1975, the armed struggle made no progress as ZANLA leaders were imprisoned for twenty months. This saw the formation of the Zimbabwe People's Army (ZIPA) in November 1975 in Mozambique. ZIPA was an amalgamation of ZANLA and ZPRA, but just in name. This was an attempt by Frontline states to bypass the squabbling nationalist political leaders and unify the armed struggle. ZIPA was also known as the Third Force.[70] Rex Nhongo, the most senior ZANLA military commander outside prison, became the leader and Alfred "Nikita" Mangena, ZPRA's commander, his deputy. ZIPA soon became a ZANLA affair after ZANLA guerrillas, with the support of the Tanzanian Defence Forces, disarmed and massacred a significant number of ZPRA guerrillas in joint training camps in Tanzania and demanded that they denounce ZAPU and its leadership.[71] At Mgagao, an unknown but considerable number of ZPRA soldiers were shot. At Morogoro, over a hundred young ZAPU fighters died at the hands of the ZANLA soldiers. Thereafter, ZPRA fighters resisted being sent to Tanzania for training. ZPRA became concentrated in Zambia and ZANLA in Mozambique and Tanzania.[72] The "old guard" in both ZAPU and ZANU treated ZIPA with suspicion. As a result, the young cadres who spearheaded ZIPA were "eliminated" by the senior nationalists in a typically authoritarian style.[73] In 1983, then Prime Minister Mugabe Robert confirmed the massacres which happened amongst liberation armies: "Unfortunately, in circumstances in which there were political divisions amongst us, it was inevitable that quarrels would occur sometimes resulting in unfortunate fights and killings. We certainly abused Tanzanian hospitality not only once but on several occasions."[74]

According to Mugabe, the first stage in the process of searching for a permanent solution to the contradictions that had combined in correcting national grievances was that of reformist nationalism of the 1950s. This stage was characterized by predominantly nonviolent means. The second stage was that of revolutionary nationalism, beginning in the 1960s and characterized by armed struggle, and which in turn produced the third stage of national independence.[75] Mugabe argued that the fourth stage was economic independence. This stage was reluctantly implemented only to be pushed for political ends, of course with consequences on human security. Mugabe tortured and killed in order to remain in power while the economy was tumbling. Overall, the war fought between 1966 and 1979 left deep scars on society. Towards the end of the struggle, in 1978–79, internal political leaders Abel Muzorewa and Ndabaningi Sithole had their own militias as well. All of the protagonists used violence to mobilize the civilians, implying that the number of civilians killed and wounded, tortured and dispossessed during the struggle was considerable.[76]

At the peak of the war from 1976 to 1978, biological and chemical weapons were used by the regime. The techniques used were poisoning wells, spreading cholera, infecting clothing used by "terrorists," and using anthrax to kill cattle and thus deny food supplies to the guerrillas.[77] In an attempt to end the war, in 1978 Ian Smith hammered out an internal settlement. A black prime minister, Abel Muzorewa, was elected through universal suffrage, but the military and intelligence apparatus firmly remained in white control. The international community refused to recognize Zimbabwe-Rhodesia, as it was known,[78] because Muzorewa was considered to be just black skin with a white mask. With the war unwinnable and white emigration on the rise, Ian Smith signed the Lancaster House Agreement in December 1979. Rhodesian losses in men and aircraft were increasing, whereas the supply of equipment and recruits to the guerrillas seemed endless.[79]

It is true that the country was won through the barrel of the gun, but none of the major players (ZANU, ZAPU, nor the Rhodesian government) secured a military victory. Only ZANU secured a strategic victory, but not in the manner intended. Moreover, the "campaign design" for each side failed. ZANU's approach stalled in Phase II of the Maoist model. Phase I is the development of local support. Phase II is organizational growth, and combat against the enemy. Phase II revolutionaries are interested in using military force for political purposes. This is low-intensity warfare at this point, so the target will likely be an individual or a small group. Phase III is the transition of the guerrilla organization into a conventional force, and the defeat of the enemy. While ZANU's Maoist strategy failed to reach Phase III, it could have been part of their strategy not to directly confront the enemy. Guerrilla tactics have become much more closely associated with progressing a program of political action designed not necessarily to result in outright military victory, but to wear down those in power so as eventually to secure the political aims of the liberation movement. The prolonged nature of the conflict implies that guerrilla warfare is not a purely military struggle.[80] Mao's phases of guerrilla warfare are thus subjective. On the other hand, ZAPU's "conventional" approach never got off the ground, and the Rhodesian military solution, grounded in mobile, air, and special operations forces, was unable to prevent infiltration and mobilization of the rural populace. They all acquiesced to the negotiations in the hope of resolving the conflict in their favor.

Conclusion

The liberation war was won by ZANU in the political arena, not on the battlefield. There are cases in warfare when a participant may realize its strategic goals not by scoring a decisive military defeat on its enemy but because the enemy decides to cut his losses and withdraw rather than risk additional damage. This was the case with the capitulation of the Rhodesian Security Forces. This also proved to be the case for the Soviets in Afghanistan when the Afghan mujahedeen just kept fighting until the Soviets wearied of the whole affair and withdrew rather than suffer the continuing agony of that prolonged war. Arguably, this has proven equally true for the Americans in Afghanistan. The guerrilla forces in Zimbabwe kept up the fight simply because the cessation of hostilities would amount to a return to the status quo that they found unacceptable to begin with. Guerrilla warfare is about exhausting the enemy; thus, shortening the conflict is not desirable. The RSF were driven to the negotiating table because it was clear to them that the war was unwinnable.

2
Conceptualizing the Development of Air Power as a War Asset

Introduction

It is now a reality that battles can be fought in the sky. The development of military aviation is proof of the fact that while change is desirable, very few are prepared to embrace it in the first instance. Modern warfare reveals the important roles that could be performed by aircraft despite the fact that its early advocates were relegated to the status of mere lunatics. From simple reconnaissance missions, air power has developed into an indispensable instrument of both conventional and irregular warfare. In view of the strategic and tactical significance of air power, this chapter traces the development of this weapon of war. The chapter investigates the development of aviation up to a time when its relevance and utility in combat were fully appreciated.

In addition, the chapter discusses the general theories of air power through the works of primarily Trenchard, Mitchell and Douhet, as well as utilizing examples from the First and Second World Wars. This is done in order to establish the efficacy of air power as it will be applied in the Zimbabwean context. Although the material used is more suited to making the case for strategic bombing, targeting of civilian centers of population, and securing support for an independent air force, it reveals the suitability of air power in conventional warfare, thereby providing the basis for analyzing its usefulness in counterinsurgency operations. Guided by the ideas of great air power thinkers who entirely focused on strategic bombing and the "moral effect" of air power in conventional warfare, it is crucial to examine the role of air power in strategic planning and at tactical level in guerrilla warfare.

It should therefore be highlighted at this juncture that although this chapter discusses the theories of air power such as strategic high-altitude bombing and the bombing of civilian populations in cities as advocated by the pro-fascist Italian Giulio Douhet, the Rhodesian Air Force did not attempt to do this, nor did it have the capacities for it. Besides, the political consequences of bombing the cities of the Frontline states would have been enormous. The contributions of air power theorists were utilized in examining the benefits of air power in warfare such as great speed, the ability to fly in any direction (flexibility) and being independent of surface limitations. Billy Mitchell, for example, emphasized the tactical use of air power such as long-range strategic bombing.

History of the Development of Air Power

Air power is defined by the British defense forces as the ability to project military force in air or space by or from a platform or missile operating above the surface of the earth. Air platforms are defined as any aircraft, helicopter or unmanned air vehicle (UAV). Air power is a broad subject, comprising all the uses of aviation in the pursuit of nations' and other political actors' power and security interests.[1] This study concentrates entirely on conventional air power. The bulk of air power literature has been shaped by two opposing views, ultimately creating what is known as the "Great Air Power Debate." One side holds that air power is on an endless journey to excellence. Put in different words, this view is hinged on the belief that the improvement of tactics and technology will continue to strengthen air power's utility as a military instrument. Ultimately, the early air-power theorists' dreams will come to fruition as air power will be able to win wars on its own. In contrast, the other view of air power, which could be described as "strategic," holds that the utility or suitability of air power is always context-dependent. For instance, strategic air power is effective in "traditional" and conventional interstate wars, such as the Second World War or the Gulf War of 1991. However, its usefulness in today's era of irregular wars is restricted. In the current security setting characterized by "new" wars and irregular conflicts, the core missions of independent air forces are increasingly being eroded, certainly downgrading air power's usefulness to a supporting role at best.[2] In line with this school of thought, this study is of the view that air power is important, but not always necessary, as demonstrated by the sophistication of guerrilla war.

The development of air power is one of the most unusual (in terms of gestation period) phenomena in modern history. The period taken by strategists to harness its impact in combat reveals the military conservatism that prevailed for decades on the possibilities of aircraft in fulfilling political and military ends. The eighteenth century failed to find a solution to the problem of flight, but produced two far-seeing prophecies which are of vital interest to the present.[3] Gray's *Luna Habitabilis* written in 1737 concluded:

> The time will come when thou shalt lift thine eyes
> To watch a long-drawn battle in the skies,
> While aged peasants, too amazed for words,
> Stare at the flying fleets of wondrous birds.
>
> England, so long mistress of the sea,
> Where wind and waves confess her sovereignty,
> Her ancient triumphs yet on high shall bear,
> And reign the sovereign of the conquered air.[4]

Samuel Johnson contemplated the implications of flying in his "Thesis on the Art of Flying" in 1759. He paradoxically questioned the safety of people on land if attacked by aircraft by asking: "What would be the security of the good if the bad could at pleasure invade them from the sky?"[5] Theoretically, Gray and Johnson played an important role in the development of aircraft by envisioning the consequences of planes when invading one's territory, obviously with dire repercussions on the attacked. The threat of an invasion from the sky was frightening to think about. These prophecies were partially fulfilled when the English Channel was crossed by air in 1909, thereby exposing the defenselessness of many countries.

In 1799, a British citizen, Sir George Cayley (1773–1857), first formulated the basic nature of a powered airplane. In 1909, exactly one hundred and ten years later, Louis Bleriot flew across the English Channel.[6] Cayley designed and constructed a glider to carry a man, but the problem of stability remained vexing. Stringfellow took up Cayley's ideas and, with the help of William Henson, made the first power-driven model airplane flight in 1848.[7] Starting in 1878, the British government allocated £700 per annum to Captain Templer to make the first British military balloon, named the *Pioneer*. He was to train Royal Engineer officers in ballooning, using his own private balloon *Crusader* to train engineers until *Pioneer* was completed.[8] While some inventors were experimenting with balloons, others were studying the flight of birds with a view to producing a kite capable of supporting man.[9]

Louis Bleriot's crossing of the English Channel in an airplane from Calais to Dover, on July 25, 1909, had as vivid and profound an effect on kings and governments as it had on the general population. English aviation pioneer Sir Alan Cobham (1894–1973) revealed how the incident impacted the military thinking of the time when he noted that the day Bleriot flew the channel marked the end of their insular safety, and the beginning of the time when Britain must seek another form of defense besides ships.[10] Still, commanders could not stomach the idea of an airplane being of any more service in war than a flying observation post. The British War Office had to cease experiments with airplanes at Farnborough "as the cost had proved too great."[11]

The first great aviation meeting in history was held in Betheny, near Reims, from Sunday, August 22, to Sunday, August 29, 1909. The meeting was hosted by the then president of the French Republic, Armand Fallieres. Following hard on the heels of Bleriot's crossing of the English Channel, Reims marked the true recognition of airplanes as practical vehicles. One of the attendees, British Cabinet Minister Lloyd George, was evidently impressed by the strategic capabilities of the airplane. He commented: "Flying machines are no longer toys and dreams, they are an established fact. The possibilities of this new system of locomotion are infinite. I feel, as a Britisher, rather ashamed that we are so completely out of it."[12] The "Great Week of Aviation" was intended to be a showcase of man's conquest of the air and progress in aeronautics.[13]

The British made efforts to engage the Wright brothers, Wilbur and Orville, who in 1903 were the first men in history to make powered, sustained and controlled flights in airplanes.[14] Despite the insistence by the Wright brothers, the Americans were reluctant to embrace the advantages of aviation technology. On January 18, 1905, the Wright brothers told their congressman, Robert Nevin: "The series of aeronautical experiments upon which we have been engaged for the past five years has ended in the production of a flying machine.... It not only flies through the air at high speed, but it also lands without being cracked."[15]

The response to the Wright brothers, signed by Major-General Gillespie of the General Staff—the president of the Board of Ordnance and Fortification—concluded: "[T]he Board has found it necessary to decline to make allotment for the experimental development of devices for mechanical flight and has determined that, before suggestions with that object in view will be considered, the device must have been brought to the stage of practical operation without expense to the United States...."[16]

The Development of the Air Power Doctrine During the Interwar Period

By the time of the outbreak of the First World War in 1914, the airplane had proven its worth. It had sufficiently advanced to be accepted by the British War Office and the Admiralty as a potential weapon of significance in 1913. The War Office decided to adopt one type of airplane designed by Geoffrey de Havilland.[17] The Royal Flying Corps and the Royal Naval Air Service had between them about 300 planes in 1914. On April 1, 1918, the Royal Air Force was born as an independent service with over 20,000 airplanes capable of reaching 30,000 feet.[18] Of all the major combatants in World War I, Great Britain was the only one that came away from the war with an independent air force. Hugh Trenchard was an important figure in the development of military aviation in Britain. He built the world's first independent air force, complete with its own institutions, ranks, uniforms, flag and tasks. Nonetheless, this involved bureaucratic dogfights with the navy and army.[19] Trenchard concluded that final victory rested on the destruction of enemy industries and on the lowering of morale of enemy nationals caused by bombing.[20]

From its very inception, the RAF was assigned strategic bombardment as a founding role. It was an air force that was very much a creature of the circumstances and personalities that had created it. The RAF came into being in April 1918, primarily in response to German attacks on London and the perceived inability of its predecessor (the Royal Flying Corps) to deal with them.[21] The air raids carried out by Germany on London on June 13 and July 7, 1917, killed 227 persons and injured 677. Throughout the war, Zeppelin and airplane attacks on English and German cities killed almost 2,000 civilians. There was an outrage when some of the bombs hit an infants' school in the East End. The British aircraft only managed to destroy one Gotha plane. This showed the impotence of the defenders. The public reacted by calling for defense restructuring, including the creation of a separate air force for both air defense and reprisal raids.[22] The British air raids on Germany in 1918 lacked impact and did little damage to German industrial output. This meant that the costs of the RAF's destroyed aircraft exceeded the expense of the damage it inflicted on Germany. There were also a lot of accidents in the British air force. Trenchard pushed the inexperienced pilots too hard.[23]

The Germans began launching air attacks against London in 1915. The first reported victim was an English child killed by a bomb dropped from a German Zeppelin. At first the Germans used airships such as Zeppelins and later on employed large bombardment aircraft. Retaliation raids by Britain were the stated purpose of the Independent Force (IF) of bombers under the command of the future leader of the RAF, Lord Trenchard. In the other theatre of war, the Italians and Austrians were enthusiastically bombing each other.[24] The most significant use of air power in support of land operations came first during the German spring offensives in 1918, when air power played a vital role in upsetting and dislocating the German advance, mainly in attacks against supply convoys and reinforcements moving up to the front.[25]

The war of 1914–18 is the mother lode for air power historians. Every significant manifestation of 20th century air power was envisioned and worked out in at least rudimentary form between 1914 and 1918.[26] The war foreshadowed what was to come in the realm of air war. Nevertheless, aviation remained on the periphery of a war dominated by colossal campaigns of attrition on the ground.[27] A perfect example was the Battle of Verdun in 1916, meant to "bleed France white." Verdun was the longest and bloodiest battle of World War I. There was a massive use of artillery and shells. Thousands of troops were deployed. The battle was a nightmare for the people of Lorraine and the soldiers themselves. Verdun epitomized the horrors of World War I. Besides being dismembered by the bullets, soldiers were prey to rats and lice. French generals never expected an attack on Verdun, so they had moved men and material to other fronts.

Campaigns of the First World War had profound effects on theorists who had direct experience in bombing operations, such as Hugh Trenchard, William "Billy" Mitchell and Giulio Douhet. Aircraft were predominantly used as extensions of the eyes of the ground commanders, just as balloons had been used during the French Revolution.[28] Air power was mainly restricted to reconnaissance, then called observation.[29] Aviation commenced the war as essentially the "eyes" of long-established land and maritime forces. It was the considered view of the military experts of the day that this was the most efficient and effective use of this new technology. The potential of this new weapon to change the face of war was left to the imagination of fiction writers.[30]

The bombardments that took place during the course of World War I planted the seeds for the development of air power doctrine during the interwar period, at least in the west. From 1926, Trenchard spent a lot of his time building, rather than defending the air force. This he comfortably achieved because his position as Chief of Air Staff had been accepted as equal to that of the First Sea Lord and Chief of the Imperial General Staff.[31] He retired from service in 1929 but during World War II his advice was still sought after by the Air Ministry. He never departed from his gospel of strategic bombing and its "moral effect." The crusade was joined by other great air-power advocates such as Giulio Douhet and Billy Mitchell. In light of the aforementioned evidence, it is apparent that the development and acceptance of aircraft as strategic and tactical weapons of war in many countries was hindered mainly by military conservatism and command and control problems. The navy and army were still considered as the first lines of defense.

In the United States, army aviation came under the Signal Corps in 1913. In the same year, pilots in the Aeronautical Division convinced members of Congress that progress in military aviation could be achieved if aviation was independent of the Signal Corps.[32] In the United States, air power was considered a valuable adjunct to the army and a second line of defense of the nation should the first line of defense, the U.S. Navy, fail. Aircraft tactical roles were supposed to be restricted but not limited to harbor and coastal defenses, where they were used for observing, and to preventing enemy reconnaissance, enhancing the accuracy of coastal artillery, artillery spotting, destroying enemy aircraft, attacking the enemy's smaller surface forces and long-range bombing.[33] William "Billy" Mitchell is regarded as America's foremost advocate of air power. Mitchell's contribution to air power encompasses his ideas on the tactical use of air power such as long-range strategic bombing, the creation of an independent air organization, and adoption of Douhet's "vital centers" arguments.[34] In 1919, Mitchell was tasked with the training and operations of the Air Service. It was during this period that he passionately initiated his campaign for an independent air force and the unified control of military air power.[35] Mitchell was mainly influenced by his experiences of the First World War. The theories of Trenchard and Douhet also captivated him.

Air power theorists General William "Billy" Mitchell and General Giulio Douhet were distinctive strategists because they demonstrated the practicability of their ideas. Mitchell is credited for playing a dominant role in the development of the American Expeditionary Forces (AEF) aviation program. Although Mitchell was not an original thinker, his ability rested in identifying and dissemination of thoughts and concepts.[36] Like Douhet, Mitchell realized that the airplane was inherently an offensive weapon, and he instilled the Royal Flying Corps with that spirit despite dreadful losses. At the end of the First World War, Billy Mitchell called for a new national defense organization in America featuring an independent air force co-equal to the army and navy. The same air unit was supposed to be responsible for all military and civilian aviation in the United States.[37] The important thing, in Mitchell's view, was not strategic bombing, but rather the centralized coordination of all air assets under the control of an autonomous air force command, freed from its dependency on the army.[38] He contended that the military high command was incompetent, criminally negligent and almost treasonable in its administration of national defense.[39] He insisted that capital ships were vulnerable to air attack. The solution therefore rested in the establishment of an independent department of aviation and a unified command of the armed forces.[40]

In justifying his argument for an independent air force, Mitchell argued: "[T]o entrust the development of aviation to either the army or the navy is just as sensible as entrusting the development of the electric light to a candle factory."[41] This, inevitably, created tension with army and naval commanders and Secretary of War Newton Baker.[42] In order to defend the need for an autonomous air force, Billy Mitchell, on July 21, 1921, bombarded Chesapeake Bay, completely obliterating the obsolete former German battleship *Ostfriesland*.[43] Mitchell's experiments demonstrated the impact of direct aerial bombs dropped from an airplane. What Mitchell did was an act of fulfillment and "vindication."[44] Chesapeake Bay acted as a military laboratory for Mitchell. He successfully proved that air power was the defensive and offensive weapon of future warfare because the tests sent several obsolete battleships to the bottom.[45] Old-line admirals took violent exception to Mitchell's claim that bombers could disable any American battleship. They reluctantly agreed to a series of tests, with Mitchell in command of the strike force. Due to the military friction that existed, naval forces were dismayed because Mitchell had prophesied and demonstrated that aircraft could indeed sink battleships.[46]

Mitchell predicted in 1923 that bombers would make warships useless, an opinion resented by Navy Admirals.[47] He was court-martialed in 1925 for insubordination. He was publicly tried in a case that shocked the nation. The trial lasted more than seven weeks and was everything Billy Mitchell had wanted—a public forum at which his ideas could be aired.[48] From 1926, Mitchell advocated for the necessity of military preparedness in the air. He continually called attention to the rapid strides being made in aviation in Europe and Asia and warned of Japanese plans to seize Hawaii, Alaska and the Philippines. He also predicted, accurately, that the Japanese would not bother to declare war formally.[49] At the time that Mitchell was being court-martialed, the Japanese were invading a city in Manchuria called Mukden. Three years after his death in 1936, the Luftwaffe was hammering Poland. He was posthumously awarded the Medal of Honor "for outstanding pioneer service and foresight in the field of military aviation" in 1946. His prophecy came true when Pearl Harbor was attacked by Japan in December 1941. Japanese aircraft and submarines attacked the U.S. Pacific fleet in its base at Pearl Harbor, Hawaii. Although the damage was very severe, the most important ships in the fleet, the U.S. aircraft carriers, were out at sea. This was to prove decisive in the outcome of the Pacific War. Japan had built up an empire in Asia and its leaders wanted Japan to become Asia's leading power. They knew that the USA would stand in their way and that war with America would happen sometime. The advocacy and experiments performed by Billy Mitchell draw our attention to the suppression of military aviation for several decades. The military leadership of the day struggled to comprehend how the new weapon could single-handedly win battles.

Overall, the period after the end of the First World War was a time of critical thinking, a time of reflection into the reasons which had led to the grim deadlock. Air-power theorists began to envision a new type of warfare involving the use of aircraft. After World War I, Douhet enunciated how air power could independently achieve political and military objectives. With respect to the military use of aircraft, Douhet was of the opinion that World War I provided no guidance whatsoever for the future.[50] His sentiments stemmed from the peripheral duties assigned to aircraft during the long campaign. Douhet argued that the nation that loses command of the air swiftly loses the means of regaining it through the bombing of her aircraft industries, or even loses the means of mobilizing and maintaining her armies and navies.[51]

Douhet's book, translated by Dino Ferrari, reveals the fundamentals of air power. Douhet revealed that when air power was first introduced, many people took the extreme position that it was impossible to fight in the air. Others acknowledged that it was only useful as an ancillary to the already existing means of warfare such as navy and infantry.[52] Air power was first employed by Italy in Libya during the Italo-Turkish War in 1911–12. It was basically used for reconnaissance and liaison purposes. At the outbreak of the First World War, air power was still in its infancy.[53] Douhet worked hard to convince his critics that airplanes could be major offensive instruments of war. The Italian elucidated the reasons why he considered air power to be the offensive weapon par excellence. He said that unlike other weapons, aircraft were independent of surface limitations, flexible (ability to fly in any direction), and possessed superior speed which was greater than any other known means of transportation. The greatest advantage of the offensive is having the initiative in planning operations—the freedom to choose the point.[54] From the foregoing, it can be concluded that the noticeable advantage of air power in a guerrilla environment is its ability to transport a substantial number of troops and a large amount of material into a theatre of operation in a short space of time.[55] In most counterinsurgency operations, poor ground transportation networks, inhospitable terrain and rampant insecurity necessitate the use of air power to quickly deliver fuel, food, equipment, and security personnel to trouble spots.[56] It is important to examine how these advantages of air power allowed the Rhodesian Air Force to meet its tactical requirements during the Second Chimurenga.

The task of developing air power doctrine in the U.S. during the interwar period was led by the Army Air Corps, in Britain by the Royal Air Force (RAF), in Germany by the Luftwaffe, and in Japan by the Imperial Japanese Naval Air Force. These four organizations were fundamental in the growth of their respective national approaches to air power during the interwar period. Despite the fact that nearly every major combatant in World War I, whether victor or vanquished, had an air service as part of its fielded military forces on November 11, 1918, it was not employed as an important weapon of war. Air power had yet to be developed. Importance was primarily attached to land and maritime forces.[57] According to Liddell Hart, the appreciation of military applications of air power was a slow process and early air-power advocates had an uphill struggle for recognition. Prior to the war, General Foch revealed his disregard for airplanes when he said: "For the army the aeroplane is worthless."[58] Critics generally argue that air power did very little in World War I because it was predominantly used for reconnaissance missions. Nonetheless, it has to be categorically stated that reconnaissance was very important in the First World War for observing troops, railheads, aerodromes, camps, supply dumps and artillery. Thousands of soldiers fatally succumbed to the machine gun. It thus became important to locate and destroy, where possible, enemy weapons, before full-scale engagement. Added to that, due to the static nature of trench warfare, aircraft were the only means of gathering information beyond enemy trenches. Aircraft were essential for discovering where the enemy was based and what they were doing. However, aerial reconnaissance was a dangerous job. Taking photos of enemy positions required the pilot to fly straight and level so that the observer could take a series of overlapping images. This certainly made pilots easy targets. Traditionally, cavalry had served as the eyes of an army, scouting behind enemy lines and reporting to commanders about troop concentrations and movements. This became impossible in trench warfare. Armies had to develop new ways of looking behind the opposing front line. Reconnaissance was made perfect by airplane-mounted cameras. The improvement of photographic technology meant that the commanders were provided with quality information.[59]

Douhet was the leading exponent of the offensive use of aircraft through his theory called "command of the air."[60] He was convinced that the first task in the air offensive was to gain command of the air. He defined command of the air as being "in a position to prevent the enemy from flying while retaining the ability to fly oneself."[61] This effectively meant crippling the enemy's ability to fly. Command of the air was achieved through bombing those areas of strategic significance to the enemy. Douhet was convinced that command of the air could be gained within a few days of the outbreak of the war.[62] The theory formed the backbone of what Douhet referred to as strategic bombing and the bombing of civilian centers of population. On the significance of bombing civilians and strategic bombing in modern warfare, Giulio Douhet argued that an air force of 50 bombing units (500 planes), each capable of destroying a surface of 500 meters in diameter, could in a single flight completely destroy 50 enemy objectives, such as supply depots, industrial depots, industrial plants, warehouses, railroad centers, and population centers, to mention but a few.[63] The Rhodesian Air Force's command of the air enabled it to embark on long-range bombardments which destroyed, but not completely, guerrilla bases in neighboring countries such as Angola, Mozambique and Zambia. These raids were carried out after Rhodesia became frustrated with endless guerrilla infiltration.

Douhet's entire philosophy pointed to positioning the enemy air force and his aircraft production industry at the uppermost of the priority list among target systems to be attacked.[64] According to Douhet, command of the air does not mean such totality of control that even the enemy planes are prevented from flying. It is rather some kind of supremacy or predominance in the skies.[65] But it would make a lot of sense if the enemy is put into such a position that he finds it difficult to execute meaningful aerial actions.[66] Giulio Douhet was apparently frustrated with the outcome of the Great War, and as such he overlooked the role that could be played by anti-air weapons, which had remained marginal in the prosecution of the war. When the Southern Rhodesian Air Force became one of the permanent units of the defense forces in 1951, its major duty in the air was artillery observation and transporting Very Important Persons. Although its use sharply contradicted what Douhet considered to be the significance of air power in modern warfare, it worked within the confines of the available resources. In addition, the principles of strategic bombing were not valid because the enemy during the war shunned conventional methods of war and did not own anything strategic.

Douhet undoubtedly had a lot of faith in the capabilities of air power in breaking deadlocks. For four years the soldiers remained stuck in the trenches with no decisive weapon to set them free. Through command of the air, Douhet believed that a nation would be able to protect its own territory from enemy aerial attack and even devastatingly thwart the operations of the enemy's land and sea operations, leading to the collapse of the physical and moral resistance of the people.[67] To this end, he argued: "To conquer the command of the air means victory; to be beaten in the air means defeat and acceptance of whatever terms the enemy may be pleased to impose."[68] Command of the air was primarily achieved through strategic bombing, that is, destroying all airplanes of the enemy either in air combat or at their bases and airports, or in their production centers. Douhet discredited the army and the navy in carrying out this important task.[69] Giulio Douhet, however, emphasized that the best method was not to seek the enemy's airplanes out in the air, but to destroy his airports, supply bases, and centers of production. Strategic bombing therefore lies at the heart of the strategic doctrine of command of the air. Scholars, students and enthusiasts of air power cannot therefore overlook the contributions of Douhet because he laid the basis for the use of air power in military engagements.

Besides, air power today plays a significant role in conflict and peaceful times. It plays an invaluable role in civilian emergency services such as rescuing accident and flood victims. The offensive nature of aircraft in warfare could be exemplified by American air strikes in the Gulf War, Afghanistan, Syria and Iraq; Israeli air strikes against Egypt, Gaza and Syria; and the European Union bombardment of Libya. Israel's command of the air in the Middle East region could be demonstrated by her endless air strikes against Gaza. The 50-day (July–August 2014) conflict between Israel and Hamas killed more than 2,100 Palestinians, 64 Israeli soldiers, and five Israeli civilians. Israeli air strikes destroyed more than 17,000 homes, 360 factories and 42,000 acres of farmland. More than 100,000 Gazans were displaced from their homes. The cost of rebuilding all this was estimated to be above $8 billion, three times more than the last conflict between Israel and Gaza in 2008.[70] An Israeli air strike on a government-held village on the Syrian side of the Golan Heights cease-fire line killed five pro-regime forces in July 2015. Israel seized 1,200 square kilometers (460 square miles) of the Golan Heights from neighboring Syria in the 1967 Six-Day War.[71] In March 2015, Saudi Arabia–led coalition jets flew over Sanaa, Yemeni's capital. In Douhetian strategic bombing style, the jets dropped bombs on the international airport, which housed the country's main air force base.[72] Saudi jets also bombed key military installations in and around Sanaa and other cities occupied by Iran-backed Shia Muslim rebels known as the Houthis.[73]

The Theory of Bombing Civilian Centers of Population

The proponents of attacking civilian targets to achieve political and military objectives were Giulio Douhet and Hugh Trenchard. To support his argument for bombing civilians, Douhet argued: "Mercifully, the decision will be quick in this kind of war, since the decisive blows will be directed at civilians, that element of the countries at war least likely to sustain them."[74] Douhet believed that a nation should be prepared at the onset to launch massive bombardments against the enemy centers of population, government and industry. It was necessary to hit first and hard to shatter enemy civilian morale, leaving the enemy government with no option but to sue for peace.[75] Douhet's theory of bombing civilian centers of population was based on the premise that a demoralized population would rise up and force the government to opt for peace. He predicted that the people would become quickly demoralized by bombardments. In the years leading up to World War II, Japan became the first country to assault civilians from the air. Japanese warplanes bombed a worker district in Shanghai (China) in 1932. The incident produced worldwide outrage. Nonetheless, the protests did not halt Japan from bombing civilian areas of other Chinese cities. In 1935, Italian dictator Benito Mussolini ordered an attack on the mainly defenseless east African country of Ethiopia. This was purely an act of revenge for the defeat suffered by the European country at the Battle of Adowa (Adwa) on March 1, 1896, at the hands of an African ruler called King Menelik. When Mussolini's poison gas and warplanes struck the capital city, causing many civilian casualties, the world again condemned the slaughter of innocent people. Victory was concluded in 1936. In 1937, German bombers and other warplanes bombed Guernica, a town of about 7,000 persons in northern Spain.⁷⁶ This was during the Spanish Civil War, which commenced in 1936. The Spanish Republic was battling rebels led by Spanish General Francisco Franco. Hitler sent a special air force unit to Spain to aid Franco and to test new military aircraft and bombing tactics. German pilots deliberately ignored a small munitions factory and other possible military targets. They aimed their explosive and incendiary bombs into the heart of the city. A squadron of experimental aircraft dropped the first bombs on the plaza in front of the railroad station filled with war refugees.

More attacks on civilian centers continued in World War II. In May 1940, the Nazis invaded the Netherlands on their way to France. Despite the fact that the Dutch defenders were easily conquered, the Germans still bombed the center of Rotterdam with explosive and fire bombs, slaughtering tens of thousands. From fall 1940 through spring 1941, Hitler's air force struck London and other English cities with frightening night bombing raids. The bombing of London, the main target of German planes, cost the lives of 30,000 people. British Prime Minister Winston Churchill was personally against the bombing of civilians in war. He avoided bombing Berlin until German bombs fell for the first time on central London on May 24, 1940. Unable to defeat the RAF and so clear the way for invading England, Germany undertook the September "blitz" against the population of London. The two-month campaign killed 14,000 civilians, and seriously wounded another 20,000, and killed only 300 British soldiers. After this, Churchill permitted British bombers over Germany to drop their weaponry on any appropriate target if they failed to locate the objective they had been assigned to attack.⁷⁷ Winston Churchill broadcast in 1941 that the Royal Air Force was making "the German people taste and gulp each month a sharper dose of the miseries they have showered upon mankind."⁷⁸ The minutes of Lord Cherwell in 1942 specified working-class residential areas as prime targets. Lord Cherwell was confident that it was practical to render a third of the German population homeless by 1943.⁷⁹

In February 1942, the British discarded their "precision bombing" strategy. For the rest of the war, they concentrated on the systematic widespread destruction of German cities by RAF nighttime air raids, a strategy called "area bombing." The clearest demonstration of the destructiveness of British area bombing occurred in 1943 during three night raids on Hamburg, Germany. On the second night of bombing, something "unanticipated" occurred. The fire bombs dropped by 731 RAF bombers started "thousands" of fires. They merged to create a huge firestorm, sucking up oxygen and generating hurricane-force winds. Many who did not burn to death were asphyxiated in underground bomb shelters. The firestorm killed more than 40,000 people in one night. Following German rocket attacks against London late in 1945, almost 800 RAF bombers bombed Dresden, a center of German art, architecture, and culture. The city had been untouched by previous Allied bombing raids.[80] On August 6, 1945, one B-29 dropped an atomic bomb on Hiroshima, creating a firestorm that wiped out 70 percent of the city and killed 70,000 Japanese. The atomic bomb attack on Nagasaki three days later was somewhat "less destructive" due to the geographical features of the city. The American air force also undertook strategic bombing campaigns that crushed and burned numerous German and Japanese cities. The Allied area bombing of civilians played a significant role in undermining the will of the German and Japanese people to continue the war. But contrary to the predictions of military strategists before the war, this did not happen swiftly. For a long time, the bombing of German and Japanese civilians only stiffened their resolve to fight on. They wanted to surrender only after their countries lay in ruins, hundreds of thousands had perished, and all hope of victory was lost. The Second World War and other wars before and after it demonstrated that civilians are deliberately targeted in conflict.

The Battle of Britain in 1940 and subsequent counteroffensives on Germany proved Douhet wrong in terms of the results that could be achieved by continuous assault on civilian targets. In 1940, the British authorities feared that the German bombing of British cities during the blitz would lead to mass panic and a collapse of civilian morale. The effect, however, was to harden British attitudes to civilian casualties. The German Air Force attacks on Britain, instead of breaking the public's spirit, rather invigorated their resistance against the Germans who slaughtered the civilians.[81] Air Chief Marshal Arthur Harris, the head of Bomber Command, threatened to bomb Berlin until "the heart of Nazi German ceases to beat."[82] Nevertheless, even when the tide of war turned against the Axis in 1943, the German people continued to give their support to the Nazi regime. The constant bombing of German cities, the threat of invasion from the Soviet Union, and the Allied demand for "unconditional surrender" actually seemed to stiffen the resolve of the people.[83]

Civilians found themselves almost as much on the "front line" in the bombed cities of Britain as had the Belgian or French refugees crowding the roads in front of Hitler's invading armies.[84] On May 30, 1943, the German communications and industrial centers were hit by air attack. The Ruhr was bombed because it was the center of steel production. Many German cities were left in ruins, though later evidence suggested that neither morale nor production suffered as drastically as was expected. As London showed under repeated bombardment, civilian morale could be stiffened rather than broken by "savagery."[85] Douhet's theories as articulated in *The Command of the Air* captivated the interests of strategists and were applied in their entirety during World War II and other wars thereafter. As a result of the influence of Trenchard, Mitchell and

Douhet, Anglo-American air power doctrine was molded around three basic tenets: strategic bombing was a war-winning, decisive strategy; the bomber would always get through, meaning that there was no defense against airplanes; and only an independent air force commanded by airmen could implement the strategy.[86] These theories of air power are vital in assessing the extent to which the Rhodesian Air Force benefited in developing its air power doctrine. Strategic doctrine pertaining to the use of air power in warfare was, in some way, applicable to the RhAF context, thereby justifying the relevance of the theories promulgated by Douhet, Trenchard and Mitchell, amongst other theorists. The air power doctrine disseminated by these theorists captivated the attention of military strategists throughout the world, and Southern Rhodesia was no exception.

In 1947, Lord Tedder, Marshal of the Royal Air Force, asserted that the Second World War (1939–1945) had proved that air power was the dominant factor in the modern world and would remain the leading factor as long as power determines the fate of nations.[87] Air power proved invaluable to Allied success in World War II. Air power theorists generally advocated for an independent air force that would not be subordinate to the army or navy. There was also emphasis on strategic bombing and attack on the civilian centers of population.[88] These theories were developed during the interwar years when air power was still in its formative stages. The likes of Trenchard, Douhet and Mitchell were theorists and advocates of military aviation (and often of civilian aviation as well), engaged not only in seeking to understand air power but also in trying to generate interest and investment in it in spite of resource shortages and organizational resistance from powerful army and naval traditionalists.[89] After World War I, aircraft were no longer for the sole use of the army. Their use stretched to targeting areas deep behind enemy lines and establishing independent operations of their own.[90] Britain became the first country to be subjected to strategic bombardment by cruise and ballistic missiles (the German V-1 and V-2). Aerial interdiction and close air support played a central role in the German blitzkrieg and in the subsequent Allied counteroffensives.[91] World War II provided far-reaching insights into the future of air power, especially with reference to psychological warfare through the bombing of cities and strategic bombing through the destruction of ports, oil plants, manufacturing industries and the centers of communication.

Although air power was born in World War I, it came of age in the conflagration of World War II. While air power can operate independently, history suggests that independent air operations, while often contributing a great deal to the conduct of a particular campaign, do not have the same effectiveness as when they are synergized with land and/or maritime forces.[92] Air power has been of critical importance when used alongside both armies and navies almost from the outset of the creation of mechanized warfare. One of the keys to German success in the early part of World War II was from the close integration of air and land assets.[93] Soviet theorist Lapchinsky pointed out the importance of strategic bombing in the mid–1920s. He did not dwell on Douhet's thesis of a strategic bomber as the be-all and end-all in determining the outcome of war. On the contrary, Lapchinsky saw aviation as an integral part of the combined arms of the country.[94] Although military technology has given air power an edge over other weapons, it is imperative to note that air superiority can be countered by anti-air weapons and radar systems. The end of World War II marked the beginning of the nuclear revolution. Air power was central to this development, being the delivery means for the "absolute weapon."[95]

Conclusion

The fact that Britain became the first country to have an independent air force reveals the importance attached to military aviation in that country. This implied that future projects that required the training of airmen were fully appreciated and supported. Rhodesia, now Zimbabwe, benefited from aeronautical developments in Great Britain mainly because the British Air Ministry valued the role of military aviation. The training of British personnel in the colony inevitably meant that Rhodesia would certainly benefit, and this happened in 1939 through the Rhodesia Air Training Group.

3
The Establishment of the Rhodesian Air Force

Introduction

The aim of this chapter is to investigate the factors which led to the establishment of the Rhodesian Air Force (RhAF). It is a fact that Southern Rhodesia benefited from aeronautical developments in Great Britain through the extension of the Empire Air Training Scheme (EATS) to the colony in 1939. Under the guidance of the Marshal of the Royal Air Force, Hugh Trenchard, Britain emerged as a military giant. An indication of this progress was the development of military aviation, a weapon whose applicability in warfare had received strong criticism from the political and military leadership of the time.[1] The study assesses how Southern Rhodesia benefited militarily as a result of the revolutionary changes in the air power doctrine in Britain. The outbreak of the Second World War in 1939 was a major turning point in the development of military aviation in Southern Rhodesia. Aeronautical developments before the arrival of the Rhodesia Air Training Group were directed towards civil aviation and very little was done to promote military aviation. Developments in civil aviation were possible because it was less expensive to establish and maintain, whereas military aviation involved huge operational costs. Overall, the chapter examines the role of factors such as Imperial defense, permanent scheme, climatic conditions and economic considerations in determining the establishment of the air training scheme in 1940.

The Composition of the Rhodesian Defence Forces and the "Neglect" of Air Power

When the British South African Company (BSAC) led by Cecil John Rhodes was granted the charter in 1889, the company was given authority to raise and equip a police force of its own. As a result, the British South Africa Police (BSAP) came into being to maintain law and order in the newly occupied territory.² The BSAP accompanied the Pioneer Column and was always considered a military force in addition to civil roles it performed.³ The police, originally composed of five corps, were used to guard the most important points within and to the north of the colony during World War II.⁴ After the formation of the Responsible Government in Southern Rhodesia in 1923, the government envisaged a highly trained and reliable standing army that would take up the responsibility of defending the colony and complement the efforts of the police force. This later proved pivotal in shaping the defense policy of the colony, but the possibilities of air power as a military weapon was neither embryonic nor envisaged.

The era of the Responsible Government in 1923 ushered in tremendous benefits to the Rhodesian military system. The First Chimurenga/Umvukela of 1896–97 still lingered in the minds of the settler regime. During the First Chimurenga, about 450 European men, women and children were killed, meaning ten percent of the white population had been slain.⁵ This therefore called for military preparedness in case of emergency. When presenting the Defence Bill to Cabinet in 1926, the Minister of Defence, Robert James Hudson, argued: "I do not think even the most rabid critic or opponent of this Bill has ever denied that we must have some system of defence, and that it would be folly and madness for us to disarm our police and rifle companies and discard all arms or military preparations."⁶ Undeniably, it became urgent for the white population to be generally prepared in terms of training so that men would always be ready when needed. Hudson further contended: "Rhodesia learned it in 1896, and it was a costly lesson, and that is why it is so essential … to provide for emergencies which may arise in this country, that you must have this body of young men in practically continuous training, as is provided in the Bill, for over five years."⁷ The bill had a provision rendering all male able-bodied adults up to the age of 60 years liable for performing service in time of war.⁸ One major issue that needed utmost attention was the reinforcement of the police force, which was regarded as comparatively small for defense purposes. Accordingly, a force which could be fielded with maximum mobility was necessary.

Before the Defence Act came into being, the Southern Rhodesian Defence Forces (SRDF) consisted of a permanent force and a volunteer force, of which the BSAP was the only permanent force. The volunteer force was composed of squads in certain centers designed to form the framework of units which could take to the field in an emergency in cooperation with the permanent force.⁹ The organization was considered unsuccessful, as men with military experience were not joining. It also consisted of rifle companies formed throughout the country and primarily responsible for the defense of the areas in which they were situated.[10] In view of the absence of a genuine defense force, the Rhodesian Parliament passed the Defence Act in 1926 to bring in a moderate form of compulsory peace training for citizens aged between 19 and 22 years for the purpose of establishing a defense force, consisting of permanent and territorial elements, plus reserves as necessary.[11] The Defence Act of 1926 came into effect on January 1, 1927, the first step being the registration of citizens between the ages of 19 and 22.[12] A total of 1,553 citizens were registered during the year. Of this number, 1,239, or about 80 percent, volunteered for service in 1927, the highest percentage of volunteers being at Umtali (Mutare).[13] Of those who registered, 91 percent were fit, four percent permanently unfit and five percent temporarily unfit.[14]

The Defence Act provided for the establishment of the permanent force, the territorial active force, the territorial reserve force and the general reserve. The permanent force consisted of the BSAP and certain staff of the defense force.[15] The territorial active force was made up of young citizens between the ages of 19 and 22 who were drawn from certain prescribed areas or towns in which they could be brought together for training. In addition, their number was laid down from time to time and could be taken in the first instance as 450, which included certain men who were not liable by age, but joined voluntarily.[16] These men became the uniformed active force and they were at liberty to take to the field with or without the permanent force. The territorial reserve force had three categories: (a) men who were trained in the territorial active force and who were elected to remain in the reserve up to the age of 45, (b) men who were liable for, but not trained in the territorial active force, and those who elected to remain in the reserve up to the age of 45, and (c) former members of the Southern Rhodesian Volunteers and others over the age of 22, who volunteered to serve in the reserve.[17] There was also the general reserve, which consisted of citizens up to the age of 60, who were not members of any other part of the defense force.[18]

The Defence Act entitled every adult European male citizen to render personal service in time of war. The defense force was strictly confined to Europeans who made up the permanent staff of some 12 officers and 54 other ranks, engaging in training, and the territorial units, in which every male European served from the age of 19 up to the age of 23.[19] The defense system of Southern Rhodesia was admired by neighboring territories which had not yet reached the same feat. K.E.W. Harris, MP for Ndola Electoral Area, urged Zambia to emulate Southern Rhodesia in overhauling its defense system when he said: "Let us look at our nearest neighbours, Southern Rhodesia, the state which we all hope will one day be linked with ours, and see what they have done in connection with defence. They have followed, as has every British Dominion, the British Government, and have today a sound, up-to-date, and excellent system of defence."[20]

The Responsible Government made the defense of the colony a top priority. Before the era of the Responsible Government the BSAP made up the first line of defense, mainly because of the conservative military policy of the BSAC and limited financial resources. Although the Responsible Government deliberated on the expansion of the armed forces, there was virtually no consideration to create an air unit in the colony. This could be attributed to multiple reasons, chief among them being the huge financial commitments involved in military aviation.

The Impact of Civil Aviation on the Development of Military Aviation in Southern Rhodesia

The Southern Rhodesian Government promoted civil aviation before the establishment of the RATG in 1940. A Salisbury (Harare) resident and member of the Aeronautical Society of Great Britain called C.F. Webb revealed in an article written in 1912 the general backwardness of aviation in the colony in a paper titled "The Aeroplane in Rhodesia—Its Practical Utility."[21] Webb indicated that some portions of Rhodesia were basically unknown and other parts imperfectly surveyed. Moreover, he observed that huge tracts of the country could now be surveyed and rivers accurately mapped in one-tenth the time and at less cost than before aerial surveying was available.[22] Despite lagging behind in terms of aviation technology, the colony still managed to attract aviation into the country. In a spectacular event, a Vickers Vimy aircraft named *Silver Queen* landed at the Bulawayo Race Course on March 5, 1920, and brought aviation to Southern Rhodesia for the first time. The pilots of the historic flight were Sir Pierre van Ryneveld and Sir Quintin Brand from England.[23] Captain Douglas Mail and Aston Redrup formed the Rhodesian Aviation Syndicate in August 1927 in Bulawayo. A year later the Aircraft Operating Company moved its main base from Northern Rhodesia to Bulawayo.[24] One pilot was a member of the territorial force with a Moth machine in 1928. Landing grounds had been established at Salisbury, Bulawayo, Gwelo and other selected sites at Umtali, Gatooma and Que Que.[25]

The Aviation Act of 1929 required the licensing of all aircraft, pilots and engineers in the colony. Capt. Roxburgh-Smith became the first to pass the tests with a South African "B" pilot's license number 1.[26] In the same year, the government introduced a pilot training scheme under which it undertook to grant £750 per annum to each flying club on condition that five initial pilots were trained to "A" license.[27] A further £50 was paid for each pilot trained and a flying grant of £30 to each pilot who obtained an "A" license in the previous year, while the balance was given to the club as a grant in aid.[28] The government scheme for training pilots was at the time only confined to Salisbury. Candidates desiring to obtain an "A" license were not privileged to use government funds for the purpose but instead they were required to train as military pilots and the period of training was to be a longer one. To qualify as a military pilot one had to stay in Salisbury until the course of training was finished.[29] The Aircraft Operating Company had two airplanes, while the Rhodesian Aviation Syndicate and Salisbury Light Aeroplane Club had a single airplane each. There were two privately owned aircraft.[30] Air transport services in Southern Rhodesia were provided by the Central African Airways Corporation, which was the sole international air transport organization in British Central Africa.[31]

The Rhodesian Aviation Syndicate in Bulawayo did much of the flying to the Victoria Falls during the tourist season.[32] The company was later incorporated into a new company, the Rhodesia Aviation Company, which was established by local and foreign capital in 1929.[33] The significant roles of aircraft in Southern Rhodesia before RATG were aerial photographing, as was required by different government departments, and transporting government officials. An Air Survey Conference hosted by the Surveyor General on August 12, 1939, unanimously agreed that photographic aerial surveys had a wide application in many technical branches of the service, and recommended that immediate steps be taken in completing the work in collaboration with the aerial arm of the Department of Defence.[34]

The Department of Civil Aviation, formed in 1930, was administered by the Department of Defence until 1936. The duties of the Director of Civil Aviation were undertaken by Commandant Territorial Forces, Colonel Parson. It was absorbed by the RATG in 1940.[35] Before the air unit was formed, Southern Rhodesia relied on airmen from private and commercial aircraft in the colony for aviation duties. Local pilots were enrolled in the Air Section of the Reserve of Officers.[36] The local aviation company was granted an annual subsidy by the government in return for which bomb racks were provided for the machines.[37] The Beit Trustees allocated a total of £50,000 on February 25, 1932, to be used between 1933 and 1934 for the purpose of providing improved aeronautical facilities in the Rhodesias.[38] A representative of the Air Ministry visited Rhodesia to advise the Beit Trustees on the best way of spending the grant. As recommended by the report, Southern Rhodesia was allotted £11,150 for 1933. The grant was mainly to improve the Cape-Cairo Air Route. Details on how the grant was spent are shown below:

Table 3.1: Distribution of Beit Trustees Grant in 1933

Landing grounds on mail route	£5,000
Wireless	2,500
Meteorology	1,000
Telephone	1,600
Truck	750
Total	**£10,850**
Victoria Falls landing ground	300
Grand total	**£11,150**[39]

Towards the later part of 1933, a company called the Rhodesian and Nyasaland Airways (RANA) Ltd. took over the assets of the Rhodesian Aviation Company.[40] RANA carried out several survey flights on behalf of the Government Veterinary Department. It also investigated the foot-and-mouth disease on the borders of the territory and carried out some flights for the Government Forestry Department. Experiments in dusting locust swarms from aircraft were carried out by planes lent by Imperial Airways, and the Union Government also co-operated.[41]

The interest to initiate an air training scheme in 1939 was also motivated but not driven by the developments made by the Colony in constructing aerodromes. The new government landing grounds at Iwa, Tuli, Chipinga and Zawi had been completed in 1933 and enlargements effected at Sengezani, Lana, Gatooma and Que Que. Added to that, drainage schemes were carried out at Salisbury, Que Que and Gwelo.[42] Private landing grounds had been built during the year, the more important being Nuanetsi, Bindura, Glass Block, Lochard, Sherwood Starr, Wiltshire Estate and the Seigneury Mine.[43] There were a total of 50 aerodromes and landing grounds in 1934, developed as 3 aerodromes, 27 public landing grounds and 20 private landing grounds.[44] Five aircraft were placed on the Southern Rhodesian register during the year and commercial aviation was carried out by Imperial Airways, RANA and Lonrho.[45] Approximately £40,000 was spent in Southern Rhodesia as a direct result of civil aviation by 1934.[46] There existed five emergency landing grounds between Salisbury and Chileka in Malawi by 1943.[47]

Table 3.2: Strength of Qualified Personnel in Civil Aviation in 1932

Class	Issued	Renewed
Pilots Class "A"	nil	2
Pilots Class "B"	nil	6
Ground Engineers	1	nil[48]

The Inspection Department issued certificates of airworthiness to aircraft.[49] The preceding evidence shows that Southern Rhodesia made some great strides towards the development of the civil aviation industry. These developments were crucial in stimulating the interest of investors, the biggest one being the RATG, which later shaped the development of military aviation in the colony. Civil aviation was essentially harnessed by the government to be part of the defense forces in times of emergency. Even in World War II, civil aviation was an important component of the RATG. This was revealed by Commander Military Forces, Brigadier Garlake, when he said: "The [Air] Unit's very existence depended therefore on the assistance of Central African Airways and the RAF, which was always forthcoming and is gratefully acknowledged."[50]

The Role Played by the Air Ministry in the Development of the Colony's Air Force

It is evident that the RATG cemented the already cordial relations between the RAF and the Southern Rhodesian Defence Forces. The RAF expressed inclination towards sharing knowledge in aeronautical activities with Southern Rhodesia by periodically visiting the colony before the outbreak of the Second World War. The cordial relations explain why the EATS was "unconditionally" accepted by Southern Rhodesia and why the RAF was willing to use the colony as an air training base. Most significant to the development of military aviation in the colony was the fact that the exchange of knowledge between the RAF and the SRDF took place long before Southern Rhodesia had a functional air unit. Five RAF Fairey Gordons of No. 6 Bomber Squadron visited the territory between April 21 and May 17, 1933, and carried out a series of exercises with the permanent and active forces in Bulawayo and Salisbury.[51] Several smaller aerodromes and landing grounds were visited throughout the colony and many prominent citizens were taken for more or less short flights.[52] By this time the facilities for learning to fly in Salisbury were governed by the De Havilland Aircraft Company. The company was registered on April 30, 1934, with a nominal capital of £5,000, and had two fully qualified pilots who were also ground engineers.[53] The company wanted to promote aviation by providing full facilities for training pupils in flying, selling flying machines, repairing flying machines and engines, and general maintenance.[54]

Six RAF machines, consisting of two Vickers Victoria and four Fairey Gordons, passed through Bulawayo and Salisbury to Nyasaland on January 7 and 8, 1934.[55] Air Vice-Marshal (AVM) Newall was in command of the combined flights and Brigadier Norman, Inspector General King's African Rifles, was a passenger.[56] Four Vickers Victorias of No. 216 (BT) Squadron and five Fairey III F's of No. 45 (B) Squadron visited the territory on March 5 and 6, 1934, and again on the homeward route from Pretoria to Cairo, from March 26 to 31.[57] Troop carrying and other exercises were carried out in conjunction with the permanent and territorial forces in Salisbury and Bulawayo. On March 28 a public bombing display was given by 45 Squadron.[58] Prior to the arrival of Group Captain Harris in March 1936, Huggins had been in communication with the Secretary of Air Ministry with regards to the possibility of aircraft being supplied to the Southern Rhodesian government at a nominal figure. Harris alerted the Air Ministry on March 18, 1936, that the whole question about the organization of the Rhodesian air unit relied on the availability at scrap price of ex-RAF aircraft.[59] Without such assistance it was conceived that the local government would not afford air training.[60] The air unit started on some old planes and then got some Spitfires at a cheap price from the Air Ministry. By then they were almost out of date, although they were good for training purposes.[61] Arthur Harris was a proponent of new views about using air power to control the empire. As such, the RAF was dispatched to help put down insurgencies in British Somaliland and Iraq during the 1920s. He also worked hard for the development of aviation in Southern Rhodesia, partly because he had lived in the colony from 1910 to 1915. At the age of 17, in 1910, Harris immigrated to Southern Rhodesia, but he returned to England in 1915 to fight in the European theatre of the First World War.

Southern Rhodesia's request for used aircraft was successful: six Hawker Hart aircraft were received from the RAF in 1937 after the unit moved to Cranborne military air field.[62] The years from 1936 to 1939 were crucial in the development of Southern Rhodesia's air unit. The development of military aviation in Southern Rhodesia precisely started in 1936 when air sections of the staff corps and territorial force were established. At that time, six young men were sent to the RAF Apprentice in Halton.[63] The first air unit in Southern Rhodesia had a composition of two RAF officers and twelve other ranks, with ten aircraft, four Audux and six Hart. The air unit arrived in Rhodesia on August 28, 1939, and trained local territorial personnel on the understanding that in the event of an armed conflict, Rhodesia would send a unit to Kenya to assist the RAF.[64]

The air unit became the Southern Rhodesian Air Force (SRAF) in 1939 and all personnel were absorbed into the RAF.[65] The policy of the British government was to train pilots up to the RAF standard, selected officers from the permanent staff and the territorial units.[66] With effect from May 6, 1949, all Southern Rhodesia Staff Corps air unit pilots began to wear the SRAF flying badge.[67] It is clear that Southern Rhodesia was determined to improve her military capabilities beyond the BSAP and territorial units. Meredith replaced Cloete in 1939 and took advantage of the EATS to expedite air training in the colony. The colony could well have been reluctant, taking cognizance of the huge expenses involved, to accept the EATS, but the program was well conceived beyond World War II through the inheritance of infrastructure and expertise for similar future projects. The table below shows the applicants already posted to RATG as of December 22, 1939:

Table 3.3: RATG Statistics

	Pilots	Air Gunners	Flying Instructors	Total
Salisbury	21	12	5	38
Bulawayo	10	5	-	15
Gwelo	1	-	-	1
Que	2	-	-	2
Umtali	2	-	-	2
Gatooma	1	-	-	1
Districts	5	-	-	6
Total				65[68]

From 1936 to 1939, the air unit did not see major structural changes but remained a small force, as shown below:

Table 3.4: Estimates of Expenditure—Air Unit

Officials 1936	Amount (£)	Posts	Amount (£)	Officials 1937–1938
1	**Headquarters Staff** 1,290			
1	900	Staff Officer-Air Services	900	1
		Clerks-Corporals: £260	390	2
	Instructional Staff 2,320			
5	1,160	Flight Lt.	700	1
		Flying officer	550	1
		Flight Sergeant	390	1
		Sgts., Filters, Laborers	680	2
6	125	Guards & laborers	252[69]	

The table above highlights the air unit headquarters (HQ) staff compliment from 1936 to 1937 and 1938. The years 1937 and 1938 saw a slight increase in the staff working for the unit; for example, the Air Ministry Headquarters staff added two more clerks, while the instructional staff remained unchanged. The staff officer was the Director of Civil Aviation, while the five instructional officers were seconded from RAF. The sum £1,160 refers to the money spent in 1936 for the remuneration of the instructional staff. The Africans occupied the lowest strata in the unit. They were employed as guards and constituted the general labor force.

Analyzing the Establishment of Southern Rhodesia's Air Training Scheme in 1940

The establishment and development of the Rhodesian Air Force experienced a major turning point following the creation of the air training scheme in 1940. It is important to note that the outbreak of the Second World War in 1939 stands out as the key reason for the setting up of air training facilities in the colony. Nonetheless, it is important to further investigate why Southern Rhodesia agreed to host this project and why the Air Ministry saw the colony as a suitable destination for this important scheme. The establishment of an air training scheme offered long-term strategic and tactical advantages to the Rhodesian military system. Although imperial defense occupied the supremacy of the air training scheme, it was genuinely prestigious and strategic to have an independent and robust air force in the colony. The Rhodesians envisaged a formidable defense system autonomous of Great Britain, to be used against unforeseeable foes. Moreover, the training of RAF personnel in the colony was facilitated by favorable climatic conditions. A lot of hours were spent on air training, and this suited well with British plans to sustain the strained war fronts. Besides, the reduced costs of air training in Southern Rhodesia were facilitated by cheap labor. Africans played an important role in the success of air training in Southern Rhodesia through the supply of labor and cash donations obtained from wage labor. As a result, local resources lessened Britain's and Rhodesia's burden for air training in the colony. In addition, Rhodesia agreed to bear part of the financial burden brought by air training.

In the early days prior to the Second World War, before RAF personnel were drafted to the command structures, a few Rhodesians—service and civilians—operated from a moderate-sized house in Montagu Avenue, and it was on this site that the real birth of the RATG Headquarters took place.[70] The year 1940 saw the establishment of an air training scheme which witnessed the influx in great numbers of ground staff, both officers and other ranks, and the arrival of the first pupils from England. Eleven clerks were drafted specifically from the United Kingdom to Southern Rhodesia to introduce the RAF system of administration to the HQ of the Training Command.[71] From the day the pupils arrived in Southern Rhodesia, the colony was poised to make its greatest contribution to imperial defense.

Imperial Defense

Although the establishment of the air training scheme enhanced the Colony's military power, imperial defense was a genuine cause. The friendship between Southern Rhodesia and Britain dated back to 1890, when the Pioneer Column set out from Macloutsie and made its way to the territory which lay north of the Limpopo River.[72] According to Major Wadman, the Rhodesians were on active service in three continents because Britain was at war.[73] The commitment to imperial defense was reiterated by the then Minister of Justice, Defence and Air, Robert Tredgold, when he stated: "It would be a substantial scheme [RATG], but I would emphasise that the benefit is purely incidental. The scheme was evolved primarily as a contribution to the war effort of the Empire at war, and that we shall benefit is fortunate but only secondary."[74] There existed an emotional affair between the Rhodesians and Britons which in turn influenced the colony to mobilize resources for the benefit of the mother country. It therefore became "mandatory" for the colony to come to the defense of imperial interests regardless of the costs.

At the outbreak of the Second World War, a new portfolio of Ministry of Air was created. Ernest Guest was appointed Rhodesia's first Minister of Air, mainly responsible for the conduct of the RATG.[75] The air training scheme in Southern Rhodesia was rapid, as highlighted on November 16, 1940, by O'Keeffe, the High Commissioner for Southern Rhodesia in London: "The fact that they [pilots] were trained within six months of the establishment of the air training scheme in Southern Rhodesia is a tribute to the rapidity with which the scheme was launched here."[76] Early on, when delivering an address at the first Informal War-time Meeting of the Royal African Society in London on May 1, 1940, O'Keeffe stressed that one of the first laws passed by Southern Rhodesia after the formation of the Responsible Government was for the compulsory military training of the youths, who were so keen to serve. As a consequence, when the country was called to participate in September 1939, they were able to supply at once large numbers of trained men for immediate active service: "I am not going to give actual figures, but we supplied within a few days of the outbreak of war, a very large number of highly-trained officers and N.C.O.s to no less than nine Colonies in Africa. In addition, we had a highly-trained mobile column ready to march, accompanied by no less than 670 motor lorries (this will give you some idea of the number of men), and, as a matter of fact, our Air Force was 1,000 miles from Southern Rhodesia on the day war was declared; so we were the first in the whole Empire to be on active service." Added to that, O'Keeffe highlighted that there were already a large number of Rhodesians on active service in England, both in the air and on the ground, and also in the Middle East, as well as in other Colonies:

> You will probably have seen in the Press something about the establishment in Rhodesia of Flying Training Schools, and it may interest you to have some particulars about the scheme, which is on similar lines to the schools now being organised in Canada and Australia, but not on the same enormous scale. It is proposed to have in all seven training centres—three Senior, three Elementary and one Observer. The Air Ministry personnel will amount to something like 4,000, and it is proposed to attract pupils not only from Southern Rhodesia, but from many parts of the Empire. It is a scheme partly financed by Southern Rhodesia and partly by the Imperial Government. I may perhaps say in passing, and I hope I won't shock you, that

our commitments for war purposes already amount to something like forty percent of our normal total revenue.[77]

Five Rhodesians were among the first party of RAF pilots trained in Southern Rhodesia under the EATS and were bound for active service. Moreover, the first pilots to be qualified in any of the joint training schemes in the Empire passed out of the training school near Salisbury on November 2, 1940.[78] The response of Southern Rhodesia reflected her wholehearted commitment to the success of air training for imperial defense. The resources were rapidly mobilized from all the corners of the country, which to an extent proved pivotal to Britain's victory in 1945. On the whole, it was an honor to come to the defense of the Empire.

On the "African front," Britain was under pressure from the Italian presence in Abyssinia, which threatened its interests in Kenya, Eritrea, Ethiopia and Egypt. A small RAF contingent in Nairobi had to leave to join the main forces in England. Rhodesia was expected to fill the vacuum in Nairobi.[79] The first unit to leave the Colony was the Southern Rhodesian air squadron, which at the outbreak of the war was patrolling the Abyssinian frontier.[80] The feats of the 237 Squadron in the Abyssinian and Eritrean campaigns, and the work of 266 Squadron which pioneered the Typhoon, were some of the remarkable exploits made by the Southern Rhodesian air unit during the war.[81] Six hundred Rhodesian troops were also drafted to west and east Africa.[82] On June 15, 1940, the RhAF attacked Agmachi, Kismayo and Jelib areas, causing damage to Italian military objectives.[83] Besides, the Rhodesian Squadron carried out valuable reconnaissance work and earned the high praise of the east African Command.[84] The RATG actually provided Southern Rhodesia with a realistic opportunity to take part in imperial defense.

In general, the outbreak of hostilities in 1939 demanded the massive mobilization of resources. Southern Rhodesia cooperated in the best possible ways to assist Britain. Bertram issued a circular in October 1939 requiring government departments to advise the Treasury (in terms of Treasury circular No. 16 of 1939) of extraordinary expenditure with which they were likely to be faced as a result of the war. Printing and stationery requirements (including rubber stamps and advertising) were dealt with by the government stationery office.[85] The office's war expenditure was as follows (all figures in pounds): advertisements required 2,500, printing and binding 2,000, stationery 500, special books 20 and subscriptions 30.[86]

Minister of Air Meredith headed a War Supplies Committee which was formed on July 3, 1940. The War Supplies Committee was initially formed to examine the resources of the colony for the manufacture of munitions and civil supplies with the object that its activities should be coordinated with those of the Technical Production Committees of the Union of South Africa.[87] The general production policy was, firstly, to assist the Union as far as possible, and thereafter to utilize the balance of the resources for the needs of the colony.[88] The War Supplies Committee was dissolved by government notice on December 5, 1941, and the Munitions Production Board was appointed in its place. A year later the Munitions Production Board was replaced by the Department of Supply. The major factors compelling these changes were mass production of practice bombs as an essential requirement of the RATG scheme, repair and manufacture to meet the increasing demands of the armed forces in the colony, and participation in the requirements of the Union for urgent Middle East spares.[89] A total of 2,000 pilots and 300 navigators were produced annually from 1941 to 1945. The manufacture of practice bombs was halted in August 1944 and all supplies for the RATG were drawn from the Union factory. The number of bombs produced in 1944 amounted to 34,940 while the total of all manufactured bombs was 281,580.[90] The assistance rendered to the Union served as a confirmation of Southern Rhodesia's commitment to ensure an uninterrupted supply of resources critical to the Union's effort in the Middle East, all for the benefit of Britain. Prime Minister Godfrey Huggins emphasized the importance attached by the colony to imperial defense when he said: "I should like to make our position in this conflict quite clear. Southern Rhodesia is at war with Germany because our King is at war, and further, as a self-governing Colony, of our own free will and accord, we are taking an active part in the war because we wish to take part in the crusade against paganism, lying and deceit, and because we wish to offer our resources, small though they may be, to help to restore international decency and to fight for the right of small nations to retain their independence."[91] Imperial defense was therefore one of Southern Rhodesia's critical priorities when she participated in the EATS, but long-term strategic objectives were already conceived.

Meredith, Air Officer Commanding (AOC) the RATG, visited Canada in May 1943 precisely to make a tour of the Royal Canadian Air Force (RCAF) training stations operating under the British Commonwealth Air Training Plan.[92] Meredith disclosed that the purpose of the visit was to see what Southern Rhodesians could learn from Canada since they were all training for the same purpose. Meredith confirmed the commitment of the colony to imperial defense when he said that the SRAF squadron was the first squadron to cross its own borders in World War II after they had left Rhodesia five days before the war started, crossing into Kenya.[93] Southern Rhodesia responded to the call to arms by the mother country and provided, proportionately to its population, more soldiers, sailors and airmen than any of the others.[94] Besides, the British government's decision to include Southern Rhodesia in the air training scheme completely changed the outlook of a country which, in parting with so many of its men to the war fronts, appeared to be destined to become one of the quiet backwaters of an Empire at war.[95]

The Air Ministry was disappointed by the lack of progress in Canada, thereby making air training in Southern Rhodesia a matter of urgency. At the same time, the British armament program that began in 1935 envisaged increasing the RAF to a level of parity with the new German Luftwaffe.[96] The Ministry argued that the Canadian scheme had been bogged down in apples because Canada had promised to meet its share of the expenses from the sale of apples.[97] In contrast, Meredith was encouraged by the Air Ministry to get whatever he wanted from the Southern Rhodesian government, to be settled later.[98] The Air Ministry showed great interest in having air training out of Britain. Canada was the initial choice and the scheme there was known as the Empire Air Training Scheme. The Ottawa Programme encompassed countries such as Canada, Australia, New Zealand and the UK. The plan was first announced in the House of Commons on December 10, 1939, and agreement was signed on December 17, 1939. Schools were set up in all the dominions while training was expected to produce no fewer than 20,000 pilots and 30,000 air crews a year, for all three dominions.[99] Besides Canada, Australia, New Zealand, South Africa and Southern Rhodesia, air training schemes were established in India, Ceylon, Malaya, Trinidad, Bermuda and Kenya. The three Southern Rhodesia squadrons of the RAF were accepted for service by the UK at the outbreak of the war.[100]

Imperial commitment was demonstrated in many ways. On the occasion of the birth of a son to Her Royal Highness, Princess Elizabeth, on November 18, 1948, Meredith sent a congratulatory message to Buckingham Palace: "The Air Officer Commanding, officers and airmen of the RATG, RAF with humble duty send their heartfelt congratulations on the birth of your son."[101] On June 2, 1953, a short ceremonial parade was held at each RATG station for the coronation of Queen Elizabeth II. The Royal salute was given on the occasion.[102] The Battle of Britain Commemoration Service was held in the Anglican Cathedral on September 16, 1951.[103] Commitment to imperial defense was also evident when twelve RRAF Vampires flew over Salisbury, Lusaka and Blantyre in September 1957 to celebrate the Battle of Britain.[104] All these commemorations were crucial in demonstrating the undisputed loyalty of Southern Rhodesia to imperial authority, and thus proved essential in reinforcing the warm relationship between Britain and her dominions and colonies. The most important characteristic of this relationship was military cooperation, which benefited both countries.

Rhodesian miners aided the war effort by purchasing training aircraft.[105] The Express Nut Oil and Soap Works Company of Salisbury offered the imperial government one hundred cases each containing eight gallons of Express cooking oil for use in the imperial war effort.[106] The Colony was the main source of chrome, essential to the production of many munitions. It was also one of the main sources of asbestos and other important minerals.[107] Donations to support the war effort were mobilized through the National War Fund. According to Major Waldman: "The Fund was established to provide an opportunity for rich and poor alike to contribute to the provision of comforts for those Rhodesian men fighting in World War II and all British and allied forces engaged on active service."[108]

An Aircraft Fund was one of the initiatives under the National War Fund which was launched to assist the purchase of training aircraft supplied to the colony under the EATS. The contribution was made directly to the British government and was remitted through the air force headquarters.[109] The Southern Rhodesia tobacco industry made contributions towards aircraft production, the initial contribution being a sum of £7,500 collected through the Southern Rhodesia Tobacco Industry Aeroplane and Munitions Fund.[110] In the first ten months of the war the government received £85,000 from private citizens.[111] On August 29, 1942, MacAllister Smith of the Inez Mine in Kadoma presented the government with a second check of £1,250 for the purchase of training aircraft under the EATS. The Rhodesia Angling Society donated £20 to provide comforts for Southern Rhodesia troops.[112] Africans "provided" two fighter aircraft, a Typhoon and a Spitfire.[113] The donations proved indispensable, especially at a time when Britain was strained by Germany's bombardments in engagements such as the Battle of Britain in 1940. The funds undeniably lessened Britain's war burden in sustaining the RATG. Some of the donations under the Aircraft Fund are listed below:

Table 3.5: Aircraft Fund Donations in Pounds

Mr. and Mrs. Milne (two planes)	2500 00
Mr. and Mrs. Barbour (one plane)	1250 00
"Slet" (one plane)	1250 00
Oxley and Company	250 00
Mr. and Mrs. Miller	150 00
Mr. and Mrs. Prior	100 00
The Mayor and Mayoress of Salisbury (Mr. and Mrs. McDonald)	50 00
Atlas Brick Works	50 00
Grieve and Gibbons	50 00
L.W. Bates	50 00
Mr. and Mrs. Godlonton	25 00
Mr. and Mrs. Rowland	25 00
Mr. and Mrs. John Dennis	25 00
Mrs. Clarke	5.5.0
W.W. Clarke	5.5.0[114]

The Impact of Climatic Conditions on Air Training in Southern Rhodesia

The British Air Ministry wanted countries with favorable climatic conditions where training centers could be established.[115] The suitability of Southern Rhodesia for air training was long admired by airmen who had visited the country before World War II. This was mainly because the air was "sharp and clear," and for seven months there was no rain to interrupt flying activities. Airmen knew that at least eleven months out of the twelve, the air was fit for flying.[116] Southern Rhodesia's climate was admirably suitable for all-year-round training and this made her a natural choice. During his visit to Canada in 1943, Meredith commended the suitability of air training in the colony by stressing: "It is a sub-tropical climate. During the summer, which is October to March, we have our own rainy season, but it is not severe enough to prevent flying training from carrying on. In the winter, nights are cold, but with no frost, and the days are bright. We are about 4,000 feet above sea level there."[117]

According to Sir Archibald Sinclair, Rhodesia's interest in the EATS was not mercenary, but it gave the people the greatest possible satisfaction that the RAF should have found such hospitable climatic conditions.[118] Air operations could be conducted at all times of the year, though visibility was impaired for short intervals owing to rainstorms, low flying scud and smoke from grass fire.[119] One cannot therefore rule out the importance of climatic conditions in the establishment of an air training scheme in Southern Rhodesia. Overall, climatic conditions in Southern Rhodesia permitted air training for longer periods.

Economic Considerations for Air Training in the Colony

The Southern Rhodesian government took advantage of the RATG to initiate military aviation in the colony, which in turn offset financial constraints which had jeopardized military aviation before. It required about £2 million less a year to train in Rhodesia than at home, thus the Air Ministry was more than eager to kick-start the project. The colony contributed towards the annual costs of upkeep, and provided the whole costs of RATG headquarters and the salaries of the school staff. The UK was responsible for the costs of technical equipment, gasoline and oil, and for the transportation and pay of trainee pilots.[120] The UK Air Ministry provided a big number of aircraft and ancillary equipment, as well as personnel to staff the schools. Planes were sent through the Cape, then assembled and flown to Southern Rhodesia. Over 2,000 men were trained every year, including 1,800 pilots, 240 observers and 340 gunners.[121]

The financial responsibility accepted by the Southern Rhodesian government as a contribution towards the allied war effort included the capital expenditure on land and buildings for the whole of the training scheme, including quarters and housing; the cost of all barracks equipment at air stations; the cost of RATG Headquarters; all pay and allowances for Rhodesian personnel serving in Rhodesia; makeup pay and family allowances for Rhodesians serving abroad; and a cash contribution of £800,000 per annum towards the operating cost of the air training scheme. All other costs, including the provision of aircraft, equipment, gasoline, oil, transport, and the pay and allowances of RAF personnel were met by the Air Ministry.[122]

Table 3.6: Costs of Air Training 1939–1946 (all figures entered in pounds)

1939–40	1940–1	1941–2	1942–3	1943–4	1944–5	1945–6
56,336	911,550	1,301,283	1,402,410	1,453,326	1,429,021	1,011,865[123]

The expenses incurred on air training from 1939 to 1946 demonstrate that each year the cost to train RAF personnel increased except towards the end of the war. This could be adequately explained on the basis of pressing war demands on the western, eastern, Pacific and other fronts during the Second World War. The total Southern Rhodesia government expenditure by September 30, 1940, was £812,077, whereas the Air Ministry liability was £77,808. The grand total expenditure by September 30, 1940, was therefore £889,885.[124] By October 31, 1940, the total Southern Rhodesia government expenditure was £980,033, whereas Air Ministry liability was £101,305. The grand total for Southern Rhodesia by October 31, 1940, was £1,101,338. A large sum of money was spent on pay and allowances.[125] According to Meredith, the Rhodesian government's total expenditure on RATG from 1939 to 1946 was £11,215,522.[126] The figures point out that the Southern Rhodesian government contributed immensely to the RATG and reduced Britain's financial obligations. At the end of the war, her contribution was invaluable because Britain managed to win her military objectives as a result of the financial assistance rendered by the colony.

The issue of cutting costs was very important for the success of the air training scheme in the colony. In the mechanical transport section of RATG, the aspect of reducing the costs was seriously valued. When requesting, or authorizing, the use of mechanical transport, and in the driving of vehicles, all ranks were required to pay strict attention to the saving of gasoline, oil and tires.[127] By June 1943, mechanical transport repair depots had been set up at Cranborne, Thornhill and Heany to provide for the needs of Salisbury, Gwelo and Bulawayo, respectively.[128] For journeys within the town area, bicycles were encouraged to be used, while journeys to towns were supposed to be kept down to a minimum and officers were encouraged to share transport. The aim was to save the mileage of vehicles and gasoline.[129]

The Minister of Mines, Public Works and Air, Colonel Lucas Guest, initiated the Air Force Housing Scheme to build houses for aircraft personnel for the three stations in Salisbury, Gwelo and Bulawayo in 1941.[130] Although the responsibility for air training rested with the UK and Southern Rhodesia, up to 1942 the pupils' accommodation was in a deplorable state. The Initial Training Wing based in Bulawayo used bed boards with no mattresses.[131] Pigpens were initially used for accommodation. Although they were condemned by the Prime Minister's office, it was decided that they should be used for accommodation purposes until new huts were built.[132] Moreover, it was initially proposed that the old government offices situated at the then Jameson Avenue and 3rd Street be used to house the Headquarters staff of the air force. However, the discussions held on February 1, 1940, between Prime Minister Godfrey Huggins, the Minister of Finance, and the Acting Minister of Defence concluded that the matter was supposed to be settled by the SRAF, Public Works Department and Treasury.[133] The proposal for spending approximately £8,000 on the old offices or "the stables" was abandoned as the offices were going to be demolished before long.[134] It was imperative that the construction of offices for the air force needed to be fast-tracked because the first draft of air force personnel was expected by the end of March 1940.

In terms of Government Notice No. 390, dated August 15, 1941, the Rhodesia Air Askari Corps (RAAC) was established as a unit of the SRAF, and the ranks and rates of pay, and conditions of service of European members of the corps were those prescribed for the SRAF.[135] RAAC structures were laid down on the principle that no European member would hold any rank lower than that of a sergeant, irrespective of the nature of his duties.[136] In terms of section 17 of the Defence Act (Chapter III), the governor drafted regulations governing the capacities under which Africans were allowed to engage: the RAAC was composed of European and native members. No native was to be enlisted as a member of the corps (RAAC) unless his engagement was voluntary, while the ranks and rates of pay and conditions of European members of the corps were those prescribed from time to time for the air section of the territorial force.[137] The corps were charged with the duties of providing armed guards and labor services at air force establishments as could be defined from time to time by the Minister of Air.[138]

The stimulation and success of the air training scheme in Southern Rhodesia was, to an extent, a result of the contribution made by the African population. Their work consisted of cutting grass for thatching purposes, digging river sand and loading it into trucks, off-loading railway trucks, felling gum trees, and any work in connection with the acquisition of materials for building purposes.[139] The RAAC assisted in ground maintenance and other duties connected to the EATS.[140] During World War II, Africans supplied labor for essential undertakings and recruits for the Rhodesian African Rifles and for the Rhodesian Air Askari Corps.[141] Africans contributed well over £9,000 to various war funds by 1942.[142] Over 14,000 Africans came forward to the service of the Empire. At the end of the war most serving personnel returned to their civilian occupations and the defense forces of the colony were reduced in size.[143]

Table 3.7: Channels of Labor Supply for RATG

Bulawayo	Gwelo	Salisbury
All districts in Matabeleland except Belingwe, Gwelo and Selukwe	Belingwe, Selukwe, Chilimanzi, Chibi, Victoria, Gokwe, Ndanga, Bikita, Gutu	All districts in Mashonaland not included under Gwelo[144]

Table 3.8: Categories of Africans in RAAC

GRADES	Group 1	Group 2
A—Garden boys, cleaners, pot washers, scavengers, grass cutters, runner messengers, batman, scullery boys, general mess hands, woodcutters, barrack room boys, aerodrome maintenance boys, compound cleaners, native cooks for natives, ablution and block cleaners	8d. to 10d. per day	6d. to 8d. per day
B—Sanitary boys, flight boys, mechanics' hand, artisans' hand, thatching boy, motor transport cleaners, greasers, waiters, cooks, vegetable boys, gasoline boys, laundry boys, fire tender boys, compound police boys	1/- to 1/4d. per day	8d to 1/- per day
C—First-class cooks, headwaiter, clerks, interpreters, first-class thatching boys, tailors, shoemakers, hospital orderlies, compound police boys (after passing through grade "B"), aircraft boys, maintenance (technical) boys, native teachers (Group 1 only)	1/4d. to 2/8d per day	1/- to 1/4d per day
D—Officers Mess head cook and first-class interpreters only	2/8d. to 3/4d. per day	nil[145]

Besides, there was a special grade in which Group 1 earned £5 to £6 per month with half yearly increments of 5/- subject to satisfactory service, while Group 2 earned £4 to £5 per month with half yearly increments of 5/- subject to satisfactory service.[146] Exploitation was rampant, especially during the early days of RATG. Mrs. Morris was employed at air force headquarters on May 20, 1940, at the rate of 10 shillings per day, while Africans employed in 1940 at Cranborne hangars such as Chiyangwa, R/C No. 9605, and Reza, R/C No. 023811, earned 22 shillings 6 pence per month. In addition, Ruzwidza, R/C 13351, and Mudepi, R/C X9168, earned 20/- per month.[147] As a result, many Africans went away without official leave and were periodically penalized.

Chemakoma, stationed at Mt. Hampden, engaged on July 27, 1942, and up until August 31, 1943, he had not gone on leave.[148] However, the issue of punishments was to some extent applicable to all races. A/C Warwick (M.413) was granted leave, without pay and allowances, from May 14, 1940, to May 28, 1940.[149] A closer look at the type of work done by Africans and wages paid shows a certain degree of semi-slavery during the EATS in Southern Rhodesia.

The EATS was acceptable to Southern Rhodesia because the Europeans relied on exploiting African labor, thereby cutting the costs. Africans were purported to be endorsing the *modus operandi* as revealed in a memo written by RAAC Headquarters to RATG Headquarters on October 29, 1943: "It is accepted by all African Forces that the lowest rank amongst Europeans should be that of a Sergeant, and it is felt that the same principle should apply to the corps."[150] Many African laborers were discharged in 1945 and were given war medals. The cessation of hostilities saw most serving personnel returning to their civilian occupations and the defense forces of the colony reduced in size.[151] An analysis of statistical data shows that discharged Africans held ranks not above private I. Very few were promoted to corporals; for example, Ruwambiwa (Regiment No. 54), who on August 1, 1948, was promoted to corporal.[152]

Africans who were trained as artisans were left unattested. Nonetheless, they were made to perform jobs restricted to attested and European personnel. To conceal the information, Meredith informed the Department of Internal Affairs that for security reasons it was considered undesirable that the text of the letter containing reference to the exploitation of Africans should be passed on to the National Industrial Council.[153] On October 18, 1943, the Secretary in the Department of Internal Affairs alerted the Secretary for Air: "My council would be pleased if you will ask Honourable Minister for Air if he is aware of, and has accepted the policy of using attested skilled Native labour for building or other skilled work on any Air Station or temporary landing ground."[154] The case emanated from one African laborer called Marimo, who was seen working at the carpenter's shop at Cranborne Air Station. Marimo was deliberately employed before attestation, possibly to pay him low wages. In reply to the Department of Internal Affairs, Meredith wrote: "It has been ascertained that Native No. 5042, Marimo, was attested on July 6th and employed in the workshop mentioned.... For a few days prior to July 6th, he was tested with a view to ascertaining whether he was suitable for employment. It is probable that this was a native observed."[155] It was a confirmed policy that no native unauthenticated labor should be employed in any workshop at RAF stations. The RATG did not also intend to use native skilled artisans for maintenance work. Although the colony shouldered the financial burden of air training, the successful development and operation of the air force in the colony was achieved through the exploitation of Africans.

Airmen were entitled to medical attention at public expense. They were also eligible for free hospital treatment at public expense wherever they happened to be in the country. The benefits were restricted to treatment in service hospitals. Where service hospitals were not available, special authority for incurring expenses was required. Their families were subject to AMOA 507/39 in case of infectious illness, and with a view to limiting or preventing the spread, would (under the authority of the Medical Officer [MO]) be admitted to service hospitals at public expense.[156] Admission to a non-service hospital at public expense was not permitted to families. Their families were allowed the privileges of free medical attention provided they lived within a reasonable distance of the station (five miles) and a Medical Officer was available.[157]

Permanent Scheme

Soon after the outbreak of World War II, it became obvious that more flying instructors were required than could be possibly supplied by Britain single-handedly. The end result was that the Central Flying School passed on its traditions to other schools. With the advent of the Joint Air Training Plan, a great part of Allied flying training spread to Canada, Australia, New Zealand, South Africa and Rhodesia.[158] Among those trained were Greeks, Yugoslavs, Frenchmen, Australians and South Africans. The upkeep of students from Australia, South Africa and Greece, along with other expenses, were recovered either from the respective governments or the Air Ministry.[159] The air training scheme was a blessing for the colony because it ushered in important long-term infrastructural developments that shaped the future of the Rhodesian Defence Forces, especially the air force. In the long term, the RhAF proved crucial to the Rhodesian war effort.

The Rhodesians were committed because it was part of their imperial commitment and above all a permanent scheme.[160] The most significant contribution came in the training of 10,000 air crew at Southern Rhodesia's expense under the EATS.[161] One important thing to note at this juncture is that the RATG was not imposed on Rhodesia. It was a purely home-grown idea. As soon as the Southern Rhodesian government agreed to host the project, a comprehensive scheme was carried out between the representatives of the two governments in London. In December 1941, in reply to a signal from Britain's Secretary of State, the Southern Rhodesian government accepted responsibility for landing grounds in Southern Rhodesia.[162] This meant breaking almost entirely new ground because there was no existing training organization in the colony. The training scheme in Southern Rhodesia was administered by the RATG headquarters while policy direction was taken from the Air Ministry in London.[163] In 1942, the Speaker of Parliament, Allan Welsh, revealed the high praise the UK gave to the air training scheme, the standard of the training achieved, and the speed with which it had developed.[164]

According to Lt. Colonel Meredith, the RATG, besides being Southern Rhodesia's main contribution to the Second World War, was one of the most important happenings in Rhodesian history.[165] Meredith emphasized that the whole effort of the RATG originated in Rhodesia. The Air Ministry saw the possibilities and got whole cooperation from Rhodesia.[166] The value of the coming of the RAF to Rhodesia, it was argued, could not be calculated in pounds, shillings and pence, but it was well appreciated that the benefit was considerable.[167]

Table 3.9: RATG Centers for Air Training

Units	Opened
Headquarters, Salisbury	5 January 1940
Elementary Flying Training Schools	
No. 25 Belvedere-Salisbury	24 May 1940
No. 26 Guinea Fowl Gwelo	8 August 1940
No. 27 Induna-Bulawayo	31 January 1941
No. 28 Mount Hampden-Salisbury	29 March 1941
Service Flying Training Schools	
No. 20 Cranborne-Salisbury	19 July 1940
No. 21 Kumalo-Bulawayo	11 October 1940
No. 22 Thornhill-Gwelo	7 March 1941
No. 23 Heany-Bulawayo	June 1941
Bombing, Gunnery and Navigation School	
Moffat-Gwelo	25 July 1941
Flying Instructors School	
Norton	2 October 1942
Initial Training Wing	
Bulawayo	April 1940
Aircraft and Engine Repair Depots	
Cranborne-Salisbury	19 July 1940
Heany-Bulawayo	June 1941
Central Maintenance Unit	
Bulawayo	1941
Rhodesia Air Askari Corps Depot	
Salisbury	1940[168]

On May 24, 1940, the first RATG, No. 25 EFTS Belvedere, was opened many weeks before the first Canadian station became operative. This was followed by an air station at Guinea Fowl, Gwelo, for flying training. RATG HQ had numerous sections such as air staff, air training, signals, armament, administration, equipment, engineering, personnel, medical and legal. Air stations increased to ten and they specialized in different tasks such as training flying instructors, air firing, bombing ranges, gunnery school and navigation.

Students who aspired to be pilots began with elementary flying training, and at the same time they were given a good deal of ground instruction. There were sixteen subjects to be studied, including armament and navigation. After a period in the elementary school, the pilots proceeded to a service school. From there they proceeded to intermediate types of training aircraft. At the intermediate stage, the ground instruction was designed to keep pace, and the pupils spent many more hours on these subjects than they did in elementary school. The next step was the advanced stage, which was undertaken at the service school. The object here was to teach the pupil how to apply to service the basic flying lessons learned in the earlier stages. When advanced training was completed, the pupil pilot passed on to a service flying until he could fly multi-seat types.[169]

Conclusion

The establishment of the air training scheme in Southern Rhodesia reflects on a number of crucial things. The BSAP constituted the first and only line of defense, thereby leading to the promulgation of the Defence Act in 1926 by the Responsible Government. The colony made important steps in aeronautical developments prior to the RATG in 1940, but none were of military significance. Flying grants were distributed to pilots and flying clubs by the government and Beit Trustees in a deliberate attempt to promote civil aviation and improve communication. It was generally believed that the trained pilots would be of significance in case of emergency in the colony. Aeronautical developments in Southern Rhodesia began with simple planes essentially for aerial surveying, investigating animal diseases, and transportation of government officials. The Air Ministry was always keen to share its military expertise with Southern Rhodesia. This was evident in 1933 and 1934, when RAF squadrons led troop carrying and other exercises with the permanent and territorial forces in Salisbury and Bulawayo. Ex-RAF aircraft were sold to the colony at low prices. This was, however, done with a view to cater for the security needs of the Empire. The establishment and transformation of the RhAF benefited from the RATG, which altered the colony's military landscape. The colony foresaw an air force that would be responsible for the defense of the country. The major turning point in the development of the RhAF was the outbreak of the Second World War. Southern Rhodesia grabbed the opportunity, primarily to assist the imperial war effort. Rhodesian miners and farmers and several other companies and individuals donated funds to purchase training aircraft. Although imperial defense was a necessity, it was vital to have an efficient and effective air force in the future. The air training scheme proved significant in laying out the base for military aviation in the country. The availability of both free and cheap African labor was another fundamental factor which allowed the air training scheme to be hastily established. African labor helped offset the huge costs that were incurred as a result of air training.

4

The Development of the Air Force During the Interwar Period

Introduction

The major aim of this chapter is to examine the development of the Rhodesian Air Force during the interwar period (1946–1965). The cessation of World War II hostilities effectively brought a halt to air training in the colony. The same period saw a series of negotiations between the Air Ministry and the Southern Rhodesian government about the prospects for continuing air training. The Air Training Scheme was closed down in November 1946 but was resuscitated in April 1947. Both the Air Ministry and Southern Rhodesia had strategic interests at stake which needed to be safeguarded. This explains the commitment and rationale for the revival of air training after virtually five months of non-activity. It is verifiable that the end of World War II in 1945 left the Southern Rhodesian Air Force on a modernization path. This chapter critically analyzes the fundamental reasons which enabled the resumption of air training in 1947 when the purpose of the Rhodesia Air Training Group had functionally outlived its usefulness. More importantly, one has to bear in mind that when the air training scheme was established, the colony envisaged a permanent air training scheme. Basing on this premise, the colony after 1945 targeted to meet its internal security requirements. From then on, military aviation was treated as a matter of policy that mattered most to the survival of the Rhodesians. Moreover, other priorities like Commonwealth defense and assisting Northern Rhodesia and Nyasaland to meet their internal security requirements were equally significant. The federal era enabled Southern Rhodesia to expand military aviation such that when the Second Chimurenga broke out, the country had one of the most formidable air units on the continent. A notable development during the Federation was that the two squadrons which existed were increased to seven, plus a parachute training school. Before the Federation, the two squadrons of the air force were being trained for use in the case of a major war as a contribution to imperial defense under the RAF.[1] The two squadrons were part of the colony's effort in conjunction with the rest of the Empire, and an important contribution towards defense.[2] Besides, the federal government gave more responsibility to the Rhodesian Air Force because it was now expected to guarantee the security of all the partners in the Federation. The interwar period afforded the researcher an opportunity to examine the ways in which Africans who served in the RhAF continued to be treated as inferiors destined to work for white superiority in spite of their commitment to imperial defense during and after World War II. An analysis of the nature of relations between the two racial groups is vital in highlighting the hypocrisy that existed in the RhAF, where every man was alleged to be equally treated despite rampant racism in the air force among other sections of the Rhodesian Security Forces.

Challenges and Opportunities for Air Training in Southern Rhodesia After World War II

When the RATG closed down in November 1946, all Southern Rhodesian Air Force records were taken over by what was called the "A" Branch. Several Royal Air Force stations were handed over to various government departments for other purposes. In addition, arrangements were made at Gwelo (Gweru) and Gatooma (Kadoma) for military buildings to be temporarily vacated.[3] RAF houses in various centers were handed down to the Municipalities, Public Works Depot and Housing Board. The strength of the Southern Rhodesia Women's Auxiliary Service was reduced from fifty-two to three persons.[4] The closing down of RATG saw the Ordnance Staff being involved in considerable extra work of taking over all furniture and barrack stores which were the property of the Southern Rhodesian government. When RATG closed down at Kumalo and Heany, the furniture and 90 houses at Heany were sold for a total sum of £10,000.[5] The furniture was intended for the British Army married personnel stationed at Heany and for replacement of furniture for married quarters in Zomba and Lusaka, as well as single messers in command.[6]

At the end of World War II, the SRAF and RATG were effectively disbanded and later resurrected in 1947.[7] Despite the challenges for air training, Air Vice-Marshal Charles Meredith disclosed that the government of Southern Rhodesia welcomed the scheme for continued Royal Air Force training in Rhodesia. He expressed his desire for the scheme to be expanded beyond the existing dimensions. Meredith supported his claims by revealing that the Southern Rhodesian government would make the airfields and buildings selected from

Heany, Cranborne, Kumalo and Thornhill available without charge.[8] Until April 1947 and since the cessation of air training under the RATG at the end of 1946, Rhodesia's air activity was dormant. The government officially approved the formation of the Southern Rhodesian Air Force in 1946 and it was duly constituted by Act of Parliament on November 28, 1947.[9] The Air Ministry agreed to replace the Southern Rhodesian government aircraft which had been taken over by the RAF at the outbreak of hostilities in September 1939. Three Anson XIX communication aircraft and two Tiger Moths were replaced and two Havards Mark II were delivered in early 1949 by RATG to complete the replacement.[10]

A meeting held in the Commonwealth Secretary Room on January 21, 1946, discussed the problems arising from the decision to wind up the RATG and the question of the re-equipment and future training of the SRAF. The UK was represented by Pritchard, Tory Lords Swinton, De L'Isle and Dudley, and Air Chief Marshal Sir John Baker, while Southern Rhodesia was represented by Sir Godfrey Huggins, Whitehead, Strachen, Ross and Nicholas.[11] Lord De L'Isle asserted that the Air Ministry was no longer justified in continuing to spend £125 million extra in Southern Rhodesia when they had corresponding training capacity going on elsewhere.[12] The Air Ministry financial adviser's analysis of the costs showed that an estimate of the overall annual costs of training would be £1,700,000. However, Lord De L'Isle clarified that this did not mean that they were no longer interested in cooperating with the SRAF, but it was simply a case of being forced by financial considerations to place first things first.[13]

The Air Ministry's financial objections were echoed by Meredith, who wrote to the Southern Rhodesian government during his visit to Britain in 1945: "Objections may be raised by financial people but all others will do utmost to convince them of desirability."[14] The Southern Rhodesian government exhibited a lot of enthusiasm in continuing the air training scheme and replied to Meredith confirming the availability of free infrastructure: "Air stations required would be available rent free and maintenance charges acceptable ... houses at present retained will be held until your discussions have reached a final stage and disposal operations will be retarded. Government strongly favours scheme and are prepared to consider any further proposals which might assist you in gaining final decision. Sufficient barrack furniture is being retained."[15]

The Empire Air Training Scheme was resuscitated in 1947 to train 350 pilots and navigators a year for the Royal Air Force and provision was made within the scheme to train Rhodesian pilots.[16] The RATG existed as an active survival from the wartime EATS to train pilots for the RAF.[17]

In 1946, the government sought aircraft from RAF for inspection of landing grounds. The Auster, fitted with long-range tanks, was considered suitable for the task.[18] When negotiations for the resumption of air training began, Southern Rhodesia bargained from a point of strength because the existing airfields, buildings and hangars were freely available. Added to that, Southern Rhodesia was supposed to contribute £250,000 a year towards the cost of the air training organization. The colony accepted the financial responsibility for all expenditure incurred in connection with African personnel, while the government of the UK took up the financial responsibility for all expenses of the air training organization while the training scheme was controlled by the Air Ministry.[19] The contribution of Southern Rhodesia in each year towards RATG included minor work services and works maintenance; fuel, light, water and sanitary services; rations in kind; and pay and allowances for African personnel.[20]

The end of the war witnessed a considerable number of properties belonging to the air unit and defense being distributed to various government departments. The rationale was that RATG had survived its utility of serving the Empire during the war. The numerous properties owned by the RATG were distributed as follows:

Table 4.1: Buildings Relinquished by Defense and Air

Salisbury

Rhodesian Air Training Headquarters	It was given to Public Works Department (PWD) for Group government offices. Headquarters of the Internment Camp Corps were accommodated in these buildings but were subsequently moved to Defence headquarters.
Belvedere Air Station	It was returned to the owners, the Rhodesia Agricultural and Horticultural Society.
Belvedere Askari Camp	Certain buildings in this camp were sold out to the Rhodesian Railways.
Guinea Fowl Air Station	It was handed over to the PWD Government Housing Board, a small portion being retained for the Communication Squadron.
Disposals Depot	It was handed over to the PWD for the Education Department and became Salisbury West Junior School.
Norton Air Station	It was handed over for use of internees.

Bulawayo

Kumalo Air Station	A large portion of this station was handed to the PWD. The balance was retained for the Air Training Wing.
Central Maintenance Unit Quarters	It was taken over by BSAP.
Central Transport Pool	It was handed over to the PWD.

Gwelo

Guinea Fowl Air station	The station was handed over to the PWD for a miners' training school.
Central Transport Pool	It was handed over to the PWD.
Military camp	It was handed over on a temporary basis to the Government Housing Board.

Gatooma
Drill Hall   It was handed over on a temporary basis to the PWD for additional government offices. In addition to the above, quarters at various centers were handed over as follows:

	Salisbury	Bulawayo	Gwelo
Government Housing Board	6	-	-
Public Works Department	69	13	3
Municipalities	10	40	-
Total- 141[21]			

Table 4.2: Houses Held by RATG

Station	Officers	Airmen	Remarks
Belvedere	13	12	7 houses and 6 flats = 13 total
Cranborne	15	71	15 officers' quarters reserved for future use by Air and Defence
HQ Housing	10	-	7 houses reserved for future use by Air and Defence
Gwelo East Township	4	-	-
Kumalo	8	64	3 officers' and 5 airmen's houses reserved for future use by Air and Defence.[22]

Table 4.3: Decorations Awarded to Rhodesians Who Served in the RAF During World War II

KBE-1	MBE-11	Greek Air Force Cross-1
CB-1	DFC-84	Royal Order of Phoenix with Swords-1
DSO-7	Bars to DFC-9	Bar to DSO-1
AFC-10	OBE-7	CGM-2
Mentioned in Dispatches-68		Commemorations-5[23]

Additionally, white personnel who had served in the Second World War received preferential treatment during the demobilization process. Crowther and Perry were given first priority by the government to buy equipment such as the Churchill lathe, universal milling machine, power saw, radial drill press, surface grinder, and "du-more" grinder.[24] The treatment was accorded to them because they were ex–RAF servicemen. RATG Headquarters wrote to the Government Disposals Officer on February 4, 1946, instructing him: "It was stated that the firm of Crowther and Perry would, as ex-servicemen, receive preferential treatment in the supply of any workshop machinery which they required, and which might be available from Air Force Stocks...."[25] Special tribute was also paid to all Defence Headquarters staff in connection with the affairs of serviceman and their dependents.[26] The RATG demonstrated in future to be the greatest successful immigration scheme since many of its products went back to stay in Rhodesia after World War II.[27]

A Defence Working Party of senior officials, consisting of the chairman of the Public Services Board, the Secretary for Internal Affairs, the Commander of Military Forces and the Director of Demobilisation was set up in 1948 to make preliminary proposals for coordinating the preparation of war plans in peacetime and reported to the Cabinet in November 1948.[28] Nearly two years after the resumption of air training, the manpower state of the SRAF had substantially improved, considering the fact that the unit had just started its revival program in April 1947. There were fifteen pilots, one wireless operator, forty technicians and two administrators at the end of December 1948.[29] The Dakota Unit proceeded to the UK in March 1948 to transport members of the staff corps to courses of instruction arranged through the War Office. The group received courses on offensive support at the School of Land Air Warfare and flying instructors' refresher courses at the Empire Flying School.[30] There were seven serviceable and four unserviceable aircraft in the colony at the beginning of 1949.[31] In an indication of improvement, more aircraft were added to make twenty-four serviceable aircraft at the end of 1949. Added to that, the RAF seconded sixteen ground crew personnel.[32] The air unit had aircraft strength of thirty-six in 1950. Of these, two were to be rebuilt at the end of the year.[33] Nine staff pilots proceeded to the UK in January 1951 together with members of the Southern Rhodesia Auxiliary Air Force (SRAAF) and ferried eleven Spitfires to Rhodesia in March.[34] In November, eight staff pilots proceeded on the seczond ferry, which resulted in nine Spitfires reaching Rhodesia just before Christmas.[35] A team of RAF testing officers from the Central Flying School in the UK visited Cranborne in 1951 and were impressed by high standards of training. The Central Fighter Establishment of the RAF also visited Cranborne and lectured on modern fighter development. In 1951, the Short Service Unit was established and recruitment for No. 1 course was opened in May.[36] The Air Ministry acted vigorously in order to ensure that air training was done at RAF standard.

The SRAF provided staff and aircraft to train the Southern Rhodesian Air Force Volunteer Reserve and Air Observation Post artillery reconnaissance pilots.[37] The air force also provided air transport for ministers and government officials, including medical officers to African clinics. It similarly provided aerial photography and reconnaissance for the roads department, Natural Resources Board, Irrigation Department, Native Engineering Department, Town Planning Office, Central African Council, and the Air Ambulance facilities to provide assistance in air search and rescue in cooperation with the Department of Civil Aviation.[38] The SRAF became one of the permanent units of the defense forces of the colony in 1951.[39] It composed of members of the Staff Corps drafted for air duties. Their key duties were to operate a communication squadron for the transport of Very Important Persons and to train members of the territorial force as pilots, but particularly as artillery observation pilots.[40] The Southern Rhodesia Women's Military and Air Service served as typists, clerks, telephone and teleprinter operators, parachute packers and the general administration of the Defence Force.[41]

Between January and March 1952, new subsections of the RhAF were established as follows:

A Group—Airframe Spares, **E Group**—Engine Spares, **F Group**—Tools and ancillary equipment, **D Group**—Aircraft General Stores and other departments such as receipt and issue, equipment provisioning and accounting, barrack and clothing, main plane store and salvage.[42] The development of the SRAF from 1948 to 1951 is attributed to the political and military will of Southern Rhodesia to modernize the air force through the acquisition of aircraft and training of manpower. The 57 airplanes available in 1951 were increased to 67, comprising twelve different types of planes, while technical manning increased from 63 to 103 men of all trades.[43] Despite being a military weapon, aircraft occupied an important position as a source of pride. Flying displays were performed at Cranborne, Karoi and Gatooma in 1951 and a record gathering of 20,000 people attended the display at Cranborne in June.[44] The government approved a re-equipment scheme for the SRAF to enable it to meet its war commitments and to replace obsolete aircraft in 1952. This involved the purchase of 55 aircraft (Vampire trainers, Vampire fighters, Provost elementary trainers and Pembroke) and spares costing about £1,800,000.[45]

Table 4.4: Schedule of Aircraft Fleet State During the Year 1951

Type of aircraft	Strength on Jan. 1	Acquired	Struck off	Strength on Dec. 31
Anson 12 VIP	1	-	-	1
Auster J1 and J5	5	-	1	4
Avro 19	3	-	-	3
Dakota DC3	1	-	-	1
Harvard, MKII &IIA	11	4 (IIB)	-	15
Leopard Moth	1	-	-	1
Rapide DH 89A	3	-	-	3
Spitfire MK 22	-	20	-	20
Tiger Moth DH82A	11	-	2	9
Total	36	24	3	57[46]

Further Development of the Rhodesian Air Force During the Federation

The full administrative and financial control of the military forces in the Federation became the responsibility of Central Africa Command on July 1, 1954.[47] The Defence Interim Act passed by Parliament was promulgated on September 10, 1954. The act established the defense forces of the Federation and compulsorily transferred all members of the forces, other than British army personnel, in the three territories on their existing conditions of service to the Federal Defence Force and introduced compulsory military training for a continuous period of 137 days for the whole Federation.[48] The fundamental purpose of the act was to establish the Federal Defence Force in accordance with the Constitution, which described defense as an exclusive federal subject.[49] By agreement with the territories and the UK, financial and administrative responsibilities for the defense forces were taken over by the Federation as from July 1, 1954.[50] Federal conditions of service were taken over and applied in their entirety to the Rhodesian army and RRAF. The dissolution of the Federation resulted in the loss of a large proportion of skilled personnel, a reduction in the number of aircraft, and a substantial cut in the expenditure.[51] The RRAF Salisbury Headquarters moved from Dolphin House to Milton Building.[52] The air unit inherited by the Rhodesians at the breakup of the Federation in 1963 was bigger and was one of the better equipped air units in Africa.[53]

Although the Federation induced important developments in the colony, Southern Rhodesia had evidently made notable progress in the military field. The Federal Defence Minister and Prime Minister of Northern Rhodesia, Sir Roy Welensky, disclosed to members of the federal Parliament that he would not claim any credit for the great efficiency of the air force because his predecessors had initiated it.[54] By African standards, the air force was regarded as a first-class service. The federal government inherited two squadrons of air force from Southern Rhodesia.[55] The table below illustrates the Southern Rhodesian Air Force infrastructure attached to the Federation in 1953:

Table 4.5: Southern Rhodesian Infrastructure Attached to the Federation in 1953

Serial No.	Description	Approx. Areas in Acres	Location
1	Kumalo Aerodrome, ex-RAF stand 4086, Bulawayo Township, portion on Bulawayo Township land	140	Bulawayo
2	Supply Depot situated in PWD Yard	-	Bulawayo
3	Guinea Fowl Aerodrome, Subdivision A, portion Divide, Subdivision A, portion Bromley, portion Divide less 182 acres Education Dept. and 10 acres Road Camp	430.1	Gwelo
4	Thornhill Aerodrome (including all houses thereon), Gwelo small holding No. 19, Sub-division A, Thornhill, Sub-division A, Small holding No. 18, Lots 12 and 13, Christmas Gift, Smallholding No. 16, Subdivision No. 20, portion New Christmas Gift	1,258.8	Gwelo
5	Heany Aerodrome, Subdivisions A, B, C, D and E, Heany Junction Farm, portion Imbesu Block and Subdivisions A and B, portion Schombu, portion of Heany Junction Farm	2,136.4	Heany[56]

Defense became the prime responsibility of the federal government under item three of the federal legislative list, which sought to raise, train and maintain military ground and air force.[57] The Federal armed forces were principally responsible for protecting the Federation against external attacks, further cementing the significance of internal security. Certain forces were available, by agreement with the UK, for use outside the Federation in conjunction with the UK forces.[58] Seven SRAF pilots underwent jet conservation courses in either the UK or South Africa in 1953. During November and December the first Pembroke aircraft and four Vampires were ferried to Rhodesia from the UK.[59] Before the Federation, Southern Rhodesia was the only country with an air unit. The SRAF had a two-day fighter or ground attack squadrons, elementary flying training equipment and a few transport aircraft. Northern Rhodesia had one African battalion, the Northern Rhodesia Regiment, while Nyasaland had two African battalions, the King's African Rifles and 1st and 2nd battalions.[60]

At the onset of the Federation, the army and air force were a composite force under one command. The proposal had long been deliberated on January 25, 1944, by AVM Meredith, who informed Honourable Sir Ernest Guest that it was inevitable that Defence and Air would have to be amalgamated again one day.[61] In September 1953, SRAF was renamed the Rhodesian Air Force upon creation of the Federation of Rhodesia and Nyasaland.[62] Her Majesty granted the permission for the air force to be renamed the Royal Rhodesian Air Force in 1954. The divisions in command were effected due to the differences in the operational techniques and approach. The RRAF was authorized to use the administrative and operational techniques of the RAF.[63] The air force changed its ranks and uniforms and began to use new ones that were similar to those of the RAF.[64] At the disintegration of the Federation in December 1963, the RRAF squadrons were well trained and equipped to fight insurgency. After the Federal dissolution, the control of the RRAF inevitably went back to the Southern Rhodesian government. Although the number of aircraft was reduced, there were few changes to the manpower establishment and the air force was basically unaffected.[65] The British allowed Southern Rhodesia to inherit the entire fighting force of the RRAF, a move that enabled Rhodesians to retain air supremacy throughout the war that was to follow.[66] The dissolution of the Federation resulted in the defense responsibilities of the RRAF reverting once again to that of territorial defense.[67] The air force was split up between Southern Rhodesia and the Northern Rhodesian Air Wing, later becoming the Zambian Air Force (ZAF).[68]

The transition from SRAF to RRAF was indicative of the fact that the force had clearly developed from a self-contained unit preoccupied with territorial defense to one concerned with the defense of the entire Federation.⁶⁹ The prefix "Royal" also symbolized the fact that the air force had acquired a wider responsibility as part of the RAF's defense commitment in the Middle East.⁷⁰ Rhodesia changed to republican status in 1970. The president was appointed commander-in-chief of the armed forces. The prefix "Royal" was dropped from the air force title and it became the Rhodesian Air Force. A new motto was adopted, *Alae Praesidio Patriae* (our wings are as the fortress to our land).⁷¹ There were numerous suggestions put forward from all levels of the force regarding the form of the basic emblem. A strong section of opinion held that the Zimbabwe bird would be a natural choice for air force use, while the flame lily and the elephant enjoyed some minority support.⁷² The overwhelming opinion swung in favor of the lion, as being representative of strength, courage and defiance. The lion and tusk was finally adopted as the Force emblem.⁷³ The motto of the air force was adopted by the Air Force of Zimbabwe in 1980.

It is evident that the RRAF grew from strength to strength. The development of the air force between 1954 and 1959 reflects the determination by the air force to develop into a formidable fighting component. The Federation worked hard to make the air force an efficient fighting force. However, the utmost disturbances were the technical challenges faced by the RRAF prior to the outbreak of hostilities in 1966. Efforts to acquire modern aircraft were successful, but the rate at which they were grounded as a result of the shortage of spare parts and manpower confirms the inherent weaknesses of the RhAF. This later became a perennial problem that hampered the effectiveness of the air force as a fighting component during the Second Chimurenga. This is supported by the Spitfires, which were practically nonfunctional in December 1954, and by 1959 they had ceased to be favorites.

Table 4.6: Aircraft Strength in 1954

Type	1 January 1954	31 December 1954
Anson	3	3
Auster	3	3
Dakota	1	3
Harvard	20	19
Pembroke	1	2
Provost	-	4
Rapide	3	2
Spitfire	20	2
Tiger Moth	14	12
Vampire FB9	4	14
Total	69	64⁷⁴

Despite the challenges in the air force, the government was determined to improve the efficiency of the Royal Rhodesian Air Force as exemplified by the aircraft strength in 1959. Pembrokes were selected to replace Anson aircraft (then obsolete and out of production) because it was the only medium-transport aircraft in current production which could: (a) carry eight passengers, bombs, and freight, carry out aerial photography, carry stretcher-cases, carry out twin engine conversion training; (b) enable standardization on one reciprocating engine and propeller as it had the same power plant used in the Provost Trainer; and (c) meet service standards required by the Ministry of Supply. This was the standard medium transport of the RAF, which meant the colony could draw spares from the Air Ministry organizations.[75] The Southern Rhodesian government wanted to reduce the number of types of engines and aircraft, which in turn reduced overall costs. Provosts were favored because they were the standard elementary aircraft of the RAF.[76]

Table 4.7: Aircraft Strength in 1959

Type of aircraft	Total
Canberra	18
Dakotas	8
Pembroke	2
Provosts	14
Vampires	29
Total	71[77]

Dakotas and Pembrokes were mainly used for carrying troops, police and civilians, while Provosts were for pure reconnaissance. The idea of introducing helicopters in the Federation was rejected by Federal Defence Minister John Moore Caldicott owing to the altitude, temperature and range limitations in the Federation. The helicopter was also considered to be militarily uneconomic.[78] In accordance with the policy of re-equipping the RRAF with jet aircraft in order to fulfill its commitment to produce ground attack pilots, fourteen Vampires were ferried out from the UK by air force pilots in 1954.[79] In addition, four Provost Trainers, two Dakotas and one Pembroke aircraft were acquired and delivered. In order that the air force may carry out its allotted internal security tasks, the urgent need for additional troop carrying aircraft was expressed.[80] However, it can be observed that various models of aircraft were suspended in 1959 because of the huge costs incurred in maintaining them.

The Rhodesian Air Force in Internal Security Roles

The development of the air force in the colony after the Second World War echoed the centrality attached to Southern Rhodesian internal security, Commonwealth Defence and the internal security of Northern Rhodesia and Nyasaland.[81] Airplanes were anticipated to play crucial roles in times of conflict.

Federal Defence Minister Caldicott stressed that both the regular battalions and territorial forces contained mobility in their own transport, and by virtue of their airlift capability which was provided by the air force. The emergency in Nyasaland demonstrated that troops could be airlifted into a trouble spot without delay.[82] Caldicott introduced the Defence Amendment Bill (No. 2) on June 29, 1961. Clause 5 of the bill gave the minister the power to require all residents between the ages of 18 and 50 years who were not already registered, to register. The minister was given discretion to call on any class of resident specified in the notice to register himself.[83] Another bill had been introduced in February 1961 to amend the Defence Act in order to enable the minister in times of emergency or threatened emergency to call up temporarily to the territorial forces all persons between those ages.[84] Residents in Nyasaland between the age of 31 and 50 were exempted from registering because the very limited trained manpower in that territory was all required for service in the regular police or the reserves, or for other essential services.[85] The RRAF won the admiration of the political leadership in the country as highlighted by Winston Joseph Field, who described the RRAF as an extremely efficient set up that everyone was supposed to be proud of.[86] By 1964, it was apparent that Rhodesia was supposed to be self-sufficient in the management of her military power.[87] The emergence of the "anti-terrorist" war and the isolation precipitated by the declaration of UDI made Rhodesia to begin thinking in terms of territorial defense.[88]

As already highlighted, the end of the Second World War provided Southern Rhodesia with an opportunity to inherit RAF administration and infrastructure for the purpose of building her own air force for internal security in case of emergency. The Commander Military Forces warned colleagues in the Southern Rhodesian Staff Corps on December 20, 1951, that they were living in dangerous times and the more prepared they became the more they were able to meet any emergency.[89] Previously, the Commonwealth meeting in 1946 had proposed that Southern Rhodesia should consider the formation of a first line combat unit while the essential minimum maintenance backing involved in the scheme was supposed to be able to support it.[90] To be able to fulfill its mandate, the Federation took up priority in reinforcing the fleet previously owned by the SRAF. Even after the dissolution of the Federation, the RRAF introduced a training program geared at ameliorating national defense in cooperation with the police and army.[91] When the initial indicators of "terrorist" activity surfaced along the country's borders, it became imperative that the country's forces were supposed to step up their preparations.[92]

White people in the Federation became increasingly preoccupied with their security as a result of the conflict in Nyasaland, which broke out in February and March 1959. A plot to murder the governor of Malawi was uncovered in 1958 and a state of emergency was declared in the Protectorate.[93] Federal Government Notice No. 39 of 1959 authorized the dispatch of a force to assist the civil power of Nyasaland in the prevention and suppression of internal disorder within Nyasaland at the request of the governor of Nyasaland.[94] The RRAF went into action for the first time on February 21, 1959, in an internal security role. The provost attacked rioting crowds with tear gas bombs while leaflets were dropped. Reconnaissance flights were undertaken for the police and the army.[95] Sections of No. 3 and No. 4 Squadrons were detached to Chileka airfield in support of the federal army.[96] During the Nyasaland Emergency, No. 3 squadron airlifted troops to Blantyre in Nyasaland.[97] A total of 1,300 Malawians were detained and over 51 killed.[98] The incident led an African representative from Northern Rhodesia to accuse the Federation of using race as a point of reference when treating Africans by arguing: "If security means that one section of the Federation is discriminated, and have people who attack us in the locations, no Defence Force is called in, but when people claim their own rights, you talk about defence. This attack on Nyasaland shows how racial this community in the Federation is. You can have trained men, make strong bridges and have helicopters but that would not stop the spirit of Africans to get freedom."[99]

It was in such typical emergencies that airplanes were expected to play important security roles. Captain Robertson, MP North-East, emphasized the importance of aircraft in such scenarios when he said: "I do suggest we have paratroopers with adequate troop-carrying planes that if trouble breaks out in a place like Fort Hill, the rapid delivery of a company of paratroopers there while the civil authority tries to get the situation under control and with the knowledge that from those planes may come tear gas bombs or paratroopers would have a most detrimental effect on the rabble rousers from that area."[100] The Nyasaland emergency proved to many Southern Rhodesians the necessity to maintain a state of readiness in the territory. Wightwick, the MP for Salisbury North, argued that the Defence Vote, which reached over £4,500,000 or 10 percent of the total expenditure, was a tremendous burden for a small country like Rhodesia.[101] Wightwick was, however, criticized by Sawyer, the MP for Salisbury Suburbs, who argued that the expenditure was justifiable on the grounds that the reaction of the Army and the RRAF in the Nyasaland emergency of 1959 was because of an efficient organization which had to be maintained at all times.[102] Sawyer defended the budget on the basis that the responsibilities of the armed forces were not limited to one territory as in the pre–Federation days, but were extended over three territories. Sawyer attributed the success in Nyasaland to the high state of organization.[103] The approximate total cost of the operation of the Nyasaland Emergency by April 1959 was £306,000, bringing cessation of normal training and routine activities.[104]

One aspect that made internal security more pertinent to Southern Rhodesia was the fact that the Rhodesians understood the resentments arising across the continent as a result of whites' activities. Against this background, any suggestions related to the cutting down of the defense services were considered a huge mistake.[105] Southern Rhodesia was aware of the fact that the world was against the oppression of the majority in Central Africa. To be able to deal with such emergencies, they were supposed to equip a force able to deal with internal and external threats.[106] In fact, the costs of the defense services were supposed to be increased despite the hardships involved. This was crucial because the activities of nationalists were stepping up. Related to this, Fox, the MP for Umniati, strongly supported the increase of the size of the army and the air force so that they would be capable of dealing with both internal and external threats.[107] The colony felt that the greatest help it was giving to the Empire was by looking after its own affairs and seeing that there was no conflict.[108]

The winds of change were generally sweeping across Africa. As early as 1957, PM Roy Welensky reiterated the need to maintain peace and stability within the Federation.[109] Reacting to the Congo crisis, Welensky emphasized that the federal government was supposed to keep everything in a state of preparedness. To this end, reserve battalions were called out and given some training to make certain that in case of emergency they would be available and fit for use.[110] The Europeans rushed to Katanga and Elisabethville in Congo to rescue their own.[111] In the same vein, Field, the MP for Mrewa, pointed out that the issue of defense and the armed forces was a very important aspect in the lives of Rhodesia in the light of the vastly changing conditions which prevailed in the world and in Africa, particularly Central Africa.[112] In view of these challenges, the MP for Hartley/Gatooma, Group Captain Harris, stressed the significance of the air force when he noted that it was still very mobile, making it the most important arsenal, not only for attack, but for defense and also for internal security.[113]

To be able to meet its internal security roles, the government decided to increase the RRAF airlift capacity by purchasing four Argonaut aircraft from the British Overseas Airways Corporation.[114] The government concluded that it would be unwise to rely on civil aviation to supplement the RRAF transport resources in times of local disturbances or war. Argonauts were well suited for internal use because a fleet of four carried in one lift approximately 250 police or troops. In addition, they had similar takeoff and landing characteristics to the Dakota and could use airstrips that in normal circumstances would be used by Dakotas.[115] With such advantages, they were a major addition to the territory's capacity to reinforce any area in the Federation on demand. However, the models had their own defects, mainly attributed to old age. For example, the engines on the RRAF Argonaut that transported the Churchill School Pipe Band to the UK had to be changed during the course of the journey in 1961. The aircraft returned to Salisbury 50 minutes after takeoff and two engines were changed.[116]

The formation of the RRAF Volunteer Reserve in 1961 was significant in providing an additional source of trained manpower to support the RhAF Regular Force in the case of crisis. Such an emergency was conceived as being an internal security situation within the Federation.[117] It was increasingly becoming apparent that a potential external threat to the Federation could develop across the northern, eastern and western borders. It was thus impossible for the regular force to provide all the necessary manpower to cope with the developing challenges.[118] Recruitment for the volunteer force started at the headquarters at Dolphin House, Salisbury, to cover both Northern and Southern Rhodesia. Two Regular officers, Wing Commander Dickie Bradshaw and Flight Lieutenant Don Holliday flew to Lusaka to establish an operations center for use and training by Volunteer Reserve members there.[119] Field, the MP for Mrewa, wanted auxiliaries to be reintroduced cognizant of the role they played in the defense of Britain in 1940.[120] The unit existed in Southern Rhodesia but was dropped. The Minister of Defence, Caldicott, rejected the proposal on the basis that it was extremely expensive. Instead, the Territorial Air Force was established.[121] The MP for Bulawayo Suburbs, Eastwood, had argued in late 1954 that the government should reconsider the question of developing an auxiliary air force apart from the permanent one instead of the one they proposed to develop, the Reserve Air Force.[122]

The Federal community gave internal security utmost importance to an extent that they imagined the possibilities of a nuclear war that had even failed to take place during the Cold War. The MP for Lusaka west, Gaunt, asked the Minister of Home Affairs in 1961 the steps that had been taken by the government to provide for civilian defense in the case of a nuclear war.[123] The Minister of Economic Affairs, Caldicott, on behalf of the Minister of Home Affairs, affirmed that neither the strategic position nor the economic factors in the Federation placed it in the line of attack in a nuclear war.[124] The interwar period is thus significant in examining the centrality attached to internal security by the Federal community.

The Centrality of Commonwealth Defense After 1945

Commonwealth defense was of utmost importance to the Southern Rhodesian government after 1945. The RhAF actively participated in conflicts involving the Empire in Kenya, Malaya, Korea, Iraq, the Middle East, Aden,

Arabian Peninsula, and Cyprus, to mention a few. Up until 1963, when Rhodesia was under Britain's rule, the force was trained, armed and structured principally to help out with imperial defense. The Colony's aircraft and manpower were regularly called upon to join the RAF in Aden, Cyprus and other war zones.[125] Part of the motivation for this was to justify settler ambitions for Southern Rhodesia to become an independent dominion along the lines of Canada or Australia. The colony's security sector was modernized to an extent that it assisted Kenya with officers from the police force who helped them in training some of their people because of the logistical challenges faced there.[126] The RAR were in the Canal Zone for some considerable time. When one of the northern battalions went to Malaya, Southern Rhodesia sent a portion of a battalion of the RAR to take their place during the four months before the other battalion returned from foreign assignment.[127] In a meeting held at the Defense Headquarters on November 4, 1949, the SRAF was assigned to meet the requirements of the Overseas Defence Committee, that is, to field one or two squadrons in the event of war. It was anticipated that in time of war, the existing SRAF would be offered to the RAF for direction throughout the hostilities.[128] In 1951, the Minister of Defence highlighted the colony's role in imperial defense when he said: "We have successfully come through a trying year and I am proud to say that we in Rhodesia are making a small, [but] important contribution in the sake of world peace. I would refer to our Squadron with the Special Air Service (SAS) in Malaya and to the draft from the RhAF which will shortly leave for the Middle East...."[129]

The government of Southern Rhodesia spent £1 million in the Korean crisis (1950–53) in 1951.[130] In the same year in March, a unit composed entirely of volunteers was dispatched to serve with the UK's forces in Malaya.[131] The cost of training and equipping the first battalion of the Rhodesian African Regiment for service in Malaya was £33,996, while the cost of transportation of the battalion from Llewellin Barracks to Beira, the point of embarkation, was £1,681.[132] Although the costs were recovered from the UK government, the Federation initially met the costs, thus signifying the level of imperial commitment. Just like internal security, Commonwealth defense was seriously prioritized by the Federation. The point was made clear by Federal PM Welensky when he said: "What good is it to say that we are capable of maintaining internal defence if the Commonwealth collapses around our ears? We are members of a club, I like to think, and I believe we should pay our membership if you want to be a member of it.... We are part of the British Commonwealth, and I hope in the not far too distant future an independent member of it. There are responsibilities on our shoulders and we have to bear them."[133] As a result of being a member of the Commonwealth, the Federation had a duty to make a contribution, no matter how small, towards Commonwealth defense. According to the Federal Minister of Defence, Viscount Malvern, the Federation had two roles: firstly to maintain good order within the Federation, and secondly to assist the Commonwealth effort in war.[134] The Minister of Defence revealed that the Federation's air effort was the only form of assistance which was surely immediate, in terms of deployment. As a result, the air force was supposed to be maintained at the standard required for it to carry out its task in the war, although it was quite expensive because for it to be operational or battle worthy, it needed first-class men, equipment and resources.[135]

The Federation started off with two Canberra squadrons which carried out exercises with the RAF based in Cyprus in September 1959. No. I RRAF Vampire squadron was sent to the support of the British forces in the Arabian Peninsula from January to March 1958 under RAF command. The squadron was again sent to Aden during August and September 1958 at the request of the UK government.[136] This inaugurated a scheme for the annual training of Rhodesian air units with Aden forces as a contribution to Commonwealth defense.[137] Vampires were preferred because of their suitability to conventional wars. Welensky justified the operations of the RhAF as part of the federal government commitment to the British forces in the Middle East in support of the Baghdad Pact.[138] In July 1958, No. 1 Squadron was dispatched to Aden to support the British forces, following a coup in Iraq. Three aircraft of No. 3 Squadron were in support.[139] Huggins argued that the problem of financing the re-equipment of the SRAF was supposed to be examined from the standpoint of imperial defense rather than as a domestic problem for the colony.[140] Trends in the Middle East revealed the significance of east Africa as a potential air base while air training in Southern Rhodesia made a direct contribution to commonwealth security.[141] In order to provide "maximum" contribution to imperial defense, the army alone had four regular battalions, plus certain independent companies which helped to defend the Commonwealth, mainly against Communism or any other type of aggression if the need arose.[142]

Although the disbandment of the Federation did result in losses of personnel, equipment and aircraft, the RRAF was not crippled because it retained most of the infrastructure critical for its survival. Below is a discussion of the squadrons which remained intact after 1963.

RhAF Squadrons

No. 1 (Day Fighter/Ground Attack) Squadron

The unit can be traced back to 1939. After the outbreak of World War II, the air unit was officially known as the SRAF. This meant that the flights on service in Kenya were designated to No. 1 Squadron. The absorption of all RhAF personnel into the RAF in 1940 meant the redesignation of No. 1 Squadron to No. 237 (Rhodesia) Squadron, and from it grew the RhAF. The squadron was equipped with Hawker Hunter aircraft. Mr. de Cock, deputy minister in the Department of the PM, presented the Jacklin Trophy to No. 1 Squadron for being the most efficient squadron of the year in May 1974.[143]

No. 2 (Ground Attack/Advanced Flying Training) Squadron

The squadron was formed in 1951. Its role was that of flying training, ground attack in close support operations, and air defense against relatively unsophisticated aircraft.[144] It was equipped with Vampire aircraft and became officially affiliated to Que Que (Kwekwe) in August 1964.[145]

No. 3 (Transport Support) Squadron

Equipped with Dakotas, No. 3 Squadron was established in 1953. The role of No. 3 Squadron was that of air support, paratrooping, resupply, sky shouting, search and rescue and air communications, including VIP transport.[146] In 1954, £29,000 was reserved for the purchase of a Dakota because the SRAF by then had only one Dakota. This was considered inadequate for the purposes for which it was required, as at any time it had to carry police or troops.[147] The unit operated continuously in support of the other squadrons, the army and police, in a wide variety of roles such as communication flying, air trooping, paratrooping, air freighting, supply dropping and several evaluation exercises.[148] It also worked closely with the Special Air Service, especially in the provision of transport.[149]

No. 4 (Light Ground Attack/Basic Flying Training) Squadron

It was equipped with Provost aircraft and formed in January 1956. The role of No. 4 Squadron was that of support of the army in internal security operations. This was later modified in 1969 with the introduction of the Trojan aircraft to include light transport, reconnaissance, forward air control, casualty evacuation (casevac) and light ground attack.[150] It was moved from RRAF New Sarum to RRAF Thornhill at the beginning of the Second Chimurenga and was affiliated to Umtali.[151]

No. 5 (Lighter Bomber/Ground Attack/Photo Reconnaissance) Squadron

No. 5 Squadron was set up on April 13, 1959. The role of No. 5 Squadron was that of bombing and photo reconnaissance. It was equipped with Canberra aircraft, moved from RRAF Thornhill to RRAF New Sarum (Manyame) in

January 1964.¹⁵² A wide variety of photographic tasks were successfully completed, mainly for the Department of Survey.¹⁵³

No. 6 (Flying Training) Squadron

No. 6 Squadron was formed in 1960 and was absorbed into No. 5 Squadron in 1963. It was resuscitated in 1967. After 1977 the roles of the squadron changed to basic training, light strike and weapons training.¹⁵⁴ It was resuscitated in order to concentrate all flying training to "Wings" standard in one unit, and to relieve No. 2 and 4 Squadrons of these duties.¹⁵⁵ The squadron was primarily responsible for flight standardization throughout the force for all basic and advanced flying training, and for the training of new flying instructors. It conducted flying instructor and instrument rating examiners' courses for qualified pilots.¹⁵⁶ It was also a training unit for students undergoing basic and advanced training in Provost and Vampire aircraft.¹⁵⁷

No. 7 (Vertical Support) Squadron

It was established on February 28, 1962. The roles of No. 7 Squadron, equipped with Alouette III aircraft, were troop transportation, casualty evacuation and battlefield support including fireforce.¹⁵⁸ They were experienced in troop deployment and casevac under all weather conditions and over all types of terrain. They also did air reconnaissance and air search while the police were assisted on a number of occasions in various areas. The squadron was affiliated to the municipality of Fort Victoria (Masvingo). It was awarded the Jacklin Trophy for having achieved the best overall progress in ground and air efficiency throughout 1964.¹⁵⁹ The helicopters were introduced in Southern Rhodesia after the RRAF had perceived the value of such aircraft in a country with rough terrain.¹⁶⁰ The advent of helicopters changed the art of modern warfare. "Choppers" were first flown during the Korean crisis and thereafter they became popular models.¹⁶¹

No. 1 Parachute Training School

A parachute evaluation detachment was sent to Rhodesia in 1960 by the RAF and a number of Rhodesian servicemen were selected for training and taught how to parachute. The RhAF Parachute Training School was situated at New Sarum outside Salisbury as a result of experiments carried out with the help of RAF personnel. Its functions were to train army parachutists and parachute jumping instructors, to keep abreast with developments in military parachuting and training methods, to develop and adapt parachuting techniques and to meet the requirements and conditions of the country.¹⁶² In December 1960, volunteers to be trained as parachute jumping instructors were called for, resulting in six young men being selected and sent to the RAF parachute school at Abingdon, Berkshire, in April 1961.[163] New members of the Rhodesian Special Air Service squadron and Southern Rhodesia Army received their basic training during 1964 at No. 1 Parachute Training School. Regular SAS training was conducted at the station.[164] The United Kingdom was the main source of supply for aircraft spares and components while France supplied Alouette helicopter spares.[165]

The Recruitment and Treatment of Africans in the Air Force After World War II

This section argues that the segregation of Africans was common in all sections of the RSF, as demonstrated by their treatment during and after the world wars. Though segregation was a common feature of the Rhodesian military system since the beginning of colonialism, its manifestation can be traced from 1914, when the Africans were actively involved in the military assignments of the colony. While the preceding chapter highlighted that the availability of cheap labor in Southern Rhodesia was crucial in the establishment of the RATG, the interwar period shows how the same people who had loyally served the Empire were relegated to low-paying jobs compared to their white counterparts. The Africans were given jobs largely shunned by the white population, including laundry duties, guarding, cooking and construction, to mention but just a few. By and large, Africans were belittled and their effort in the development of the RhAF went largely unrecognized. This analysis is important because it helps us understand the reasons why the Rhodesians underrated Africans' effort during the war, describing them as "aimless terrorists" bent on making the country ungovernable. After more than a decade of warring, the Rhodesians found their losses escalating despite possessing a reasonably efficient air force. Toward the end of the war, the nationalists negotiated for independence from a point of strength.

The Rhodesians' recruitment and remuneration policy towards Africans could well be understood from a broader picture of the white man's attitude towards Africans as backward and uncivilized. When congratulating one of the centenarian pioneers (Orlando Baragwanath) in 1972, the PM of Rhodesia, Ian Douglas Smith, said: "People like yourself came into the wild interior of Africa to establish the outposts of our modern civilisation, and it is because of the dedication and enterprise of our pioneers that Rhodesia has thrived and prospered."[166] Smith stated that the whites strove to persevere with western civilization on the southern corner of the African continent.[167] Federal Minister of Defence Roy Welensky echoed Smith's sentiments by adding that the regulations under the Defence Act empowered the commander to accept a recruit of a standard of education, and the standard was normally not less than Form III. No minimum education requirements were laid down for European recruits, but were posted to the African battalions when they were fully qualified in the rank they held.[168]

Educational standards for the RhAF required candidates to pass a minimum of five subjects at grade five or above at GCE Ordinary level, including English language, mathematics, physics or general science.[169] Welensky held that the following attributes were prerequisites for a place in the RhAF: intelligence, a sense of responsibility, tenacity and determination, personality, power of expression—both verbal and written, physical fitness, sound military knowledge, and qualities of leadership, except for specialist officers.[170] Using these yardsticks, the minister informed the Parliament that no suitable African candidates came forward.[171] The type and level of education offered to Africans indicates that they were destined to join the military for the sake of European pride. While it is true that recruitment in the air force was guided by professional standards, racism was nonetheless widespread in the recruitment process. Some whites failed to qualify in the SRAF because they lacked physical fitness. Examples included McDiarmid William Parker, number M2213, who was officially discharged from the SRAF on July 31, 1943, after being attested at Salisbury on July 21, 1943.[172] Parker served for only eleven days, the reason being lack of physical fitness. The same applied to Mackenzie L.R. Kenneth, number M2278, who was discharged on February 8 after being attested at Salisbury on January 20, 1944. He served for nineteen days with SRAF before being discharged as physically unfit for any form of air force duties.[173]

The subsequent federal debate between Federal Defence Minister Welensky and Wellington Chirwa, specially elected African Member of Parliament for Nyasaland, reveals how whites sought the entrenchment of their privileges in the Defence Forces. Chirwa argued that the government could not take any account of and could not claim to represent Africans.

> CHIRWA: Does the Minister of Defence intend to appoint some Africans to the commissioned ranks?
> MINISTER OF DEFENCE: Not at the present time, Mr. Speaker.
> CHIRWA: Why does he not intend to appoint some at the present time?
> MINISTER OF DEFENCE: Because there are none qualified, Mr. Speaker.[174]

Davies, Specially Elected European Member, Southern Rhodesia, viewed Africans as a retrogressive race, claiming: "The trouble today, Mr. Speaker, is that the vast mass of Africans in the Federation cannot be said to have any opinion. For centuries the people of Africa had no opportunity whatsoever, they were at the mercy of the slave trader and their despotic kings. Since people from the west have come to Africa, that opportunity has been granted to them."[175] The Europeans considered themselves superior to Africans, whom they viewed as primitive and semi-primitive people.[176] The minds of Africans were viewed as unsophisticated and easily molded,[177] a perceptual error that exposed the Rhodesian military system during the Second Chimurenga. Policy formulation was motivated by the aims of institutionalizing colonial state hegemony, perpetuating perceived African inferiority and undermining the creation of an informed African political community.[178]

There is plentiful evidence to demonstrate the contribution made by African soldiers in imperial defense during World War I and World War II. Nonetheless, their role was seriously undermined in both wars. The Rhodesia Native Regiment served in East Africa during the Great War, but after the war African veterans were ignored and forgotten. At the same time, white veterans of the war were hailed as Rhodesian national heroes and histories of their wartime experiences were published, beginning in the 1920s.[179] The RNR fought with distinction against General von Lettow-Vorbeck in German East Africa, but the loyal service of the RNR during the Great War was conveniently forgotten by 1939.[180] The RAR was formed in 1940 under Major Wane (nicknamed Msorowegomo). The regiment was given subsidiary task of guarding the 25th Indian Division's lines of communication in 1944.[181] After the war the regiment was disbanded and forgotten.

During World War II the RATG had an African unit called the Rhodesian Air Askari Corps, essentially formed to provide armed guards and non-armed labor under the command of Wing Commander Price. There were 2,000 armed Askari for guard duties and about 3,000 for general duties such as working in the hangars and workshops, and as cooks, waiters, messengers, groundsmen and cleaners.[182] To attain sufficient manpower, special recruits' visits to various chiefs were paid by Price.[183] There were a lot of embarrassments in the military as a result of ill-treatment, low wages, and labor-intensive duties with very limited chances for promotion or long-term career advancement. At times African chiefs were bribed or forced to provide recruits and ordinary men were always vulnerable. The Africans constituted a fairly big number of the Federal Defence Force, as illustrated below:

Table 4.8: Strength of the Federal Forces in 1959

Army	Europeans	Colored/Asians	Africans
Regular forces	787	-	3,038
Territorial forces	2,634	277	-
RRAF	487	-	-
Total	3,908	277	3,038[184]

The table illustrates that the growth of the Defence Forces was proportional to the marginalization of African soldiers. This is true because the federal population had 95.9 percent Africans, 3.7 percent Europeans, and 0.4 percent Asians and coloreds in 1959.[185] Dr. Palley inquired from Minister of Defence Jack Howman in 1969 the number of coloreds, Asians and Africans respectively, who held commissioned ranks in the Rhodesian Army and the RRAF. It emerged that none had such a rank.[186] The Africans supplied labor to various Rhodesian industries but were paid meager wages, which again reflected the racist nature of European rule. Likewise, Morar and Patel, who were Asians, applied for entry to a technical training wing course in 1960 in RRAF but they were refused admission because technical training was only open to European personnel.[187] The table below shows how Africans were poorly remunerated despite constituting the vast pool of labor.

Table 4.9: Average Earnings in the Federation Per Annum (£) (case of Southern Rhodesia)

Race	1954	1958	1959	1960	Compound rate of increase since 1954 (%)
Africans	56	79	82	84	7
Europeans	875	1,070	1,081	1117	4
Asians and coloreds	424	532	558	569	5[188]

The white population opposed the arming of Africans for many reasons. They viewed it as a gateway to the "extinction" of the white man in Rhodesia, and they reminded their colleagues about the First Chimurenga, which had ravaged the country in the past decades. White farmers were also afraid of depletion of labor, an issue raised by the Rhodesian Agricultural Union on June 18, 1940, which said that if natives were recruited for the native regiment there would be no spare labor left in the reserves to form labor gangs to assist farmers.[189]

Conclusion

The interwar period is one of the most important periods in the development of the Rhodesian Air Force as a modern instrument of war. Despite the challenges encountered in the resumption of air training, Southern Rhodesia convinced the Air Ministry to come back again. The availability of relevant infrastructure inherited from RATG made the whole job easier. The RAF continued to play a significant role in empowering the SRAF through offering refresher courses and selling ex-RAF aircraft at subsidized prices. Defense became the principal responsibility of the Federation. The deployment of the RRAF to the Middle East to back British forces in the Arabian Peninsula and Aden in 1958 shows the consistent loyalty of the colony to imperial defense. Even if Commonwealth defense stood up as a priority, the end of the war in 1945 presented a strategic shift whereby the development of the air force was primarily geared towards securing the internal security of the Federation. The importance of aircraft in internal security was apparent in 1959 in the midst of a plot to murder the governor of Nyasaland. The RRAF provided the advantages of air power such as speed and flexibility. They swiftly carried troops to Malawi for various tactical roles such as firing tear-gas bombs and reconnaissance flights. The Nyasaland emergency was an eye opener to the importance of internal security in the three territories. The defense budget reached 10 percent of the total expenditure in an effort to meet the defense requirements of the Federation. Events in Central Africa and the country demanded the country to be more attentive to internal security issues.

The Federation was exceptional in developing the RhAF by increasing squadrons from two to seven. The models were reduced to cut down the costs of purchasing spare parts. The army and air force commands were separated in 1954. This meant that the air force now possessed its own independent structures which were different from those of the Army. The air force took a wider responsibility other than defending Southern Rhodesia alone. The interwar period witnessed an influx of aircraft and personnel to operate them. Besides, the air force made some remarkable improvements in enhancing the available fleet; for example, there were 64 airplanes in 1954 and 71 airplanes in 1959. This signified that the RhAF was ready to take over the security requirements of the Federation and Commonwealth. Air power was important because it was the quickest means of transport available to the Federation. The interwar period also reveals the challenges faced by the RhAF as a weapon of war. This was evident in the critical shortage of spare parts, while the lack of manpower became a permanent problem. More so, despite the Africans' sacrifice in imperial defense during World War II, they received very little recognition.

5
The Impact of the Rhodesian Air Force During the Second Chimurenga

> To achieve command of the air means victory; to be beaten in the air means defeat.... Any diversion from this primary purpose is an error....[1]—*Giulio Douhet*

Introduction

The aim of this chapter is to assess the tactical impact of the Rhodesian Air Force on the operations of guerrilla armies, that is, the Zimbabwe African National Liberation Army and the Zimbabwe People's Revolutionary Army during the Second Chimurenga. When the Second Chimurenga broke out, the Rhodesian Security Forces never anticipated the war to stretch for more than a decade because they had sophisticated weaponry in the form of one of the most efficient air forces on the continent. But it would be an overstatement to suggest that the Rhodesian military strategists had the "short-war illusion" common in the war planners of the First World War. The availability of advanced weaponry convinced European generals that the war would be over by Christmas of 1914. In the case of Zimbabwe's liberation war, the operations of the Rhodesian Air Force were enhanced by the flawed early infiltration tactics of the guerrilla armies. The Rhodesian Air Force played a significant role in responding to guerrilla incursions mainly through facilitating the deployment of other units such as the Selous Scouts, Special Air Service, Rhodesian Light Infantry, British South Africa Police, Rhodesian African Rifles and Rhodesian Defence Regiment. The RhAF was able to master the art of airborne warfare but the odds were highly stacked against it. On the whole, this chapter assesses the impact of the RhAF operations such as air strikes, troop transportation and casualty evacuation in the conduct of guerrilla warfare.

The colony immensely benefited from the experiences of airmen who returned to Southern Rhodesia after the Second World War. World War II proved that air power could achieve impressive results in the battlefield. Hitler's blitzkrieg strategy left a huge and remarkable impression as to the efficacy of air power in conventional warfare. Rhodesia had "natural" command of the air because she totally controlled the skies without any serious challenge from the guerrillas who lacked superior anti-air batteries until late in the struggle. Moreover, the guerrilla armies lacked air support to back their activities. The RhAF was a force to be reckoned with at the breakup of the Federation due to the RATG, which had modernized the force. The air force was also able to violate the air space of Frontline states harboring guerrillas. Although guerrilla tactics needed perfecting, from 1970 the tide was turning against Rhodesia's military machine. This was revealed by legislators who argued that Rhodesia was not prepared enough to meet the challenges posed by the insurgents. Hope Hall, the MP for Highlands South, moved a motion in Parliament in 1972 emphasizing readiness: "Should we not more fully harness our manpower now rather than late so that we have at least the best chance of meeting and overcoming any dangers? My point is that when the whole of southern Africa is so obviously threatened by outside forces and at the same time when our own neighbouring governments give warnings about these dangers, then I believe it is our duty to do everything in our power to prepare for these sorts of eventualities by mobilising our manpower to make quite certain that, unlike Britain in 1940, we are not caught with our pants down."[2]

Internal security, long emphasized during the interwar period, was now a living reality. But one thing that emerged was that the manpower state of Rhodesia remained ever turbulent thereby giving leverage to the guerrillas who poured in their thousands.

How Did the Rhodesian Air Force Affect Guerrilla Operations?

Tactical Mobility and Casualty Evacuation

The skills of the RhAF were beyond doubt especially in the transportation and tactical deployment of forces to various parts of the country occupied by guerrilla armies. The RhAF was undoubtedly the most overstretched unit of the RSF because the high infiltration of the guerrillas catapulted its role. Initially limited to border patrols, the function of the RhAF substantially increased to troop tactical deployment, transportation of troops, equipment and rations, casualty evacuation, air reconnaissance, air search, air strikes and terror missions. The guerrillas suffered multiple challenges as a result of the activities of the RhAF. Transport aircraft from No. 3 Squadron were employed extensively in the redeployment of personnel and the transportation of vital equipment and rations in the border areas and between permanent bases.[3] Aircraft from No. 4 and 7 Squadrons were crucial for security force members in need of urgent medical attention and to fly numerous civilian mercy missions, many of which were accomplished in the most difficult flying conditions.[4] In addition to their other roles, the Trojan and Alouette III helicopters were effective in close support and in improving the mobility and flexibility of the ground forces.[5] In 1977, Wing Commander Gaunt was delighted with the progress made by No. 4 and 7 Squadrons: "I would like to congratulate in particular those members of No. 4 and No. 7 Squadron of the RhAF who form the backbone of the air force effort in combating terrorism. Their tremendous contribution to the overall security situation in this country will probably never be fully appreciated."[6]

Casualty evacuation took precedence over all other work for No. 7 Squadron.[7] Other duties of No. 7 Squadron in the operational areas were to provide logistical arrangements to troops and tactically deploying men as requested by the security forces, primarily the army and police.[8] The operations of No. 7 Squadron buttressed the significance of mobility in warfare. The active role of the squadron provided the much-needed mobility of troops and supplies. Their operations made a difference in responding to the insurgents. According to the Joint Air Power Competence Centre (JAPCC), air power is important in irregular warfare for tactical mobility. The deployment of helicopters for tactical mobility constitutes one of the features of post–World War II counterinsurgency operations. The use of helicopters for air transport remarkably improves the mobility of the infantry.[9] Helicopters also facilitate in protecting the land forces from ambush in the usually challenging environment favored by the guerrillas and enables small land units to conduct operations over a wide terrain.[10] During the Algerian War of Independence (1954–1962), the French Air Force mainly concentrated on rapid movement of men and material and on surveillance.[11] During the Second Chimurenga, mobility was very important in facilitating the element of surprise. The RhAF was able to swiftly respond to guerrilla incursions and this was really a challenge to guerrilla warfare in general.

Helicopters were experienced in troop deployment and casualty evacuation under all weather conditions and over all sorts of terrain. These abilities proved vital in ameliorating the depleted Rhodesian manpower. In December 1977, trooper Craig Borne (then 22 years of age) was hit on the leg by the guerrillas while on patrol on the border with his Rhodesian Light Infantry colleagues.

However, immediate casevac ensured that within three hours Borne was receiving medical care at Andrew Fleming Hospital (now Parirenyatwa Hospital).[12] On the other hand, guerrillas perished in the bush. Twelve guerrillas were killed in air-supported ground fighting in the northeast of the country in June 1974.[13] Even if there were victims who could survive, there was no transport to take them to a hospital. Helicopters were also used for casualty evacuation at the Battle of Samanga in 1977, in Honde Valley. Samanga was a homestead where the guerrillas had camped. Honde Valley, or the homestead in particular, had its own strategic advantages because it was covered by banana trees that gave protection to the guerrillas and civilians alike. The battle took about four hours. The RSF suffered because mist hindered the provision of air support.[14] In contrast to this, the mist worked to the advantage of the guerrillas because they ended up occupying a highland, thus gaining advantage of the terrain. Similarly, in 1978, there was a battle at Chief Mutasa's homestead, which led to the deaths of some white forces. The RSF took two days to evacuate their forces because it was a semi-liberated zone.[15] Helicopters were later deployed to evacuate troops who had been killed by about seven guerrillas.[16] Casualty evacuation was also extended to those civilians in danger. The RRAF carried out valuable work in relieving the flood victims in Kenya, as well as the work they did in Kuwait.[17] An underground explosion on June 6, 1972, at Wankie (Hwange), No. 2 Colliery, left the lives of 468 mining personnel underground in danger.[18] The Minister of Defence provided aircraft of the RhAF to ferry rescue personnel provided by the parent company and other sectors of the industry, together with proto-rescue apparatus, to Wankie.[19] Troop deployment and casualty evacuation revealed the importance of mobility in warfare. The guerrillas found themselves under constant harassment because the RhAF was always prepared to act when called to do so.

Effects on Recruitment, Deployment and Operations of the Guerrillas

This section examines the impact of the operations of the Rhodesian Air Force on guerrilla recruitment and deployment. The RhAF facilitated the implementation of the operations organized by other forces. Cross-border operations started in 1976 with a raid on Nyadzonia in Mozambique in which the Rhodesians killed over 1,200 guerrillas and captured huge numbers of weapons.[20] The air force undertook cross-border operations mainly to fulfill Special Air Service (SAS) long-range reconnaissance missions. In addition, the air force had an additional role as a quick-reaction force and the capability for direct-action missions such as cross-border operations.[21] The tactic to hit cross-border targets was referred to as "hot pursuit" by the Rhodesian authorities. Hot pursuits aimed at tracking down "terrorists" operating in Rhodesia who sought sanctuary in Frontline states.[22] The bombardment of neighboring countries was done to threaten these countries that their economic and social infrastructure would be demolished if they continued supporting guerrillas.[23] It was also an endeavor to scare black Zimbabweans to accept white rule as invincible, as even the mildest form of opposition was punishable by death. There was also need to internationalize the war within Rhodesia so as to get military and financial support.[24] In addition, the bombing of targets in Zambia and Mozambique was expected to make people revolt against their governments. Demonstrations from the public in these countries would then lead to the ejection of guerrilla armies.[25]

During the attack of Teresera base in January 1973, the camp was obliterated, leading to the deaths of about 1,000 recruits and some trained guerrillas who could not match the RhAF firepower. Even FRELIMO's assistance could not help the situation.[26] Although Nyadzonia was an exploit of the Selous Scouts, it deserves mention to exemplify how the RSF were determined to cripple guerrilla resistance. The RSF felt justified in their attack on the United Nations High Commission for Refugees (UNHCR)–supported Nyadzonia in August 1976 because they believed that Nyadzonia refugee camp had many potential recruits for the guerrilla army, even though none of them had yet received any military training.[27] In contrast to the stated figure of 1,200 people killed at Nyadzonia, Fay Chung argues that only 600 refugees were killed while 500 were injured. Nonetheless, the crux of the matter is that all of these were potential recruits, thus the recruitment base was disturbed. As chronicled by Easygo Mamboininga (pseudonym), one of the survivors of the Nyadzonia attack who escaped through the river, many people died in Nyadzonia River because they did not give each other time to cross the river using the makeshift bridge.[28] It is imperative to highlight at this stage that ZANLA bases were strategically positioned along water sources so as to have a reliable water supply for the guerrillas and refugees inside the camps. In Mozambique, many of these bases were located along the Pungwe River.[29]

In view of the Chimoio and several other raids conducted by the RhAF, it is clear that the air strikes negatively impacted the recruitment and deployment of guerrilla armies, considering the carnage of prospective and trained recruits who were supposed to be deployed to the front. The Director of Air Intelligence (DAI) reported to the Director-General on all aspects of air and naval intelligence. DAI provided aerial photography of external training camps or possible targets for sabotage operations and provided naval intelligence on the port of Beira and inland water traffic on Lake Kariba.[30] DAI provided efficient photographic interpretations which were of utmost importance in planning external operations such as the raids against Chimoio, Tembwe and Nyadzonia. SAS operations were executed after consulting the DAI.[31] Chimoio and Tembwe, among other bases, held recruits on their way north for training and provided launching pads for trained guerrillas re-entering Rhodesia.[32] Attacks on large guerrilla camps such as Chimoio, Luso, Mulungushi and Tembwe resulted in the deaths of thousands of guerrillas and the capture of supplies sorely needed by the Rhodesians.[33] Chimoio had a limited number of trained personnel as the majority of casualties were untrained women, men and children.[34]

It became a matter of policy for the Smith regime to destroy all guerrilla training bases in order to cripple the resistance especially from outside. This also emanated from the failure to deal with insurgency at home. Ian Smith made it clear in the late 1970s: "When terrorists operate from foreign bases you cannot knock them out completely without knocking out the countries from which they operate. That is, in our case, Mozambique and Zambia."[35] This inevitably meant that the guerrilla bases in neighboring countries were supposed to be razed to the ground. Surprise attacks on these bases killed thousands of recruits. Chimoio was one of the deadly surprise attacks during the war. The bombardment was also a clear indication of the poor intelligence gathering techniques of African armies during the war. Every time, the guerrillas were caught with their pants down. According to Prussian philosopher Carl Von Clausewitz, surprise is the most powerful element of victory.[36] The rapid arrival and buildup of aircraft near or in trouble spots provides a visible sign of presence and intent.[37] During the war, the guerrillas could not beat the element of surprise, but rather devised tactics to deal with surprise attacks. At Chimoio, ZANLA guerrillas were caught unaware during their morning parade at around 8 a.m. At this time the recruits were gathered for a briefing. The attacks came at a time when the guerrillas had absolutely no weapons to defend themselves.[38]

A number of guerrillas were killed at Chimoio because they did not expect the air raids.[39] One of the claimed survivors, Oppah Muchinguri, explained how people were caught unaware: "We saw planes, about ten initially, flying towards the camp. We did not suspect anything as we thought they were Mozambican."[40] Muchinguri's explanation concurs with the version given by another Chimoio survivor, Benz Chavhundura, who said that they thought the initial spotter plane that flew across was a Mozambican plane carrying patients from Tete to Maputo.[41] The situation was worsened by the fact that the type of planes used were not heard approaching until after they had already dropped their bombs, and these were later supported by helicopter gunships. Upon realizing that they were under siege, one person from the command post came to the parade and ordered people to quickly disperse.[42] In less than five minutes after dispersal, there was a spotter plane that flew across showing red lights, a signal to the other planes that they could start bombing.[43]

Envelopment strategy was employed to trap people inside the camps. Paratroops were deployed in all directions to curb the inward and outward movement of people at Chimoio. No resistance was offered as the guerrillas were on parade and there were no weapons at the site. In fact, the trainees at Chimoio used wooden guns. Such was the pathetic situation of the ZANLA guerrillas, who depended on Chinese support. It is crucial to stress that the lack of weapons was a problem amongst guerrilla armies. Sadly, there was also a shelter with a single anti-aircraft gun. Overall, there were no significant weapons at Chimoio.[44] Chimoio was attacked together with other various camps inside Mozambique, such as Parirenyatwa clinic; Chindunduma school complex; Zvidozvevanhu transport section; Wampuwa (later renamed Herbert Chitepo), specializing in political education; Nehanda, which was a women's base; Takawira I for male residents; Takawira II for training; Percy Ntini rehabilitation center for those wounded on the war front; Chaminuka security base; and Mudzingadzi for agriculture/production.[45] The attack resulted in about 20 mass graves and FRELIMO soldiers helped in burying the dead.[46] More than one thousand people were killed. The huge number of casualties was caused by the massive deployment of aircraft to bombard Chimoio. The air armada consisted of 42 helicopters, eight Hunter, six Vampires, three Canberra, six Dakotas and twelve Lynx.[47] Bombs were dropped from the Canberra, and DC-8 maintained security of the aircraft.[48] Some survivors were left mentally deranged as a result of witnessing the horrors of the attack.[49]

Despite certain myths, Chimoio was not a refugee camp, although there were civilians who had run away from the brutal Smith regime. The base was a well-established training center and all able-bodied persons at the center were awaiting training. The recruitment base perished in the attacks, but more tragic was the loss of trained men and women awaiting deployment to various parts of the country. Again refuting claims that Chimoio was a refugee camp, RSF argued that the ZANLA camp was not listed by the Mozambique authorities as a refugee camp.[50] Furthermore, according to war veteran Margret Makomva, Chimoio was a training base but there were settlements for refugees, and that is where she received her military training after staying at Nyadzonia and Doroi.[51] Chimoio was situated on a farm donated by the Mozambican government. Food from the farm was used to feed the guerrillas and recruits.[52] A glimpse at the figures of dead people at Chimoio and other guerrilla camps gives a picture of how ZANLA and ZPRA were affected in their operations as a result of the RhAF raids.

The raid on Chimoio was followed by over 30 cross-border strikes.[53] The

RhAF supported SAS in an attack on the Mozambique port of Beira in which oil installations were destroyed.[54] During the attack of Mudzingadzi Camp in Mozambique in 1978, the guerrillas were also caught unaware. According to a witness, the late Kumbirai Kangai, the Rhodesian forces bombed the garage first because they thought by this time the guerrillas would be repairing vehicles, but there was no one in the camp although there was heavy bombardment.[55] Surprise attacks dominated the tactics used by the RhAF to disrupt guerrilla mobilization. Indeed, it is practical to launch surprise attacks when possessing the advantages of speed and flexibility provided by air power. There is a nexus between mobility and surprise in warfare and the Rhodesians took advantage of this practical consideration. The speed of aircraft provided tactical challenges to guerrilla warfare. The RSF had observation posts that facilitated quick communication whenever there were signs of guerrilla presence on the terrain. The air force was thus able to make quick responses to guerrilla activities. This again shows the importance of communication in warfare.

Bombings also occurred at Mapai, one of the strongest FRELIMO bases in the Gaza Province. When Mapai was bombed, the striking force decided to airlift military equipment. When the helicopter was about to take off, it was hit by a FRELIMO soldier who had come from Pafuri camp.[56] The incident was confirmed by the then Dakota captain, John Fairey of 3 Squadron (RhAF), who said that a South African Air Force (SAAF) Puma was shot down by some sort of rocket, killing all on board, including three South African aircrew and eleven Rhodesian soldiers.[57] Mapai was one of the hot zones during the Second Chimurenga because the RSF believed that it was a major supply center and a staging post for guerrillas bound for Rhodesia.[58] In spite of these challenges, the Rhodesian Air Force played a very important role in Rhodesia's civil war. It was an indispensable component of the Rhodesian war effort. The RhAF executed assault and terror missions throughout the Second Chimurenga and inflicted big losses on guerrilla forces and civilians. Air strikes without ground support played an important factor in increasing insurgent casualties. Around mid to late 1979, a ZANLA holding camp at Nhangau, north of Beira, was bombed, leading to the deaths of about 600 casualties.[59]

On the ZAPU side, the RSF had a case of the Viscount to settle with ZPRA,[60] as evidenced by the words of Joint Minister of Transport and Power William Irvine that the claim of responsibility by Joshua Nkomo demonstrated that he was an "evil murderer and savage barbarian without any pretence of humanitarian civilised standards."[61] Irvine stressed that the country would not let the dead go unavenged when he pointed out that the security forces were hunting leaders of the Patriotic Front staying in Lusaka and elsewhere.[62] The slaughter of the defenseless civilians aboard a Viscount aircraft was portrayed as more barbaric "than anything that can be read in the annals of Genghis Khan."[63] The Rhodesians were very angry with ZPRA, and they sought to avenge the Viscount *Hunyani* and Viscount *Umniati* tragedies. Air Rhodesia's Flight RH 825 flying between Kariba and Salisbury was shot down on September 3, 1978, when a heat-seeking SAM-7 Strela missile hit near the inner starboard engine; the plane crashed and exploded in the Hurungwe Tribal Trust Land.[64] Five months later, on February 12, 1979, another Viscount airliner, the *Umniati*, was struck by a Soviet Strela heat-seeking missile and turned into a fireball in the sky, killing instantly all 59 on board.[65] The *Umniati* was struck in the jet pipe of the inner port engine, causing the plane to plunge directly to the ground.[66] ZPRA's downing of the Viscounts killed a total of 107 white persons.[67] ZAPU leader Joshua Nkomo argued that it was justifiable to attack Rhodesian civil aircraft because the airliners were equally used for carrying passengers and for carrying troops. Nkomo further claimed that Rhodesia Television had screened pictures of Viscount aircraft owned by Air Rhodesia carrying paratroopers.[68] Nkomo's claims cannot be denied because the shortage of material and personnel in the RhAF forced the defense unit to engage the services of civilian aircraft. The *Hunyani* was shot down immediately after Smith's troops had carried out a brutal attack on the Chimoio camps.[69] Moreover, Nkomo defended the downing of the second Viscount by claiming that the target was General Peter Walls, who ZPRA intelligence had indicated was on that plane.[70] It happened, however, that Walls had swapped the planes and boarded the second one.

In response to ZPRA's downing of the Viscounts, the RSF launched more raids on guerrilla bases, successfully avoiding air-defense systems and the Soviet MiG-17s based in Mozambique. Between October 18 and 20, 1978, ZPRA camps at Chikumbi (Freedom Camp) and two camps in the Mkushi area were bombarded by heliborne troops.[71] According to the RSF, about 1,600 "trained terrorists" and other ZPRA members were killed.[72] Information on Freedom Camp was gathered through aerial photographs, reconnaissance, and interrogation of captives.[73] The Hunters, helicopters and Canberra that attacked Freedom Camp used the deadly alpha anti-personnel bombs designed in Rhodesia.[74] ZAPU estimated that about 420 ZPRA comrades were killed by the Rhodesians at Mkushi Training Camp in Zambia on October 19, 1978.[75] The Rhodesian forces killed hundreds of trainees and trained cadres, leaving several hundreds injured.[76] Dakotas from Squadron No. 3 were employed during the attack on Mkushi.[77] The horrors suffered at Mkushi were described by a ZPRA woman guerrilla, Gertrude Moyo: "The day I will never forget is on the 19th October 1978 at around 11:00 a.m. when the enemy, Rhodesian forces, bombed our camp Mkushi. When they started raiding most of the women just got into the river and were eaten by crocodiles alive. Very few managed to swim across the river. Those who managed to get to the gathering points were also killed."[78] The bombings confirm that the RhAF external raids had a bearing on the conduct of the guerrilla war. Although the guerrillas faced numerous challenges, they registered success on numerous occasions. One helicopter crashed at Mkushi, injuring its two-man crew, while one soldier was killed in action.[79] A Rhodesian helicopter was also shot during a raid at Victory Camp in 1979.[80] It is thus noticeable that the RhAF's external operations disrupted guerrilla strategy in a number of ways. Recruits died before and during training and this inevitably derailed the fighting process, both morally and militarily.

Surprise air attacks on guerrilla camps such as Chimoio, Teresera, Mapai, Mkushi, Freedom, Victory, Mulungushi and Boma impacted negatively on the recruitment base of the guerrillas. It is a fact that many Zimbabweans who crossed over to the Frontline states took shelter in refugee camps before enlisting for military service. It was important for the Rhodesians to bomb these areas so as to paralyze the nationalist war effort because fireforce operations inside Rhodesia could not stop guerrilla infiltration, but rather exposed the weaknesses of Rhodesia's military machine. The bombing of refugee and military camps was fundamental in curbing guerrilla recruitment and deployment, but this did not totally hinder guerrilla resistance, since recruits were pouring out in large numbers. The RhAF claimed they were responsible for the biggest number of kills among the RSF and that their operations made the bulk of other formations' successes possible.[81] Nonetheless, in 1978 it was also becoming evident that purely as a method of inflicting insurgent casualties, outside operations were not as effective as they were initially.[82] From 1977 to 1978, ZANLA casualties resulting from such raids totaled 3,500, while the number of active insurgents in eastern Rhodesia had risen from 1,200 to more than 8,000.[83]

Huge Casualties Among Guerrillas as a Result of the Gap in Military Technology

At the beginning of the Second Chimurenga, the guerrillas were predominantly armed with AK-47s and semiautomatic rifles. Although the semiautomatic guns were improved models, these guns lacked rapid firepower because they released one bullet at a time.[84] These weapons were effective against ground targets, but planes could only be shot by chance. The guerrillas started to use big guns from 1977 onwards.[85] Although the guerrillas had anti-aircraft guns, they were comparatively inferior to the weapons used by the Rhodesians. This was evidenced in a series of battles, among them the attack of Mudzingadzi Camp. At Mudzingadzi, the guerrillas did not exchange fire immediately because they realized that the bombing intensity was just too strong.[86] More importantly, the adoption of guerrilla warfare as a strategy was born out of the realization that the enemy was technologically superior. According to former ZPRA cadre Peter "Chris Nyati" Mhizha, the guerrillas lacked huge weapons while the enemy had superior weapons, hence the hit-and-run tactic was the only way to ensure survival.[87] Except for a few machine guns, the small weapons were incapable of shooting down airplanes.[88] Margret Makomva admitted the difficulties they faced in downing the RhAF. The lack of superior firepower emerged as the dominant reason.[89] At the Battle of Ruwani fought on May 18, 1973, the Rhodesian forces started off by dropping bombs and firing at the guerrillas from their planes. This compelled the guerrillas to retreat because of heavy losses incurred.[90]

The Rhodesians were able to manufacture guns locally. They introduced home industries under Import Substitution Industrialisation (ISI) in a bid to reduce dependence on foreign countries after sanctions were imposed on them. The regime continued to develop sophisticated arms and munitions in their own industries in response to the regime's demand for guns and ammunitions. Imported weapons were expensive and scarce. Among the locally produced weapons were Rhoguns, Rhuzis, Jumbo shotguns, Mamba pistols, R76s, M77s, P78s and Cobras.[91] The Rhuzi was a semiautomatic pistol designed to fire 9mm parabellem (automatic) ammunition fed from a vertical magazine contained in a butt.[92] The ammunition industry was born in 1976 and by 1978 the managing director of Northwood Developments, Roger Mansfield-Scaddan, said that the standard of locally produced weapons was high by international standards as all had to be approved by the Standards Association of Central Africa before being sold. Each weapon was carefully tested before leaving the factories by firing both high-pressure and normal rounds.[93] The Rhodesians were militarily superior and well-equipped to fight a struggle which in Ellert's terms was "a war of Black Liberation and a war of White survival."[94] The introduction of homemade guns went a long way in sustaining the Rhodesian war effort, especially at a time when the country was under economic sanctions.

The capability to export weapons reveals the fact that the Rhodesian military industry was a big threat to poorly armed guerrilla armies. It is possible that a weapon revolution in Southern Rhodesia was facilitated by the EATS, which benefited the colony, thereby placing the country in a position to market munitions. In 1944, Halsted, the director of the Department of Supply, indicated that an order of 500,000 hand grenade center pieces had been received from the director general of supplies in the Union of South Africa, which were to be produced at the rate of 84,000 pieces per month. Production commenced in November 1944.[95]

During the "Battle of the Honde" in late 1976, the reason why the guerrillas exchanged fire with the air force was that they wanted to disperse the airplanes; anything above that was considered bonus.[96] The weapons used by the guerrillas, such as AK-47s, bazookas, light machine guns (LMG), mortar bombs and grenades, were light compared to the armored cars, machine guns and airplanes used by the RSF.[97] Bazookas were mainly used against helicopters while small rifles were effective when aiming at the pilot himself.[98] The Vampire was so maneuverable that it could spin, leading the guerrillas to believe they had shot it down, yet it would still be dropping bombs.[99] The lack of superior weaponry enabled the guerrillas and trainees to put up very little resistance during the attacks on camps such as Chimoio, Mkushi, Mudzingadzi and Freedom Camp, to mention but just a few. According to a war veteran called Nyanga, it is very doubtful if the alleged machine gun at Chimoio was ever used and whether it was the type they were using in 1979 obtained mainly from East Germany.[100] In 1979, as the war increased even more in intensity, the Rhodesian army was able to take delivery of eight T54/55 heavy tanks, which the South Africans had confiscated from a Libyan freighter when it mistakenly docked at Durban while en route to Tanzania.[101]

The Impact of Fireforce Operations on Guerrilla Strategy

The development of fireforce was one of the major achievements of the RhAF and the Joint Operations Command (JOC). One of the tactical accomplishments of Rhodesian strategists was to harmonize the qualities of the fighting forces. The military history of the Second World War proved that air power is a weapon par excellence as envisaged by Douhet, but if only combined with the other forces. Air Vice-Marshal Hawkins noted in 1967 that a spirit of harmony and cooperation prevailed among the army, the police and the air force, strengthening mutual confidence and improvement in working relationships.[102] Even though the statement was too official to contain any credibility, the operations of combined forces revealed the cooperation that existed amongst the security forces. Valuable experience was gained in actual counterinsurgency (COIN) operations, as well as from the several combined training exercises held throughout 1967 and beyond.[103] The cooperation was facilitated by the establishment of the Joint Planning Staff, which ensured the strategic coordination of military affairs to fight insurgency. The RSF exploited the natural advantages of air power to harass the guerrillas, and the consequences were really felt throughout the campaign, but were not adequate to give them victory.

The original fireforce typically consisted of four Alouette III helicopters, each manned by a pilot and technician/gunner. Three of the helicopters, referred to as "G-cars," were used to transport four fully equipped troops, while a fourth helicopter, called the "K[for kill]-car," carried a pilot who was the senior Air Force officer, a gunner-technician, and the Army unit commander, who directed the operations below. The "K-car" could also be used as a gunship when required. The four helicopters were supported by a fixed-wing aircraft equipped with rockets and machine guns.[104] Later in the conflict, the regular fireforce unit was expanded to six helicopters and was referred to as a "Jumbo Fireforce."[105] Other fireforces were named Alpha, Bravo, Charlie, and Delta. In view of the intensification of the war, there was a need to create highly mobile strike units to spread over a vast terrain. Each fireforce became an integrated unit that could move about the country when necessary.[106] The entire RLI and most of the RAR were airborne qualified.[107] By virtue of its flexibility and its high technical role, the air force could support the two ground forces, as one of its minor roles, and it was able to render the support quite impartially. The main role was considered to be the defense of Rhodesia's air space, counterstrikes and other tactical duties.[108] Fireforce was a unique and lethal blend of air and ground units, operated with maximum skill, inflicting enormous casualties on the "terrs." Once the guerrillas were located by observation groups, a fireforce reaction group manned by the RAR, RLI or both were called in and the enemy would be subjected to a vertical envelopment by helicopter-borne combat troops.[109] As a rapid reaction force, it could be also scrambled whenever any ground forces required support. This was a huge confidence builder for the average soldier, who knew that assistance was only 30 minutes away at the most.[110] Operational flexibility was further improved by the establishment of additional airfields, including some semi-permanent bases.[111] It is evident that the RhAF was prepared for counterinsurgency in Rhodesia in terms of the requisite equipment and strategic doctrine, but they had difficulties in conducting the type of warfare confronting them.

At a briefing held at New Sarum base in November 1976, Commander Air Force Air Marshal McLaren emphasized the importance of fireforce operations when he pointed out that their role was to combine with the police and army in maintaining law, order and stability within Rhodesia whilst the politicians sorted things out.[112] From January 1, 1976, to October 1976, Squadron Leader Brand, Officer Commanding No. 1 Squadron was involved in 27 operational strikes. Four of these were in direct support of ground forces that were in close contact with the guerrillas.[113] The police force equally attracted the admiration of the political leadership for its role in fireforce operations. Senator Strong commended the police for being totally involved with the army and the air force in security operations.[114] Police duties in the operational areas were tough, especially the Police Anti-Terrorist Unit (PATU), which comprised of small groups of police referred to as "sticks." These were responsible for patrols, ambush and observational work and were to call the army for assistance. In certain circumstances, time would not allow that; thus, they engaged the guerrillas alone.[115]

The appointment of General Walls as Commander Combined Operations in 1977 meant that for the first time there was unified and centralized control of all operational units in the field.[116] Air Marshal Wilson argued that the main reason for combined operations was to reduce the time factor between the decisions and execution, and to facilitate the concentration of effort, which is the primary principle of war.[117] The executive staff responsible for the control was combined operations headquarters, which absorbed the existing Joint Planning Staff organization. This meant that operational control was no longer a function of individual service headquarters. Consequently, air and police members officially became advisors to the army commander, rather than as commanders in their own right.[118] According to Flight Lt. Rob McGregor, second in command of No. 7 Squadron, the point was to speedily deploy troops to guerrilla zones, normally after the "terrorists" were located by a security forces observation post.[119] According to Air Marshal Wilson, events in the country were at a stage that control and direction of ground theatre operations on all fronts would benefit from the ready attention of a single authority, established immediately below the Joint Chiefs of Staff.[120] The response of the fireforce rapid enough to give the guerrillas numerous challenges at the front. According to the editor of *Bateleur*, Sqdn. Leader Cockle, a "terrorist" captured in 1976, had written in his diary: "The problem is air force. If you attack anywhere, it doesn't take time for air force to come."[121] Other documents captured by security forces in Mozambique raids revealed that "terrorist commanders" were complaining that "comrades at the front are always running up and down being harassed by aeroplanes."[122] The tactical benefits of helicopters in counterinsurgency operations are their ability to overcome the difficulties presented by terrain.[123]

The effects of fireforce operations were expressed by a ZPRA platoon commander operating in the Gokwe area at that time when he said that the introduction by the RSF of airborne fireforce tactics against the lightly armed guerrillas seriously disrupted guerrilla efforts in the north of the country.[124] The operations of the guerrillas were also derailed by poor communication. Fireforce operations were easily carried out because the combatants lacked very high frequency radios (VHF) for communication. By contrast, the guerrillas depended on sound or sight of the airplanes for action. These methods were highly unreliable.[125] If efficient communication had existed, some of the attacks could have been curtailed or minimized because groups would have alerted each other about imminent attacks. Fireforce maneuvers had their own challenges, as presented in the next chapter, but this is not to discredit the impact of fireforce operations in prolonging the conflict. The RhAF played a crucial role in supporting ground operations during the Second Chimurenga. Combatants and equipment were directly delivered into target areas and this enabled troops to be well supplied during the war. This operational flexibility offered the RhAF a distinct advantage over a vast area during the war.

Effects on Morale

The RhAF used bombs that fragmented as they exploded. This severely exhausted the guerrilla forces, who tried to run away from the air force.[126] Whenever airplanes conducted raids or flew past areas where guerrillas were gathered, panic was generated, especially among the new recruits who had little experience. Furthermore, the noise of a plane itself was enough to create pandemonium. The word "ndege!" or airplane was enough to scare some fighters.[127] The new recruits were the most affected. This was evident during the bombardment of Teresera base in January 1973. According to war veteran Wereki Sandiani, most recruits died because they panicked and tried to run away, thus making them easy targets.[128] In order to send a strong signal to those opposing the regime, the Rhodesian forces at the Battle of Ruwani picked one guerrilla who had died in the battle, tied him with a rope under one of the helicopters, and flew with him all the way to Dotito in Mount Darwin to show the *povo* (peasants) the consequences of being a guerrilla.[129] During the attack of Mkushi, the women had to take off their clothes after napalm bombs had been dropped on them. They were rescued by neighboring communities.[130] The impact of air power in paralyzing the morale of fighters was made clear in 1962 by Group Captain Nelson, MP for Hartley/Gatooma, when he highlighted that the advent of helicopters was important in the sense that it was not pleasant to find something coming down on top of you, even if it is not actually going to hit you.[131] In light of such troubles, it was very important to raise the morale of the guerrillas after any attack. After the Chimoio attack, *pungwes* (all-night indoctrination vigils) were held so that the fighting spirit would be kept high.[132]

Challenges Faced When Crossing Borders

In the northeast, the RSF realized that the effective strategy to minimize guerrilla infiltration was to take them out at crossing points such as at the Zambezi River. ZPRA, coming from Zambia, had the tough Zambezi to cross. The river was a strong first line of defense for the Rhodesians. Although Zambezi was a natural fortress, the guerrillas developed various strategies to cross these rivers. They offset the barrier by using rubber canoes. In spite of the initiatives, the RhAF's retaliatory tactics were deterring. In October 1977, Flight Lt. Beaver attacked guerrillas attempting to cross the river by boat.[133] From that point onwards, a trap was set by jet aircraft on "terrorist" positions adjacent to the crossing point.[134] Added to this, the whites wounded the hippos and crocodiles so that they became hostile at various crossing points.[135] This meant more trouble for the guerrillas coming from Zambia.

Conclusion

Since the evolution of the air power doctrine during the interwar period (1919–1938), the art of war has revolutionized. The advantages of air power have had profound effects on the conduct of war. The situation in Rhodesia revealed that the country naturally had what Giulio Douhet termed "command of the air," thus giving guerrillas multiple setbacks. Particularly, the RhAF even went to the extent of violating the air space of neighboring countries in an attempt to thwart guerrilla activities. One of the most notable strategic considerations by the RhAF during the Second Chimurenga was to establish fireforce operations. Since the outbreak of World War II in 1939, the integration of forces achieved outstanding results compared to the independent use of the air force. Fireforce operations gave numerous tactical problems to the guerrilla armies, especially given the fact that they were caught unaware by the quick reaction to their presence in various operational zones. No. 7 Squadron equipped with Allouette III aircraft was so instrumental in providing the troops with swift transportation, casevac and battlefield support, including fireforce. This gave the air force an edge over the other forces while at the same time mounting the challenges of the guerrillas. While the guerrillas had difficulties in accessing immediate medical attention and were often left rotting in the bushes, the RSF enjoyed the services provided by the RhAF.

In fulfillment of hot pursuit operations, the RhAF undertook several external raids against the guerrillas. Such operations were mostly offered by services of Transport Squadron No. 3. These raids emanated from the realization that the war was escalating. The downing of two Viscount aircraft by ZPRA equipped the Rhodesians with a more reasonable excuse to attack ZPRA's external bases. Thousands of guerrillas perished as a result of external raids on guerrilla camps such as Chimoio, Nyadzonia, Tembwe, Freedom, Nhangau, Mkushi, Mulungushi, Boma and Victory, among others. These raids exterminated many recruits who were supposed to be deployed upon completion of training. What this implied is that the recruitment base was seriously depleted. Deployment by air meant that the RSF reached their targets within a few minutes, with disastrous consequences for the guerrillas, as evidenced by the casualty roster at various camps. The little resistance put up during numerous attacks against guerrilla camps acts as evidence to the inherent weaknesses of the guerrillas in purely military encounters. The institutionalization of fireforce operations by JOC was a milestone insofar as the execution of the war was concerned. Fireforce operations led to the deaths of many guerrillas in the operational zones, and the rapid deployment created some tactical puzzles at the front. The study reveals that fireforce operations were effective because the guerrillas lacked communication equipment to alert each other of imminent attacks, and were usually caught unaware. Indeed, the reaction rate of airplanes was also superior. It is indisputable that the RhAF operations had effects on the morale of the guerrillas. This was mainly as a result of the types of bombs used. The effects on new recruits were immense. Aircraft were also used to trap guerrillas at various crossing points such as the Zambezi River.

6
Guerrilla Counterstrategies to RhAF Operations

Introduction

This chapter investigates the strategies that were developed by guerrilla forces in their war against one of the branches of the Rhodesian Security Forces. Military strategy is something that has always evolved since the origin of mankind. Humanity has ever been dynamic when it comes to warfare in an effort to overcome perceived and real foes. From the Stone Age, strategies and tactics have been developed and perfected in order to gain relevance in the contemporary age of military technology. From simple blunt stone tools, we now live in the nuclear age characterized by all sorts of automatic weapons and missiles with awesome range, accuracy, firepower and lethality. Despite the existence of dangerous weapons, the history of human beings is a history of adaptation to warfare. Through the years leading from a bone to a nuclear device, man has shown an amazing capacity to adjust and to live with the weapons of his time.[1] He has fought in everything from snow to blinding desert sandstorms; he has lived through tremendous naval bombardment, and has gone on to fight even against armies that have used poison gas.[2] The guerrillas suffered multiple setbacks as a result of the operations of RhAF, but they were able to devise an array of counterstrategies which enabled them to resist the Rhodesian military machine up to 1980.

Shifting Bases

During the bombing of Mbwende I base in Mberengwa in February 1977, the Vampire came surveying the base in order to identify the actual position of guerrillas. The helicopters then followed while the Dakota dropped soldiers armed with FLN guns. The contingent consisted of one Vampire for reconnaissance, three helicopters for bombing and one Dakota carrying paratroopers. About five people died and eight were injured (including guerrillas and civilians). Recalling this battle, war veteran Dhliwayo explained: "At around 09:00 hours we shot down a helicopter and other planes spent the whole day searching for the comrades. We killed about two soldiers of the Rhodesian Front. Around 18:00 hours they flew back to their Gweru base." After the bombing of Mbwende I base, the guerrillas who had survived changed their base and started to operate from Matibi 2.[3] After the attack of Nyadzonia in 1976, the base was changed to Doroi, and from there people were recruited for training.[4] After the bombing of Chidziva base in Chipinge South, the guerrillas and *mujibhas* moved to Mutii base.[5] These movements were strategically done so that the enemy would not make further attacks on the identified bases. However, not all bases were changed.

Utilization of the Available Weapons

During the Second Chimurenga campaign, the guerrillas had undoubtedly inferior weapons compared to the RSF. Nevertheless, they managed to maximize the weapons at their disposal, though they did not match the superiority of the RSF. The guerrillas had limited anti-aircraft guns and missiles to match enemy weapons. Only much later in the struggle did they obtain superior models. Although the helicopters had the advantages of flexibility and speed, proximity to the fray had its own perils. After the commencement of "Operation Hurricane" in December 1972, a helicopter was hit while dropping an army "stick."[6] The aircraft succeeded in landing some distance away, but the pilot was injured in both legs and the right arm.[7] In 1977, a chopper pilot called Flt. Lt. Cook had his helicopter damaged by "terrorist" ground fire, wounding a crew member in the process. The pilot was forced to crash-land the aircraft, in the process sustaining injuries to the face, arm and foot.[8] On November 23, 1977, Air Lieutenant Phil Haig's aircraft was struck by ground fire while flying on an operational sortie in the Umtali area. Phil chose to carry out a forced landing which destroyed the aircraft and killed him.[9] During a reconnaissance mission in the Gaza zone, an area where ZANLA camps were suspected to be, a Canberra was hit by a SAM-7 missile which brought down the plane, leading to the death of Captain Robert Sidney Warracker.[10] It is thus a fact that the guerrillas indeed shot down aircraft belonging to the Rhodesian Security Forces.

On August 14, 1974, a contingent of ZANLA Forces in the Bindura district engaged the RSF in an approximately two-hour battle in which the RSF employed both air and ground personnel.[11] The battle resulted in the death of

15 RSF soldiers, including the commander of the operation, Major Ernest C. Adams (employment code number V2021). Two enemy aircraft were also damaged by ZANLA ground fire.[12] During the hard-won "Battle of the Honde" in mid–November 1976, the security forces underrated the guerrillas, and it was a hard-won battle. After a day-long struggle, about 31 "terrs" were killed as a result of the cooperation between the air force and the army.[13] Four helicopter pilots and their technicians spent a total of 25 hours in the air. The crews involved included Flt. Lt. Chris Wentworth and Sgt. Tony Merber, Flt. Lt. Thomas and Sgt. Brian Warren, Flt. Lt. Trevor Baynham and FS Ted Holland, Air Sub-Lt. Nick Meikle and Sgt. Hans Steyn.[14] Among the ground troops involved in the battle were 3 Commando, RLI, RAR, men from the 4th and 10th Battalions (the Rhodesia Regiment).[15] However, the forces were strongly repelled by the guerrillas. The crew came under fire almost immediately when they flew into the contact area and were under sporadic fire through most of the day.[16] The pilot of a Police Air Wing aircraft was seriously injured by ground fire in December 1978.[17]

The Battle of the Honde was arguably one of the fiercest battles on the "eastern front" during the Second Chimurenga. While little is known about this battle from an African perspective, one of the survivors of the battle called Easygo Mamboininga highlighted that the battle took place at Honde Valley Mission on Hwahwazira Mountain.[18] The battle was fought for three days, as opposed to the single day given by the Rhodesians. It resulted in the death of a number of guerrillas, possibly confirming the figure provided above. A guerrilla called Kid Mawrongwrong (pseudonym) was also captured. Among the casualties were civilians, *mujibhas* and *chimbwidos* (male and female guerrilla aides during the war). According to Mamboininga, there was one "miraculous" thing that took place in the encounter which has not been explained to this day. There were two helicopters that were destroyed, but without being shot down by the guerrillas. His argument was that it was just spiritual.[19] It is therefore apparent that although the guerrillas were outmatched in terms of the quality of their weapons, they managed to bring down aircraft belonging to the RhAF and killed thousands of RSF.

Detection Strategies

The guerrillas knew the functions of various aircraft used by the RhAF. At a *pungwe* held at Chidziva-Makoho base in Chipinge South in 1977, most of the civilians escaped before the bombings occurred after being alerted by the guerrillas. The first airplane, called "Maswerasei/Magumbu" (Vampire), was responsible for surveying the area to be bombed. The second aeroplane was the helicopter which dropped bombs.[20] Connected to this, a war collaborator named Amon Dhliwayo stressed that the guerrillas became conversant with the operations of the RhAF as the war progressed. This helped to save the lives of civilians gathered at *pungwes*. During the attack of Kodorodze base in Chipinge South in 1977, only two airplanes were used by the RSF.[21] After the arrival of the Vampire, the guerrillas instructed the *mujibhas*, *chimbwidos* and civilians to relocate to the main base called Rukangari. Only a single *mujibha* was killed during the raid as a result of failing to "follow instructions."[22] However, although the RhAF tried to deceive the guerrillas, the latter had "mastered" its operations. Linked to this, Themba Nyati noted that the attack of Rupuwu base in 1977 revealed one of the deceptive tactics of the RhAF which the guerrillas were now familiar with: "At first came the Hunter to survey the actual position of the base around 09:00 hours. After the Hunter had gone, it took an hour for the helicopters to come but the comrades escaped after seeing helicopters flying from afar on "top" of a mountain. About two soldiers died during the clashes and there were no comrades or civilians shot or wounded. The following day the soldiers came to collect the bodies of their fellow fighters. The bombs that were dropped at the base had little effect."[23] As indicated above, the guerrillas devised the strategy of shifting bases after an attack by the RSF. Soon after the bombing of Rupuwu base in Benzi (Zaka district) in 1977, the guerrillas transferred the base of operation to Gava base near Mashoko Mission in Bikita District.[24]

One of the battles that demonstrated that the guerrillas had "learnt to live with the air force" was the attack on Mavhonde Ammunition Base in Mozambique in October 1979. The attack took place around 10:00 a.m. The guerrillas were alert as a result of the bombings that had taken place at Chimoio military base in 1977.[25] More importantly, the base was strategically situated in Mavhonde Mountain, which was densely covered by vegetation. Besides, the location of the base allowed for the guerrillas to put defensive guns on top of the mountain. The base was specifically meant to supply ammunition to the freedom fighters.[26] The RhAF parachuted soldiers around the base, but some guerrillas had dispersed after spotting the airplanes from afar.[27] Only the guerrillas who were on top of the mountain did not disperse. When the soldiers realized that the base was empty, they tried to airlift a Land Rover truck to the base using a helicopter, but the plane was shot during takeoff. Like Chimoio, the base was not shifted.

The guerrillas came up with various strategies to alert people about the arrival of aircraft. Mupunzarima, Mumbengegwi and Chademana, who had come to Mudzingadzi Camp to study and familiarize themselves with the war situation, were told by Kangai that if they heard someone shouting "ndege!" they were supposed to know that the base was under attack.[28] Because they lacked modern weapons to detect the movement of the RhAF, the guerrilla fighters benefited from chimpanzee actions to counter Rhodesian aerial reconnaissance and strikes.[29] The animals became unsettled at the sound of aircraft, thus leading the guerrillas to make advanced preparations.[30] The point was cemented by Edmore Zvenyika, who highlighted that animals such as baboons and birds played a very important role in the war.[31] At the same time, birds such as crows had a twin effect because they could "sell-out" when scavenging around garbage, thereby alerting the enemy.[32] Besides, the guerrillas used *mujibhas* to gather intelligence. The *mujibhas* usually climbed on top of mountains for general scouting.[33] This was important because there was no equipment to identify enemy aircraft.[34]

Exploiting the Advantages of Terrain

A land system analysis of the Second Chimurenga based on aspects of vegetation and geology shows that the RhAF was disadvantaged by the nature of Zimbabwe's terrain. Nevertheless, the RSF had detailed knowledge of terrain thanks to advanced air photographing in the colony since the 1920s by the Aviation Operating Company. Terrain is a very important factor in modern warfare to an extent that it can influence the outcome of battles and campaigns. Aspects of terrain are considered at two scales: in strategic planning, usually reflecting the gross spatial distribution of major elements such as seas and mountains; and at the tactical level during action, making the best use of ground in the furtherance of the strategic aims of the campaign.[35] The guerrillas protected themselves by fighting in restrictive terrain where the adversary could not bring his firepower to bear. The critical key for the guerrilla, of course, was to retreat rather than fight when attacked by a stronger opponent. Terrain per se is not the be-all and end-all of military success but a vital contributory factor to military campaigns.

Guerrilla warfare is suitable in all terrains. The most important thing is attacking the enemy when he is least expecting it, the paradox of victory without losses. Support from the population is a cutting edge against a strong adversary. Clearly, the RSF were adequately familiar with the terrain of Rhodesia. Nonetheless, it was very difficult to locate the "terrs" throughout the war. It thus becomes apparent that terrain played a critical role in determining the outcome of the Second Chimurenga. Barbara Cole's description of the Malaya campaign reveals the advantages of guerrillas fighting in their own terrain:

> With the terrorists' detailed knowledge of the terrain, and hit-and-run tactics which they had down to a fine art, they clearly had the upper hand. The dense jungles, tall grass and endless

swamps of inland Malaya where the water was full with tree roots and snakes, was certainly a terrorists' paradise. The conventional troops kept to the fringes of the jungle, seldom making contacts with the bandits. For the few who did continue to make soldiering their career, the Malayan experience had provided a tremendous grounding. Malaya had been a valuable experience and they had learned the elementary principles of counter-insurgency warfare like tracking and ambush.[36]

In Zimbabwe, Cole observed: "The Rhodesians didn't always get things their own way. The wild countryside dotted with huge kopjes, the thick bush, long elephant grass and endless Msasa trees were an enemy too, providing ideal cover and at times giving the terrorists the edge in the hide-and-seek game of life and death. It all went to make the task of ground troops trying to hunt and flush them out, fraught with unseen dangers."[37]

Vegetation was clearly important in providing cover to the troops while the uneven slopes provided the guerrillas with tactical positions to counter the Rhodesian military prowess. In the Zambezi Valley, the government destroyed all vegetation to deny cover and food to the insurgents. The defoliation scheme had some disturbing side effects because the children fell ill and could die. The doctors ascribed this to the spraying of vegetation with defoliants.[38] The dense forests in many parts of the country impeded the effectiveness of air power operations, and winter was greatly welcome for strategic reasons as hinted by Lardner-Burke: "However, with the onset of the dry season, it is to be expected that their [guerrilla armies] difficulties would increase, whereas the mobility of our security forces will increase and I expect a high measure of success in the coming month."[39]

In 1979, the RhAF opened up about challenges imposed by Rhodesia's terrain during the rainy season: "For you it means nothing but problems. The terrs will have more cover and more water; your job will be harder."[40] Overall, the defoliation strategy failed to yield the desired results owing to the vast operational zones of the guerrillas. The Rhodesians could not defoliate the whole country after assessing the costs and benefits coming out of their strategy.

The RhAF was ideally ineffective in areas without noticeable physical features because it was very difficult to locate targets, unlike in areas with identifiable physical features such as mountains, valleys and rivers. Air strikes were efficient when aimed at a specific target such as town or village. This explains why guerrilla bases outside the country were easy targets. In plain areas, guerrillas could take cover in simple bushes.[41] One utmost advantage the RSF possessed was effective intelligence. The RSF had agents who collected information on the names of rivers, valleys and mountains. The information was primarily obtained from the civilians.[42] Terrain intelligence refers to the collection of information on the military significance of natural and man-made characteristics of an area. In fact, it is the study of the physical features on the ground for military operations. Therefore, intelligence on the terrain and its properties, to be used as an operating environment, was critical.[43] Terrain also limited the operations of the Air Force of Zimbabwe during the Mozambican Campaign from 1982 to 1992. In ZANLA's Gaza province, most of the terrain was very flat, in particular the southeast, which had very few prominent roads, thereby creating navigation problems.[44] Some parts of Manica and Sofala provinces are highly mountainous and well covered by trees. Trees provided some thick canopies (called *Masimbiti* or Iroon wood) that rendered observation from the air very difficult in a number of cases.[45] It was difficult for the RhAF to locate guerrillas in mountains and dense and thick forests. It rather relied on information provided by agents. During the bombing of Rupuwu base, the guerrillas fled to Manyiri Mountain, where there was sufficient cover.[46] Similarly, during the attack of Mudzingadzi, the guerrillas took cover in a dense forest where the helicopter failed to locate them.[47] It is also significant to note that the guerrillas established bases at strategic places where they were not prone to enemy attack. In Mberengwa, the guerrillas set up bases near rivers in order to get cover from trees and easy access to reliable sources of water. In the event of an attack, they fled down or up the river. Examples of bases situated near Lundi River in Mberengwa were Mbwende 1 and 2, Matibi 1 and 2, Musaverema and Pazimani.[48]

Belief in Ancestral Protection/Spirit Mediums

During the Second Chimurenga, the guerrillas attributed the continuation and sustenance of the war to the assistance given to them by the ancestors of the land. As such, attacks from enemy forces were conceived to be "ineffectual" in the sense that the struggle would always move on. An ex-combatant called Maphosa revealed that the Second Chimurenga was a "spiritual war" because before the attack they would receive a sign hinting the presence of danger in the shortest possible time.[49] This was mainly in the form of *chapungu* (bateleur eagle). In deep-rooted Shona beliefs, the bird is a good sign, bringing protection and good fortune to a community. The Shona have created a sarcastic simile likening stingy people to the bateleur eagle—*anonyima sechapungu chisingadonhedzi munhenga* (he or she is stingy like the bateleur eagle that rarely drops feathers).[50] During the war, these birds would emerge in the direction where the enemy was going to come from, and within minutes, the attack would happen.[51] In this regard, war veterans admitted that the spirit mediums assisted in the war of liberation. According to some war veterans, a memorable incident was during the Nyadzonia attack in 1976 when fish eagles "forewarned" them about the impending danger. Margret Makomva said that before the attack, the fish eagles appeared in the vicinity, flapping their wings.[52] Makomva also claimed to have dreamed of the attack when her grandfather instructed her to feign illness the following day so that she would be excused from daily training. She did not tell anyone about the dream because she was only 15 years old when she joined the war; thus, she expected no one to take heed of her advice.[53]

Makomva allegedly had another dream about the attack of Chimoio. She visualized being told to vacate the camp. As a result, she carried a tin under the guise of taking water to the wounded persons at Parirenyatwa camp. In a few minutes, Chimoio was under attack. While running away from Chimoio, Makomva claimed that another big "miracle" happened. She and others with her met a swarm of bees on their way to a new hive. The bees then started to sting people, supposedly in order to change their direction because the camp was barricaded by Smith's ground force. The bees "carried people" to a certain depression where the guerrillas underwent a deep sleep and woke up at around 6 p.m.[54] About 15 guerrillas were saved this way. The belief in spirit mediums arguably had a psychological effect on the guerrillas, who saw imminent success throughout their operations. A lot of fighters believed in the prophecy made by the "heroine" of the First Chimurenga (1896–97) called Charwe, who was possessed by the spirit of Nehanda. While on death row, Nehanda allegedly told the whites that her bones would rise again (*mapfupa angu achamuka*). When the Africans took up arms in 1966, they claimed to be fulfilling the prophecy made decades earlier. War veteran Sandiani highlighted that before they crossed the Mozambican border, they were taken by trained guerrillas to a spirit medium called Parangeta for guidance. Besides, spirit mediums could participate on the war front. Examples included Sekuru Chipfeni and Sekuru Chidyamauyu.[55] The role of religious leaders in the war was even revealed by Lardner-Burke, the Minister of Security, when he said: "Through exploitation of the spirit mediums the terrorists were able to achieve a spiritual hold over primitive tribesmen. As a result no information was being volunteered to any government agency."[56] Despite incessant attacks from the Rhodesian Air Force and other security agents, the African armies took comfort in the idea that the guardians of the land were shielding them. Whether this was a myth or not, it boosted morale and invigorated the spirit to liberate the country.

To acknowledge the importance of spirit mediums in the country's liberation history, two streets in the country's capital of Harare were named after the "heroine" and "hero" of the First Chimurenga, Mbuya Nehanda and Sekuru Kaguvi respectively. Another hero, Mkwati, was honored through the naming of government buildings after him. Nehanda's "influence" is still visible decades after independence. When First Lady Grace Mugabe occupied parts of Manzou farm/estate in Mazowe (Mashonaland Central Province) in 2015 for the sake of extending her business empire, she displaced a lady called Mary Kazunga, who claimed to be possessed by the Nehanda spirit. Grace destroyed homes belonging to hundreds of families, and Kazunga was dumped in Rushinga, her original home village. However, Grace had to bring "Nehanda" back to her place. She rebuilt her houses they had demolished after certain "complications" were taking place in the area. Nehanda further reassured people that they should stay put at their farms under siege from Grace Mugabe. The words were said at a traditional ceremony held in Mazowe. Everybody in the area had to contribute rapoko for brewing beer as per tradition.[57]

Deserting Camps During the Day

At times the guerrillas spent most of their time in the bush rather than at the camps for fear of attack. This strategy of deserting the camps was significant because it saved them from the RhAF surprise attacks.[58] Only those with heavy guns would guard the camps while those in the bush would return in the evening. This was relatively safe because the RhAF did not attack during the night. Consequently, fire or light was not allowed during the night as it gave away the guerrillas' camping spots to the RhAf. Thus, any form of disobedience was heavily dealt with.[59] Light was not allowed because it gave signals to the RhAF.

Propaganda

The insurgents, particularly ZANLA, countered incursions by the skillful use of the media. The Rhodesians disregarded international law and the boundaries of the five black nations that had proclaimed themselves Frontline states: Botswana, Zambia, Mozambique, Tanzania, and Angola. The publicized violation of Frontline states' borders greatly negated the military benefits the Rhodesians derived from such operations. The international reaction became hostile and was intensified by the number of noncombatant blacks who were killed and wounded during cross-border raids. Besides, ZANLA reported events as if they were on the battlefield.

Conclusion

The guerrillas did not remain docile in the face of RhAF attacks. As one of their responses, they tactically relocated their bases after an attack. In addition, the guerrillas employed weapons at their disposal to shoot down airplanes. This, however, demanded expertise on the part of guerrillas to aim at the parts which were susceptible to fire, or else shoot the pilot himself. Wild animals were not taken for granted because they alerted the guerrilla fighters about the presence of an enemy. The guerrilla aides also took important reconnaissance missions although such missions were highly dangerous. Terrain worked to the advantage of the guerrillas. The rainy season was the most problematic for the RSF air operations because it meant more cover and water for the guerrillas. The belief in ancestral spirits also had psychological effects on the operations of the guerrillas. War is not thus a one-sided affair. Strategy leads to counterstrategy. Nevertheless, the air force, though important at tactical level, did not achieve the desired results, especially after 1972, due to the high infiltration of guerrillas, combined with social, political, economic, cultural, religious, and even psychological factors.

7

Challenges Faced by the Rhodesian Air Force During the Second Chimurenga

Introduction

Rhodesia had one of the finest air forces by African standards. Following the disintegration of the Federation in 1963, her infantry battalions, the Rhodesian Light Infantry and the Rhodesian African Rifles, were best equipped to deal with a purely military conflict. In light of the challenges faced by the guerrillas due to the RhAF operations, this chapter analyzes the factors which led to the failure by the air force to achieve its military objectives during the Second Chimurenga. The chapter categorizes the challenges faced by the RhAF into two types: external and internal. The external section assesses the challenges faced by the Rhodesians as a result of guerrilla strategy. The internal section evaluates the problems within the RhAF which affected its aim of thwarting insurgency. Aspects such as the weaknesses of fireforce operations, manpower shortage, aircraft accidents and low morale in the forces are analyzed. A number of factors contributed to the effectiveness of air power operations. Any air force depends on three main factors: machines with which it is equipped, the quality of the men who serve in it, and the excellence of the training that these men receive.[1] Whyte Beverly echoed the same point when she stated that the individual weapon of any air force is the aircraft and its crew.[2] Using these factors as yardsticks to measure the quality and effectiveness of the RhAF, it is clear that the air unit had problems. The machines were old. The situation was compounded by the shortage of spare parts and manpower. Men who served in the air force lacked the much-needed experience, as seasoned pilots deserted for more rewarding work in civil aviation. Most of the pilots were trained for shorter periods just to meet the demands of the war without flying adequate hours to gain experience.

"External" Factors

External factors cannot be isolated when one is analyzing the role of the air force during the Second Chimurenga campaign. The external factors played a crucial role in inhibiting the effectiveness of the air force.

ESCALATION AND SOPHISTICATION OF GUERRILLA TACTICS

Despite possessing sophisticated weaponry in the form of air power, the whites had problems in dealing with insurgency, as revealed by the Commander of Joint Command, General Peter Walls, when he said: "I made it clear when I became Commander of the Army in 1972, that one cannot win this war by purely military means."[3] The guerrilla tactics of sabotage, surprise attacks, ambush and support from the civilians presented numerous challenges to the RSF who were masters of conventional warfare. Moreover, they were alienated from popular support. The RSF were frustrated and depressed by guerrilla tactics, as underscored in 1969 by the Minister of Law and Order, William Lardner-Burke:

> During February and March (1969) there have been a number of incidences of internal subversion. There have been attempts to derail trains. For instance, explosives were found near the Gleneagles fly-over bridge and an unsuccessful attempt had been made to destroy the railway line. Further explosives were found in the vicinity. Other attempts to obstruct railway communication were perpetrated at the Marimba fly-over bridge where concrete road markers were thrown on to the line and near Gwelo where wooden sleepers were placed on the line. There were some stonings of motor vehicles and trains in the Matabeleland area. In the Belingwe area two miles of fencing were cut down and political notices were found attached to the fence. A further incident occurred when an illegal gathering of some 150 people demonstrated by singing political songs, shouting slogans and stoning passing cars.[4]

The intensification of guerrilla tactics was evident when Lardner-Burke further admitted that despite setbacks, the "terrorist" organizations presented an offensive capability.[5] Beginning in the 1970s, the guerrillas were now concentrating on improving the quality of the men available rather than the quantity, as evidenced in improved tactics employed.[6] Joint Minister of Internal Affairs Hayman concurred with Lardner-Burke on the challenges presented by guerrilla tactics: "The terrorist war has, in the main, been fought in the Tribal Trust Land (TTL), it is the intention of communist inspired terrorists to destroy the services, the communications, the administration and, in fact, the development within those areas and to create a state of anarchy which will result in a situation for communist takeover. For this reason, terrorists have sought to destroy the dipping service, the African Councils system, the schools, the bridges, the roads and the marketing organisation within the tribal trust land."[7]

What that means was that the RSF had very little success in curbing the acts of sabotage perpetrated by the guerrilla fighters. The guerrillas tried as hard as possible to conceal their operations. What remained visible was the damage. Guerrilla warfare is thus beyond the grasp of many conventional armies. Members of the People's Caretaker Council (PCC) led by Joshua Nkomo destroyed cattle dips, fences and bridges, cut telephone wires to disrupt communication, and derailed railroad traffic. They also destroyed farmhouses, killed livestock, and burned crops.[8] The guerrillas continued their attempts to disrupt civil administration in the TTLs by attacking administrative and educational facilities.[9] Africans who protected colonial interest were not spared by the guerrillas. An example was Constable Joweti, who was killed in June 1972 while on duty guarding a dip tank in the Zaka area.[10]

Due to the sophistication of the guerilla strategies, the RSF ended up with a severely strained workforce. A political crisis surfaced in Rhodesia in 1978 when the opposition Rhodesian Action Party (RAP) accused the ruling Rhodesian Front (RF) of conceding defeat. This was revealed in the *Herald* of December 19, 1978, which published a story titled "The PM should retire now, says RAP."[11] When asked in Parliament whether they were winning the war, the Prime Minister admitted that the guerrillas were stepping things up: "I do not think we can honestly say that we are, but we can hold the position. For a long time most thinking Rhodesians have accepted that the final solution is a political solution. In order to achieve this we must hold the security scene and we have held it for a long time. I want to assure you that if need be we can go on holding it for a long time, in spite of the fact that the terrorists are trying to step things up."[12] In all earnestness, Smith was giving people a clear picture of where things were headed. This he made plain when he said: "But in all honesty one cannot make irresponsible claims, and for me to have claimed that we were actually winning the war, and that I could see the end in sight, would be devious and misleading to the Rhodesian people."[13] Although Smith claimed that defeat was the last thing he would accept, he saw a political situation as the only answer to what was going on in the country. In this regard, the war was creating real challenges for the RSF and the air force in particular. This runs contrary to the long-held belief that the RhAF was a superior weapon during the war. The guerrilla fighters gained a lot of ground starting in the 1970s. This sharply contrasted with the manpower situation and quality of equipment owned by the RhAF. At a time when General Peter Walls was adamant in saying, "We can go on thumping the hell out of them [guerrillas]," Smith replied: "I agree. I believe we can do that and we are doing that. But that does not mean to say that we can win the war...."[14] Equally important was the fact that Walls accepted that in order to bring the war to a successful conclusion, they needed a political solution backed up by the military because the military could not do it purely as a military.[15] The Rhodesians thus admitted the hurdles they suffered during the prosecution of the conflict despite possessing state-of-the art machinery. The Prime Minister of Rhodesia and General Peter Walls all admitted that the war was not going in the direction they anticipated. Guerrilla tactics were a stumbling block in the efficiency of Rhodesia's armed forces.

The Impact of the Support Offered by Frontline States

The guerrillas obtained important support from African countries, particularly the Frontline states such as Mozambique, Zambia, Botswana, Angola, and Tanzania. The aim of the Frontline states was the political liberation of southern Africa. The coup in Portugal in April 1974 fundamentally changed the direction of the nationalist struggle throughout southern Africa. Rhodesia and South Africa lost a firm ally in the Portuguese army in the struggle against liberation movements in southern Africa. The decolonization of Mozambique, in particular, enabled ZANLA guerrillas to pursue the war more vigorously inside Rhodesia.[16] ZPRA was based in Lusaka and had been built up as a conventional force, while ZANLA, based in Mozambique, waged a Maoist-style campaign in the countryside.[17] Minister of Law and Order Desmond William Lardner-Burke informed Parliament in 1969 about the strong support offered to the guerrillas by African countries: "There is no indication whatever that there has been any change in the attitude of the Organisation of African Unity (OAU) and the so-called Liberation Committee which it sponsors."[18] This consequently meant that the whole of Africa was behind the liberation of the continent. Ghana, Algeria, Egypt, and Ethiopia were some of the countries which supported the contribution of Frontline states.

The Rhodesian government was worried by the support offered to guerrillas by the FLS during the war. The independence of southern African nations such as Botswana, Mozambique, Tanzania and Zambia gave the struggle more impetus as the guerrillas got more bases to operate from. Lardner-Burke highlighted the impact of FLS on the government's efforts to thwart guerrilla operations when he said:

> The hostile attitude of the Zambian government remains unchanged and that country continues to act as a base for terrorist infiltrations into the whole of southern Africa. Zambian Cabinet Ministers have not denied the fact that they allow terrorists to pass through their territory to Angola, Mozambique, South Africa and Rhodesia. Holding camps are maintained

in Zambia by the terrorist organisers and on more than one occasion the Zambian government has offered Zambia as a base from which British troops could attack Rhodesia. It cannot be denied that the present Zambian attitude poses a threat to the general security of this country. We know that large numbers of trained terrorists are available to the organisers in Zambia and Tanzania.[19]

The borders of the country became porous to a level that the RSF could no longer contain the large numbers of guerrillas flocking into the country. The Rhodesian Ministry of Law and Order noted that the main threat to the maintenance of law and order during 1968 was the infiltration by Communist-trained terrorists from Zambian bases.[20] The infiltrations presented a major setback to the operations of the RSF because the RhAF, which had earlier been confined to border patrols, was moved to the battlefield. In June 1972, the President of Rhodesia, Clifford Dupont, highlighted that the continued use of Zambia as a base for terrorists, trained for operations against Rhodesia in contravention of the Third Geneva Convention, required the security forces to maintain vigilance and to undertake constant and extensive border patrols.[21] FRELIMO leader Samora Machel made it clear in Cairo in 1972 that he was going to assist the "Rhodesian" guerrillas.[22] Lardner-Burke was also worried that Communist aid in the form of arms and money continued to pour from the OAU to the "terrorist" movements, while the World Council of Churches (WCC) and certain left-wing organizations in the west and Scandinavia gave morale and financial support.[23]

Early in 1969, Lardner-Burke informed the House of Assembly about the threat of guerrilla activity in Zambia when he said: "We know the numbers are there—and there are many—and for the moment they have been there for some considerable time and we have to prepare in case they decide that they wish to infiltrate here for their nefarious activities."[24] Air Marshal McLaren confirmed, in 1974, the threat posed by guerrilla infiltrations when he said: "We accept that the threat of terrorism will always be present as long as countries such as Zambia harbour and train terrorists, and give them weapons, succour and safe passage to our borders."[25] Air Marshal Wilson noted in August 1976 that the guerrillas were receiving more active and sophisticated backing from Russia and its followers, thus changing the whole scene in favor of the guerrillas.[26] Guerrillas in Rhodesia thus benefited from the sanctuary, material, advisory and financial support not only from the African continent but globally. The rising insecurities led to the unanimous adoption of the Defence Procurement Bill by Parliament in June 1972. Frederick Simmonds, MP for Mtoko, noted that the continuous movement of sophisticated armament into the north of the country was a great concern to many.[27] As a result, Rhodesia was prompted to apply drastic measures that would enhance her military capabilities in light of the attitude of her neighbors. The then Zambian Prime Minister, E.H.K. Mudenda, stated that Zambia, Botswana and Mozambique shared a common burden in the struggle for the liberation of Zimbabwe.[28]

"Internal" Challenges

CHALLENGES FACED BY THE RhAF FIREFORCE OPERATIONS

It is justifiable to argue that the military leadership of Southern Rhodesia was greatly influenced by the conduct of previous wars such as World War II, in which Hitler's blitzkrieg strategy led to the quick and decisive defeat of Poland, Norway, Belgium, Holland, Denmark and France. On September 1, 1939, the lead units of the invading Germany army (the *Wehrmacht*) crossed over the border into Poland. The operation, code-named Case White, was the world's first experience of a devastating new type of mechanized warfare. Highly mobile German formations, spearheaded by mass columns of tanks and working in close cooperation with the German Air Force, attacked on a very narrow front, making deep penetrations into the Polish defenses within hours.[29] During World War II, it was typical of modern warfare that air power was most effective when coordinated in its purpose with other fighting units. In October 1942, General Montgomery, commander of the British Eighth Army, defeated the German commander Erwin Rommel's *Afrika Korps* in North Africa at El Alamein through a mighty combination of land, sea and air.[30] Prime Minister Churchill regarded the victory as a turning point of the whole war for Britain.[31] Combined operations produce better results compared to the independent use of air power as advocated by Douhet and Mitchell.

In the case of the Second Chimurenga campaign, the capacity of helicopters to swiftly transport troops to the area of operations was evidently manifested after the beginning of the "fireforce" model in 1974.[32] The concept involved a highly mobile force, maintained at constant readiness to react instantly to any notified presence of "terrorists."[33] When a report was received calling for the fireforce, the entire equipment could be airborne "within three minutes," en route to the terrorist locale.[34] Although the reaction was swift, it did not achieve the intended results, as revealed in this discussion. Fireforce operations revealed the innovativeness of the RSF, but the challenges inherent in their execution were numerous. It is significant to highlight that the RSF acknowledged the difficulties they faced during fireforce operations. Operation Teak of 1970 is a good example. The operation was triggered by an attack on the Victoria Falls airport and the South African Police camp at Spray View Hotel in Victoria Falls. The South African Police camp and Victoria Falls airport building were attacked on the night of January 16, 1970.[35] Air Lt. Ed Paintin carried out a rocket strike on the group of "terrorists" without apparent success. In fact, his aircraft was hit by ground fire.[36] The Rhodesians actually acknowledged the limitations of fireforce operations: "The terrorists that took part in both Operations Teak and Operation Birch were better organised. They were better trained in anti-tracking measures. They worked in smaller groups of four or five and attacked at various points at the same time causing the security forces to spread their strength."[37]

To complement the above, fireforce operations were not always as successful as depicted by the RSF and white historians and journalists. The lack of helicopters prevented the creation of more fireforce units while at the same time the insurgents escalated their operations. To alleviate the situation, a stick of paratroopers was added to each fireforce crew. Furthermore, demand for fireforce swelled during the closing years of the conflict, to the point where it was normal for a crew to be deployed as often as three times a day in certain heavily contested areas.[38] As revealed by Flight Lt. Rob McGregor, out of ten fireforce call-outs, nine were what they called "lemons." In the event that one of those ten alerts resulted in a slaughter, then they felt they were really doing a good job.[39] This sharply contradicts the assertions given by Air Marshal McLaren that the air force was capable of hitting very hard and accurately.[40] The resources of the RhAF did not stretch enough to meet the numerous calls made on them.[41] Besides, according to Ken Flower, the then head of the Central Intelligence Organisation, Rhodesia was losing the war at home and the military planners in Combined Operations turned out in frustration, to strike beyond the borders where the inhibitions that restricted the army fighting on its own ground were curtailed.[42] However, Flower was against external raids on the basis that it would involve the neighbors and internationalize the conflict.[43] It is factual that combined operations gave immense tactical problems to the guerrillas. But an important fact that has been ignored by successive military historians, especially Rhodesians who documented the operations of the RSF, was and still is a deliberate attempt to deny the ineffectiveness of fireforce or air force in general. If the operations had in fact been successful, the complexion of the war would have been vastly different.

Manpower Shortage in the Air Force and Its Impact

According to Air Marshal McLaren, the efficiency of the air force was measured by two things: manpower and material resources, and the existing levels of training and experience. He further emphasized that the regular force was very small even though it was reinforced by units such as the territorial force, the general reserve and the volunteer reserve.[44] McLaren also revealed that the air force suffered many difficulties in procuring material.[45] A scrutiny of these hitches highlights the challenges faced by the RhAF during the war. As highlighted previously, the breakup of the Federation affected the RhAF in retaining all the aircraft and qualified personnel. As a result, crash courses were undertaken, and by 1965 No. 1 Ground Training School at New Sarum was at least able to address the challenges created by manpower shortages.[46] In 1967, Air Vice-Marshal Hawkins pointed out: "An increase in the number of premature retirements by air crew, prompted by the higher remuneration on offering in the field of civil aviation, especially from abroad, was evident."[47] In 1968, Hawkins further reiterated the shortage of manpower in the air force when he said: "Although sufficient recruits for training are coming forward, it will be sometime before a really satisfactory balance between experienced and inexperienced manpower, especially technical ground staff, can be achieved. The situation was aggravated further by a general shortage of highly skilled manpower of the required calibre, and thus financial inducements from civilian enterprises continued to attract service personnel, newly qualified technicians and middle bracket aircrew primarily affected."[48]

Dr. Palley, MP for Highfield, questioned Minister of Defence Howmann on November 14, 1969, on how many persons, and of what rank, had resigned from the army and air force in each of the years from 1964 to 1969.[49] Of importance was Howmann's response: "The pattern of resignations from the Defence Forces has remained constant since 1964 and before. However, as these resignations, while normal, have a bearing from time to time on the strength and state of training on the Defence Forces, I am not, under present circumstances, to give detailed figures as it would be not in the public interest to do so."[50]

The shortage of flying personnel in the operational squadrons meant that their utilization was slightly lower than they expected.[51] This could be verified using the statistics put forward by the Minister of Defence, Sir Malcom Barrow, that the utilization per aircraft as a force average for the year ended December 31, 1961, was 275 hours per aircraft. No. 3 Transport Squadron utilization was 354 hours per aircraft, and for the operational squadrons it was 252 hours per aircraft.[52] In 1960, Gaunt, MP for Lusaka west, demanded assurance that the air force would not be neglected. In response, Minister of Defence Caldicott highlighted that the air force flew to a planned program based on requirements to bring the force up to its operational efficiency.[53] This was unrealistic in light of the 1961 statistics given by Barrow that the air force was underutilized as a result of the shortage of pilots. AVM Hawkins complained in 1968 that the workload had increased as manpower resources were stretched.⁵⁴ The problem of flying personnel was further articulated by Commander Air Force Wilson when he lamented in 1972: "Regrettably, as in the past years the overall air crew strength remained just below strength."⁵⁵ This shortage was further confirmed by Air Vice-Marshal McLaren in 1977, when he revealed: "Regrettably, this country has not been able to afford a trained air force reserve and thus we have to stretch the available regular resources to meet the increased operational demands-apart from a very small capability to call on retired air force pilots and the utilisation of some civil effort in the specialised field of transport operations."⁵⁶

It was evident that civil aviation was more rewarding compared to the RhAF. The following Short Service Unit (SSU) personnel of the RhAF left the Federation for employment in other air forces or civil flying capacities by April 1959: 16 to RAF, one to Royal Canadian Air Force (RCAF) and 15 to civil airlines.⁵⁷ The benefits in civil aviation were as follows: the widow of a RRAF officer with three years' experience was paid £341 a year while his opposite in Civil Aviation got £410 and Central African Airways (CAA) £468.⁵⁸ A widow of a pilot of six years in the air force got £364, Civil Aviation £510 and CAA £585. With nine years' experience an air force widow got £390, Civil Aviation £525 and CAA £624. With twelve years' experience RRAF widows got £403, Civil Aviation £525 and CAA £663.⁵⁹ In early 1973, Holland, MP for Salisbury North, confirmed that the security forces had lost a great many experienced officers because of the salary structures.⁶⁰ Against this backdrop, it becomes clear why airmen from the air force joined civil aviation. The pilot soldiers were obviously concerned about their future, and therefore deserted. The air force was thus deprived of experienced personnel, thereby resulting in numerous accidents and a strained manpower. The RhAF thus lamented: "We are so small, and so indispensable to the war effort, that we cannot afford second best. We are all professionals in a highly unforgiving environment and our operations demand precision and skill if they are to succeed."⁶¹

By African standards, the Rhodesian Security Forces were formidable, ranking second only to South Africa in the entire continent. These were the forces that were used in the counterinsurgency campaign.⁶² The intensification of the armed struggle after 1972, and its sharp escalation from 1976, divided the whole country into designated operational areas and compelled military call-ups which strained the manpower requirements beyond the resources supplied by the whites.⁶³ The RSF were expected to deal will all types of emergencies generated by the operations of the guerrillas. On the night of April 16, 1979, Thornhill Fire Section received a call from Combined Operations reporting that "terrorists" had attacked and set fire to the fuel storage tanks in Fort Victoria (Masvingo).⁶⁴ The blaze was finally extinguished at 5:30 a.m., whereas Thornhill had left at 1:30 a.m. and arrived at 4:00 a.m.⁶⁵ In 1977, Wing Commander Gaunt concurred with Minister of Combined Operations Hawkins on the persistent shortage of manpower in the RhAF when he said: "We are extremely short of specialised air crew and I feel it would be a tragic shame to lose the services of certain of our skilled pilots and technicians merely because at the end of their 10 years' service they feel they would like to get hold of lump sum of money and put it aside for a fairly ill-defined future."⁶⁶ Gaunt further emphasized: "There is no doubt in my mind that the single and most inhibiting factor of this war is the shortage of manpower."⁶⁷

The intensification of the war meant that the soldiers were now spending more time on the battlefield. This had adverse effects on white morale, as seen in the Christmas Message sent by General Walls to the forces on December 24, 1976: "The traditional Christmas greeting hardly seems appropriate within the Army in these momentous times, when determination to rid our land of terrorists precludes our determination to our dreaming of a peaceful Christmas, and prevents so many of us from being with our families."⁶⁸ Though racial discrimination was rampant, it was a tradition of the RhAF to recruit personnel with the highest qualities and experience.⁶⁹ Pilot vacancies were being filled up with men who had previous experience as flying instructors. The pilots were then used to train the volunteer reservists during weekends, and also to perform normal communication squadron duties.⁷⁰ This highlights the manpower shortage that existed in the RSF, let alone the RhAF.

The opening up of many war fronts strained the various branches of the RSF. The shortage of manpower ran opposite to the rate of guerrilla infiltration into the country. There were minor infiltrations in 1969 but the trend did not carry forward into 1970 as small bands of heavily armed "terrorists" entered the country at widely separated points on the northern border, with the objective of both perpetrating hit-and-run attacks on selected targets or fomenting subversion in local communities.⁷¹ The security forces nominally constituted of 4,700 regular army and air force personnel supported by 10,000 white territorials, 8,000 members of the BSAP (three-quarters blacks), and 35,000 police reservists (three-quarters white) in December 1972.⁷² As early as 1975, the military forces of Rhodesia were working flat out to combat the "terrorists." This certainly put a considerable burden on available manpower.⁷³ Minister of Defence Van der Byl revealed in 1977 the desperate situation which existed in the RSF: "I call on every soldier, whether Regular or Territorial, to make his contribution by giving even more of his best in this fight, to put beyond doubt that responsible government and a guarantee of a prosperous and peaceful future, for all our communities, will be maintained in our country."⁷⁴ In order to address the critical manpower shortage, Air Marshal Wilson urged Rhodesians from diverse backgrounds to combine their activities, talents, spiritual and moral qualities in a united and determined effort to rid the land of guerrillas.[75] Colonial legislation stipulated in 1970 that only Rhodesians, members of the Commonwealth, British citizens, and South Africans, were liable for military training, provided they had resided in the country for six months and fitted within the prescribed age groups.[76] Amendments were also made in the Defence Act so that aliens, or in Howman's words, "new Rhodesians," irrespective of their nationality, were liable for national service training and for subsequent service with the territorial terms and the reserve.[77] Aliens were required to register within six months of arrival in Rhodesia, but they were liable for call-up after one year in Rhodesia. It was assumed that if the aliens were allowed to settle, their English would improve. Credit was also given for military service elsewhere.[78] All of these were attempts to solve the vexing problem of manpower shortage. In addition, in an attempt to fix the manpower scarcity faced by the country, Rhodesia went to the extent of forcibly enlisting white personnel against their will. Manpower became so depleted that members of some religious sects who did not believe in military service were compulsorily recruited. John Alexander Mutter, who was a Jehovah's Witness convert from Umtali, was sentenced to one year's imprisonment with labor for failing to report for military call-up on July 16, 1977.[79] In his defense, Mutter told magistrate Jones that he did not comply because he was a Jehovah's Witness and that his aim was that of "neutrality." Jones ruled that the security situation in the country had deteriorated to an extent that the court felt a fine, especially on a third conviction, was not appropriate.[80] Related to this, Jones convicted another Jehovah's Witness "offender," Jacobus Erns Kotze of Umtali, for a $200 fine or 50 days' imprisonment with labor for failing to report for call-up.[81] Jones supported his judgments by pointing out: "It is well known that manpower resources in the country under the present circumstances are stretched to their full limit and it is in the interests of the country that every man capable of service, who is required to do so, should do his bit as far as security is concerned."[82]

The Minister of Defence Howmann believed that Jehovah's Witnesses were actively canvassing members of the territorial force and reserves in order to induce them to object to continued military service on the grounds of the beliefs held by the sect.[83] The sect was the only one in Rhodesia that encouraged objections on religious grounds to military service for the "maintenance of peace or public safety in the defence of Rhodesia." Such objections contradicted the law which required every able-bodied European, colored and Asian to fulfill service, training and operational obligations.[84] The sect was described by

Sutton-Pryce, the MP for Salisbury City, as a "pernicious organisation with no foundation for and no justification in their attitude towards military service."[85] In addition, Air Marshal Wilson was very concerned that too many young men were being exempted from national service on what he called relatively trivial disabilities purely on medical grounds.[86] He argued that the government, medical officers and doctors ought to face the facts and be prepared to recognize that a man's ability to render service to his country lay not in his medical category but in the inner heart and in his spirit.[87] Prime Minister Abel Muzorewa's speech during the Wings Parade at Thornhill on August 10, 1979, when No. 32 Pilot Training Course received their wings and commissions, further verified the persistent challenge of manpower shortage in the RSF during the Second Chimurenga: "The Air Force maintains exceptionally high standards and the hurdles to be overcome are many. Those on parade today have completed a gruelling 18 months and have every reason to be proud. However, they, as is the case with every member of our security forces, cannot afford to be complacent."[88]

The shortage of manpower did not only affect the RhAF but all branches of the RSF. The guard force, which was used purely for protection of the protected villages, was removed from this work to look after the lines of communication. The other million went to the air force for supplying ammunition.[89] In addition to the manpower woes faced by the RSF, it cost about $100,000 a day to get rid of one guerrilla. It was therefore suggested that the guard force be amalgamated with the regular force or territorial army, although the Minister of Defence, Roger Hawkins, was quick to point out that the functions of the guard force were separate from the functions of the army and territorial army.[90] The guard force was mainly responsible for guard duties, whereas the territorial army performed combat duties.[91] The manpower shortage forced members of the South African Police to patrol villages in Chiweshe Tribal Trust Land where "protected villages" had been established.[92] Lardner-Burke campaigned for drastic measures in order to improve the manpower situation in the country. The Ministries of Law and Order and Defence initiated a review of pay allowances and other conditions of service for the BSAP and the armed forces, with particular regard to the lower and middle ranks, with a view to attracting and retaining experienced men.[93] The motor industry was also affected by call-ups, as revealed by President Ward of the Rhodesian Motor Industry Employer's Association, who said: "Whatever the security situation, repeated call-ups have placed a great strain, particularly on the repair side of the industry."[94]

The manpower shortage in the RSF was also exposed in the "cordon sanitaire" (or Corsan) strategy. The RSF introduced cordon sanitaire as a physical obstacle to prevent insurgent infiltration. During May 1974, construction began on the first border minefield obstacle and was completed in April 1976. It stretched from the Musengezi to the Mazowe River. The initial efforts entailed the use of an electronic alarm system and a reaction force, but these were phased out. Eventually, cordon sanitaire merely became a border minefield obstacle. Restrictions in manpower and finance left the security forces unable to cover it by observation or fire, or to patrol or even maintain it. Despite the fact that this soon proved impractical, however, by 1978 border obstacles of various descriptions had been constructed along virtually the entire eastern border with Mozambique, as was the section of the Rhodesian border with Zambia from Victoria Falls eastward to Mlibizi.[95] From the beginning, however, its efficiency was problematic and little was done to amend its flaws. The intention was to create a depopulated, mined, fenced, and patrolled area that would either deter insurgent infiltrators or at least make it easier for intruders to be discovered and tracked from footprints left in the soft, raked earth. In practice, however, mines were often detonated by animals or uncovered by rain, rendering them ineffective.

The reason for the barrier's failure was mainly due to the lack of manpower committed to patrolling it. Thus, even when insurgents detonated mines, the remainder of their infiltration party was often able to escape back across the border before security patrols arrived. The insurgents even found ways of breaching the corsan by digging trenches across it that similarly went undetected because of infrequent security force patrols.[96] The manpower shortage therefore had adverse effects on the operations of the RSF, whereas guerrilla forces poured in by their thousands. So dire was the manpower situation that white farmers formed reaction sticks because there was no adequate manpower to meet the security needs of the white community. The farmers spent a third of the year in the bush. Most of them were in their 50s and 60s.[97] The employment of police reservists in their 50s and 60s as a striking force was criticized on the basis that a man's reaction time once he got to this age was not as quick as that of a young man.[98]

Manpower Shortage in the Air Force and Its Impact

The shortage of manpower impacted heavily on the efficiency of the RhAF during the Second Chimurenga. The recurrence of aircraft accidents was attributed to lack of experienced airmen. In particular, novices took up the challenge of fighting tough guerrilla fighters. Accidents in the air unit can be traced back to the period before the outbreak of the Second Chimurenga. On July 3, 1943, there was an accident to aircraft Harvard Mk IIA in Kezi District, Bulawayo, which led to the death of Air Commodore J.W.B. Grigson.[99] The primary cause of the accident was attributed to the fact that the pilot was off track, probably due to an unexpected difference in the wind direction as the flight progressed, which caused him to encounter adverse weather conditions in the vicinity of his destination.[100] The secondary cause of the accident was considered to be that the pilot broke through cloud when the base was at a very low altitude.[101]

The Secretary of Defence elaborated that the police were to be responsible for guarding wrecked civil aircraft just as they would attend any other accident involving civilian property.[102] The duties of the guard were to protect all civil property, to permit the immediate removal of deceased or injured personnel after identification, to keep spectators at a reasonable distance, and to admit none but officially interested personnel to the immediate accident area. The guard was also obliged to prevent needless handling or disturbance of the wreckage or parts thereof and to take all practical steps to prevent destruction of any ground marks caused by the aircraft until it could be examined, mapped and photographed by the investigators.[103]

The first fatal accident to the SRAF after World War II occurred to Sgt. Major Love, who was killed in a flying accident in France.[104] Flight Lt. Bergren was tasked to carry out a formal investigation into an aircraft accident involving Harvard FX 255, at No. 5 Flying Training School, on January 23, 1952.[105] Bergren was supposed to ascertain the cause of the accident and extent of damage, to allocate responsibility and to apportion blame (if any).[106] AVM Bentley reported the destruction of two aircraft through flying accidents in 1964.[107] There were also a number of resignations in the same year.[108] Although aircraft accidents happened before the Second Chimurenga, they became a serious problem during the liberation war mainly because of the demanding task at hand: "We have had more aircraft accidents than we can afford involving younger pilots and this has led to speculation that inexperience was the root of the loss." From January 1 to March 31, 1979, there were 32 accidents, but 16 were unavoidable.[109] On September 1, 1978, Divaris, MP for Belvedere, admitted that many of the fighting forces were either hurt or killed because of accidents.[110] Quite a big number of pilots had limited hours of training before being send on active missions due to an ever-increasing demand for pilots. The length of basic training was minimal. In this regard, it was important that their instruction was easy to understand. This short training led to heavy losses, as inexperience in the air often proved fatal.

The table below shows the number of accidents suffered by the RhAF from 1951 to 1980:

Table 7.1: Mishaps in the RhAF

Type of Aircraft	Number of Mishaps
Allouette III	28
Bell 205	3
Genet	2
Canberra	6
Hunter	3
Vampire	8
Trojan	5
Provost	5
Dakota	4
Baron	1
Islander Lynx	1
Lynx	4
Total	**70**

Adapted from http://www.rhodesianforces.org/AircraftIncidents.htm (Accessed 17 April 2012).

One cannot therefore cast a blind eye on the impact of aircraft accidents on the operations of the RhAF during Zimbabwe's liberation war. This evidence also helps us realize that the air force faced a host of challenges which prevented it from achieving its military objectives.

PERSONNEL AND MATERIAL CHALLENGES IN THE TECHNICAL BRANCH OF THE AIR FORCE

The Rhodesian planes were old, and this sapped the potential of the RhAF. Acquisition of aircraft spares, particularly for the older aircraft types, continued to be difficult. The problem of aging aircraft applied equally well to aging road transport.[111] Most of the aircraft were so old that they had reached the limit of their useful life. The determination to maintain and fly such old aircraft was diminishing.[112] It became expensive to maintain an obsolete fleet. The Battle of Mapai exemplifies the impact of aircraft shortage in the operations of the RhAF. Several air raids were concentrated at Mapai, but the RhAF, even with the support of the South African Air Force (SAAF) Canberra, lacked adequate aircraft to dislodge the defenders.[113] In order to solve the challenge of old aircraft, the Minister of Defence, John Hartley Howmann, presented a Defence Procurement Bill in 1972, the purpose being to establish a body corporate known as the Defence Procurement Board, which would regulate a fund to be known as the Defence Procurement Fund.[114] The fund was responsible for raising money for defense purposes, subject to the endorsement of the minister and the agreement of the treasury. Howmann felt that there were many parties and individuals involved in the production and supply of defense equipment who were inhibited from, or who preferred to avoid dealing through, the accepted channels or subjecting themselves to systems of control normally used by the government for the raising of money.[115] The minister expected that the initiative would help tap sources of funds and attract money that was not attracted through the normal channels. The board was supposed to be composed of the chairman (Secretary of Defence) and three other members appointed by the Minister of Defence.[116]

The air force faced numerous technical challenges which impeded its efforts to counter guerrilla incursion. The RhAF was not as efficient as portrayed by its admirers.[117] The challenge of obtaining spare parts that gripped the RhAF during the Second Chimurenga could plainly be traced back to the interwar period (1946–1965). After the Second World War, the colony never got adequate manpower and equipment to make the RhAF an efficient unit. The air unit found it difficult at times to provide sufficient aircraft to meet the steady increase in the demands of government departments in 1948. Towards the end of 1948, flying activities virtually ceased when it was found necessary to ground all the Arson aircraft which had developed an engine defect common to all this type of aircraft.[118] The new fleet that arrived was inadequate in both number and type to replace the old fleet on the training task.[119]

After World War II, the Technical Squadron of the air unit faced shortage of spares and tools.[120] A sizeable number of aircraft could not fly at the end of 1951 as a result of difficulties in obtaining spares. Spares production in the UK fell off steadily and in some cases ceased. The agreement to supply spares was canceled by the Air Ministry in June 1951 without notice.[121] It is apparent that the RhAF entered the war a relatively troubled side. The technical side of the air force experienced many challenges as a result of the shortage of ground staff and certain servicing tasks were put out to civil contractors.[122] In addition, the Unilateral Declaration of Independence declared by Ian Smith on November 11, 1965, prohibited the RRAF from procuring new equipment in its usual markets. It also lost the usually available technical experts it used to get from foreign countries.[123] The pilots were encouraged to be resourceful in their methods of prosecuting the war. The airmen who wasted fuel or stole office stationery were often considered as doing as great a disservice as the soldier who writes off a truck.[124] More importantly, soldiers were obliged to be responsible in order to maximize savings.[125] Some types of aircraft were not economic, and thus they affected the effectiveness of the RhAF during the Second Chimurenga. Disturbances in Nyasaland demonstrated the weaknesses of the Provost aircraft in two particular capacities: they needed quite a lot of runaway, and they only carried one person besides the pilot. This was opposed to other models such as Beavers, which took up very little runaway and carried three or four persons such as military personnel for reconnaissance and other things.[126]

Just like pilots, technical personnel were resigning more quickly than they could be replaced. Two senior officers and 40 technicians left the force during 1972.[127] The total number of flying hours continued to mount. This did not tally with the amount of personnel required to service, maintain and repair these aircraft.[128] Some officers left on normal retirement package but the majority of the technician resignations and retirements occurred in the higher non-commissioned officers (NCO) ranks at an earlier stage.[129] The years of training invested were not easily recouped. Moreover, officers and men sent for advanced training in electronic degrees were a direct loss for three to four years to their branch.[130] The problem underlined the need for a review of conditions of service, pay and pension schemes.[131] During the Rolls-Royce parade held on October 28, 1976, Air Commodore Bradshaw, the Director General of Supporting Services, addressed the parade, stating how the guerrilla war had strained the Technical Branch of the RhAF: "The Technical Branch of this air force enjoys an enviable and well-deserved reputation, probably second to none, for the manner in which the most difficult circumstances with a relative handful of technicians in comparison to other forces. High technical skills and expertise alone have not produced this happy state of affairs. Rather it is the spirit and dedication of our men of their constant willingness to do just that little bit extra to ensure success. You are now full members of that team. I am sure you will all respect and enhance its traditions and reputation."[132]

Similarly, Wing Commander Simmonds highlighted the challenges faced by the RhAF technical side: "Unless we can induce our trained technicians to stay, then it will be impossible to keep the air force as a viable entity in itself. I would urge Government to do everything possible to try and maintain not only the numbers in our defence forces but the very high standard of knowledge that is so essential if we are going to maintain it at the standard to which we have become accustomed."[133] These challenges occurred at a time when members of the RSF unanimously agreed on the significance of the RhAF to the prosecution of the war. The chief of Rhodesian intelligence, Ken Flower, admitted that the air force had developed into the most efficient weapon in counterinsurgency. He strongly believed that its absence could have resulted in a loss.[134] Air Marshal Mussell concurred with Flower when he highlighted that without the aircraft from No. 7 Squadron, antiterrorist operations in Rhodesia would have taken a very different course.[135] Air power made the difference because it gave the defense forces their distinct advantage over the enemy.[136]

On the 29th anniversary of the founding of the RhAF, on November 28, 1976, army commander General Peter Walls acknowledged the pivotal role that was being played by the air force: "The army holds the air force in the highest esteem, and with good reason. The unfailing co-operation and close liaison that exists between us is something that many countries must envy, and could well emulate to their own advantage. From this co-operation has sprung a great mutual respect, and many firm friendships have been formed between all ranks of the Browns and Blues, both Regular and Territorial."[137] In order to minimize resignations in the security forces, Brigadier Keen, the MP for Arundel, advocated the soldiers to be paid what he called the "X" factor so as to attract people to stay in the army in an effort to save money on recruiting and training. By "X" factor Keen referred to the hardships and disadvantages of a soldier's life compared with the comforts of civilian life.[138] The argument was that a man was supposed to be induced to re-enlist on the basis of pay, plus on re-enlistment he could get a bonus or a bounty and his pay would go up by that much for the next re-enlistment so that a man would be induced to stay until he was about 40 to 45 years old.[139] The other thing was that a soldier did not have much of a future after 40 and this would make people reluctant to make it their lifetime service. As a result, there were supposed to be pensions that the ex-soldier could fall back on, and the government was supposed to reserve jobs, as was the custom in other countries, for old soldiers, such as traffic wardens or messengers of the police, to mention a few.[140] From the foregoing discussion, it is clear that the RhAF faced many technical challenges which inhibited it from effectively carrying out its duties. Its importance to the prosecution of the war is well appreciated but its challenges should be clearly spelled out.

The Impact of Low Morale in the Forces

From the advent of colonial rule in the colony, races not white were not fairly treated. The Federation of Rhodesia and Nyasaland did not do any better to improve the situation of the "natives." The "natives" were prevented by Federal legislation from obtaining the same technical training in the air force as was available to Europeans. Kennan, the Secretary in the Cabinet Partnership Implementation, remarked: "The implementation of partnership in the sphere of defence is particularly difficult at present time due to the largely racial divisions that still exist in the approach to political and constitutional questions."[141] Kennan recommended that the constitution be given time in order to amend the relevant regulations so as not to bar the recruitment of persons of any race for technical training in the RRAF.

Pay discrepancies represented one item on the long list of grievances raised by nonwhites in the Defence Ministry. An Asian serving in the northeast border during the Second Chimurenga argued that it was grossly unfair to be treated on the basis of the color of the skin because a bullet knew no color.[142] Nonwhites could rarely attain a rank higher than that of a noncommissioned officer (NCO) even though they were highly qualified and merit commissioners. According to a Rhodesian-Asian: "When I did my training we were not allowed to swim in the pool at Llewellin Barracks. Instead, we were driven several miles to swim in a Coloured suburb of Bulawayo. This is typical of the petty discrimination which exists in the Army today."[143] A nonwhite sergeant major got a daily basic rate of $2.80 and his European counterpart got $4.[144] This alone shattered the morale of the other fighting forces in the RSF. Discrimination irked some African parliamentarians who advocated for the same pay for both Africans and whites. The differences apparently showed that there was little or no cooperation in the security forces especially if the forces had different access to facilities with discrepancies in salary and uniforms.[145] The MP for Kariba, Peter Mhletshwa Nkomo, thus complained: "I wonder if the Minister paused and considered how much duties are involved and the burden laid upon an African soldier.... Then it surprises me that when it comes to rank, an African is always graded low, yet he is doing exactly the same duties as his colleagues, a white soldier."[146] The MP for Lowveld, Alford Dzingirai Chademana, similarly lamented about discrimination when he said: "But when they come to the benefits, they do not enjoy the same benefits.... It would far be better if all those who are fighting in the war had the same privileges on their salaries. They should have the same privileges, and when they come home we see that the European comes to a home that he is fighting for, but the African soldier who dies in the war, when his family comes home they have nowhere to sleep, no gardens at home, so why should they fight and why should they die?"[147]

The resentments, however, did very little to ameliorate the situation of the African soldiers because it was the deliberate policy of the whites to alienate nonwhite races. Minister of Justice Lardner-Burke, on behalf of Minister of Defence Howmann, indicated in 1969 that the policy of separate development in the armed forces of Rhodesia was to stay.[148] He noted that the Ministry had no intention of departing from the principles that traditionally governed the recruitment and command of the Defence Forces.[149] Black soldiers lived off other people's leftovers. In real terms, the recruitment system and the treatment accorded to Africans in particular was a tactical blunder by the Rhodesians. The Africans' morale in the police, army and air force was largely low as a result of the racial parameters used in the recruitment, promotion and rewarding processes. In a sense, this actually helped to facilitate African soldiers to desert the Forces in favor of the guerrilla armies during the Second Chimurenga. It is worthwhile to point out that no one wants to be treated like an outcast. It is practically challenging to lead an army made up of demoralized soldiers. Morale in the military sense is that conditioned quality, in the individual soldier and in the unit of command, which holds the soldier and the unit, to the performance of its duty despite every opposing force or influence. It involves quality and condition of the mind, body and spirit.[150] Napoleon's dictum that "in war morale forces are physical as three to one" was buttressed by Colonel Foertsch, the military theoretician of the German High Command, who believed: "The final word regarding victory and defeat rests not on arms and equipment, nor in the way which they are used, nor even on the principles of strategy and tactics, but on the morale of the troops."[151] This demonstrates that the outnumbered, ill-equipped, or even outmaneuvered may triumph if the morale is markedly superior.[152] Accordingly, Frederick the Great made sure that his troops received clothing every year, for both summer and winter use, and were never without bread.[153] The fact that the coloreds and blacks were despised meant that they lacked the zeal that motivated the white forces to give their all.

The Africans were regarded as unsuitable to join the air force, although the rejections were based on purported "professional" reasons, as enunciated by the Joint Minister of Combined Operations, Hawkins: "The honourable member complained that there were no African pilots in the air force but it is a fact that the wide range and fairly strict aptitude tests which are applied to applicants for the air force to determine their potential as pilots so far have not been passed by any African who has applied. So it is not a matter of racial discrimination: it is a question of attaining the necessary standards required."[154] White officers refuted the use of race in the air force on the basis of their acceptance of the individual for what he was, and on intolerance of racial prejudice, when they argued: "It matters not whether a man is a pilot or clerk, whether cook or technician, it matters not whether he works with his hands or his head. It is enough that he is part of the team, that he does his job and that we are all, in some way, dependent on him. It matters not whether he hails from Liverpool or Lalapanzi, from Odzi or Oudtshoorn; it is enough that he is a Rhodesian now."[155]

The Rhodesians were "mistaken" about the level of morale in the African units, as revealed in 1969 by Air Vice-Marshal and Chief of Air Staff Wilson, who said that: "The level of morale throughout the year has been high and a sense of genuine achievement prevailed. The regular periodic reviews of conditions of service have proved to be an important factor in maintaining morale."[156] It is true that the level of morale was high for white personnel who had their conditions of service periodically reviewed. For the Africans, it was a different story because they were treated as inferior. Evidence points out that a day in the life of an African serving in the RSF was not rosy. Africans' experiences in the RSF were actually unpleasant in a force which desperately needed their services as a result of the shortage of manpower.

Disunity was also common amongst the white population. According to Godwin and Hancock, the Rhodesians of the 1970s were not socially or ethnically homogeneous and more self-misguided than is often supposed. The overwhelming majorities were either migrants or had been born in the country since World War II. Throughout the 1970s the Rhodesians were preoccupied with the largely material needs, activities, and desires of a people living in a semi-detached western society.[157] Very little attention was paid to the needs and wants of the majority population, as revealed by Moorcraft: "Rhodesians paid more attention to their roses, their Currie Cup cricket, their horses, their dogs and the level of algae in their pools than to the black people whose land they shared in unequal proportions."[158] The effects of the war led many Rhodesians to run away to South Africa, where they joined the apartheid regime. Most of them found joy in the fact that they were accommodated in the economic and military spheres.

Conclusion

The RhAF faced numerous challenges as a result of guerrilla tactics of sabotage which the air force could not effectively deal with. Strategic infrastructure was destroyed, thereby indicating the limits of air power in guerrilla warfare. The political leadership admitted that the guerrillas were stepping up their strategies and the RSF were not able to counter these operations. The guerrillas also benefited from the support rendered by Frontline states in the execution of the war. This undoubtedly impacted the Rhodesian war machinery. Support for the guerrillas was generally coming from all directions, as evidenced by the active role of the churches and various left-wing organizations. As opposed to scholarship which depicted the Rhodesian Air Force as a super weapon that defied all the odds during the Second Chimurenga, this chapter highlights the fundamental weaknesses of the air unit in carrying out its operations. Evidence from various official documents produced by the Rhodesian government reveal that the RhAF faced an array of challenges as a result of guerrilla operations. Although fireforce operations were very swift, they were not decisive.

8
Challenging "Air Supremacy" from Outside: Analyzing the Feasibility of ZPRA's Conventional Plan

Introduction

The aim of this chapter is to evaluate the factors which could have worked against the execution of ZPRA's Zero Hour Plan during Zimbabwe's war of liberation. Besides the insights provided by an insider, Jeremy Brickhill, there is very limited documentation on how the plan was going to achieve its stated objectives in light of the strengths and achievements of the Rhodesian Air Force in conventional operations. In addition, due to lack of finer details from the Zimbabwe African People's Union, the architects of the plan under discussion, there are no fine points articulating how the plan was going to be precisely executed. What remains widely understood is that the guerrilla party had a strategy to shift to conventional aerial warfare during the course of the liberation struggle. The strategy entailed the "massive" use of air power in order to "annihilate" the Rhodesians, who had stubbornly maintained their grip on power. This chapter attempts not to delve much into the basics of the envisaged strategy but critiques the pragmatism of the plan in view of the organization and exploits of the Rhodesian Air Force in conventional warfare since 1940. It is factual that the air force failed to defeat guerrilla units during the war, but it could have been a different story if ZPRA had executed conventional aerial warfare. The RhAF proved its mettle by conducting cross-border bombardments, much to the chagrin of the guerrilla forces and the neighboring countries.

After more than a decade of warring, the Zimbabwe People's Revolutionary Army strategists sought for a strategic transformation by shifting from guerrilla warfare to conventional warfare. This strategic rebirth could be linked to the need to unlock the deadlock which had characterized the guerrilla war.

Nothing seemed to come out except bloodshed. What boggles the mind is that although the Zero Hour Plan was widely publicized, strategies and practicalities for its implementation remain conjectural up to the present. While the author might appear pessimistic about the abilities of ZPRA as a military force, the odds were certainly stacked against them. The fact that the plan failed to see the light of the day sums up ZPRA's attitude towards the Rhodesian Air Force.

Without refuting the effectiveness of ZPRA's military machine, it must be noted that the Zero Hour Operation could have been one of the greatest disasters in the military history of Zimbabwe. The conventional approach of ZAPU to the war involving the use of airplanes could have been disastrous considering that Salisbury had command of the air, which would have "certainly" crushed such an undertaking.[1] Up to the present there is scattered evidence on the composition and strength of the so-called ZPRA Air Force. Nonetheless, ZPRA's intelligence proved its competence by identifying how the downed Viscount civilian aircraft were used for military purpose.[2] Unlike the Zimbabwe African National Liberation Army, which failed to fire a "single" shot at Chimoio during a raid by the Rhodesian Air Force in 1977, ZPRA's military abilities were demonstrated several times during the course of the war. They were better trained and possessed state-of-the-art machinery. There is adequate evidence to demonstrate that the ZPRA military machine was very formidable during the Second Chimurenga. The ZPRA guerrillas made some notable exploits which facilitated Zimbabwe's independence. ZANU PF's patriotic history only talks about ZANLA and forgets that ZPRA played an indisputable role during the war. Some top politicians even go to extent of saying that Joshua Nkomo was a sellout. The role played by ZPRA cadres such as Joshua Nkomo, John Nkomo, Joseph Msika, Nikita Mangena, Lookout Masuku, Dumiso Dabengwa, Jason Moyo, Akim Ndlovu, Robson Manyika, Abraham Nkiwane, Ambrose Mutinhiri, Gordon Bushe, Walter Mbabo, Nicholas Nkomo and Phelekezela Mphoko is well documented. Nevertheless, the author concludes that the Zero Hour Plan overlooked a number of pertinent things if it were to be successfully executed in 1979 or any other date before or after 1979. The Rhodesian Air Force boasted several decades of military experience since the second Great War and the Malaya days. Besides, the air force undertook several missions in Korea, Iraq, the Middle East, Aden, the Arabian Peninsula and Cyprus in its imperial defense missions. In addition, the Federal era ushered in tremendous benefits to the army and air force while neighboring South Africa provided a helping hand in repelling insurgency. There were also critical divisions in the guerrilla camps which could have worked against the intended operation. All of these factors cannot be taken for granted if one is to seriously evaluate the dangers faced by ZPRA's Zero Hour Plan.

Brief Explanation of the Zero Hour Plan

The challenges faced by anyone attempting to account for the Zimbabwe People's Revolutionary Army's conventional strategy were revealed by an insider, Jeremy Brickhill, when he said: "The little that has been written of ZAPU's military strategy in the latter part of the war has been grossly misleading. ZAPU was never able to offer its own account and thus the disinformation has gained credence. Even serious academic studies have presented caricature and unsourced generalisations as evidence of ZAPU's military strategy."[3] Nonetheless, the lack of in-depth detail cannot stop academics and commentators from evaluating the feasibility of the Zero Hour Plan. There is a belief that ZPRA's goal was to invade Rhodesia with a conventional army it was building and thereafter consolidate its control over the country and wipe out its rivals in ZANLA.[4] The plan, regarded as the "turning point" and/or the last stage of the war, was supposed to take place during the period of the traditional *Inwxala* (first fruits festival) ceremony during the rainy season in the summer of 1979 to 1980. Militarily, it involved a conventional army in cooperation with its guerrilla forces and the paramilitarized black ZAPU members.[5] The plan was a top secret only known to ZAPU leader Joshua Nkomo and senior ZAPU leaders.[6] As put forward by Eliakim Sibanda, ZPRA had its own air force based in Angola, and this was supposed to seize the Kariba and Wankie airfields before squaring off with the RSF. Sibanda was quite convinced that ZPRA had the capabilities to achieve these military objectives because it had proven its bravery in the field, augmented by adequate manpower, a well-trained conventional army plus a militarized civilian population.[7] The invasion plan envisioned using two motorized columns, supported by tanks and jet aircraft, entering Rhodesia from Chirundu and Victoria Falls and then converging on Salisbury.[8] The war was supposed to be transformed from a guerrilla operation into a full-scale conflict in an effort to match the RSF's armor and independent air force.[9] According to the then ZPRA chief intelligence officer, Dumiso Dabengwa, the Soviets were not involved in the birth of the plan. It was something that originated from ZAPU and was endorsed by the ZAPU Revolutionary Council. Soviet advisers were there to give advice on the application of the plan.[10]

Why the Plan?

There are basically two major reasons advanced to explain why the Zero Hour Operation was hatched. ZAPU's official version is that the operation aimed to shorten the war which had dragged on for so long.[11] The other explanation is that the conventional plan was developed in order to regain the military initiative that Nkomo had lost to ZANLA in 1969–1976.[12] It can therefore be accepted that the planned ZPRA operation was to be a concerted bid by Nkomo and his Soviet backing to forestall ZANU (i.e., Chinese) political or military victory. Planning included Angola, which was to provide the aircraft for a typical Warsaw Pact–type operation.[13] It is also argued that Nkomo was hoping that Rhodesia's Security Forces would drain themselves in the demolition of Mugabe's forces, at which point Nkomo would march into Salisbury over the skeletons of his black and white rivals.[14]

Analyzing the Feasibility of the Zero Hour Operation

As revealed in the previous chapters, the RhAF underwent several stages of development, and this symbolized its "maturity" to an extent that it became one of the most advanced air units in Africa. As already explained, the story of the establishment and development of the RhAF mirrors the strategic challenges faced by the political and military leadership of the 20th century in incorporating the services of aircraft in warfare. Whereas the establishment of the air force in countries like Great Britain was derailed by military conservatism, Southern Rhodesia's dire financial situation was an obvious hindrance. The fact that the police were the first line of defense compelled the colony to enact the Defence Act in 1926 in an effort to overhaul the defense system. What is particularly interesting about the Defence Act is that the idea of establishing an air force was not even conceived except to endorse the Aviation Act in 1929, which regulated the operations of civil aviation. The Act, of course, was of little significance to military aviation. After some agreements, the Air Ministry gave help to the colony, thus enabling the low-scale training of pilots until 1939, when the scheme was revisited to meet the prevailing security challenges. In 1951, the air force became one of the permanent units of the defense forces. The Federation of Rhodesia and Nyasaland (1953–1963) ushered in tremendous developments in the air force. At the break-up of the Federation, the air unit had significantly developed to fight any insurgency.

Impact of Rhodesian Intelligence

The envisioned Zero Hour Operation reminds one of Adolf Hitler's Operation Sea Lion executed in 1940. A prerequisite for the operation was the establishment of air superiority under the German Air Force. On July 10, 1940, there was heavy bombing of southern England, and the main targets were shipping and ports, airfields and London.[15] Evidence demonstrates that the RhAF had command of the air and ZPRA was supposed to challenge it from outside. It also remains difficult to ascertain if the operation was going to be covertly executed, cognizant of the fact that the RSF had one of the most effective intelligences under Ken Flower. The CIO's Branch II was in charge of almost all external intelligence-gathering operations, while the Special Branch and Selous Scouts were more active inside Rhodesia. The CIO was made up of two branches: Special Branch, responsible for internal security, meaning the Selous Scouts fell under its wings; and Branch II, responsible for external operations.[16] Apart from external operations, Branch II was also responsible for propaganda, disinformation, covert ops, and psychological operations. Branch II had an extensive network of agents supplying intelligence from Zambia, Botswana, Mozambique, and even Angola. The agents in Zambia included people living along the border, many of whom belonged to tribes which were hostile to the Zambian government. These agents supplied substantial information on ZPRA bases in these areas. CIO also mounted a concerted intelligence-gathering effort against the Soviet and Peoples' Republic of China embassies in Lusaka, Zambia. The triumph of these operations, nevertheless, was more the result of Russian and Communist Chinese underestimation of CIO's intelligence-gathering abilities, leading to lax security, than of CIO's sophistication.[17] Agents in Angola and Mozambique included Portuguese nationals who had remained in the country after independence. Added to that, all-important external intelligence on Soviet and Chinese contacts with ZPRA and ZANLA was obtained from the American CIA, Britain's MI-5, and other western intelligence organizations. The enmity that existed between the Rhodesian and British governments after UDI, for example, did little to affect intelligence exchanges between the CIO and MI-5 or MI-6. The British services were unsympathetic toward ZANLA and ZPRA because of their ties to various Communist countries.[18] Rhodesia's intelligence learned of ZPRA's conventional war strategy and preempted the invasion by periodically attacking ZPRA's staging bases in Zambia. Accordingly, ZPRA was forced to recommence its infiltration tactics based on guerrilla doctrine.[19] Nonetheless, although Rhodesian intelligence systems kept abreast of guerrilla activities, they were not always effective. Some of their operations failed as a result of poor intelligence, such as the April 1979 attempt to kidnap ZPRA leader Joshua Nkomo.[20]

In the early 1970s, the Rhodesians turned to a concept called "pseudo operations" (pseudo ops) by creating the Selous Scouts in 1973. These were placed under the auspices of the Central Intelligence Organisation's Special Branch. Security personnel would dress as insurgents and infiltrate rural communities seeking out real insurgents. When they found the actual insurgents, they could go for an engagement or call in their position and allow other army units, notably the RLI, to come in. In the first days, highly trained white officers of the SAS were used for the operations. But language barriers and the distinct physical facial features of the whites necessitated the use of black Zimbabweans. To do this, injured or captured insurgents were "turned" and made to serve the Selous Scouts.[21] To avoid confusion and prevent other government forces from mistaking the Scouts for actual insurgents, any area they were operating in was "frozen"—that is, no other security forces were allowed in the vicinity.[22]

It is also a reality that the split of ZAPU in 1963 had an enormously damaging effect on the nationalist struggle. Though inconclusively proven, it is assumed that the Special Branch may have exploited the rivalry between these two movements whenever possible, using agents of influence strategically placed in both organizations combined with various disinformation tactics. In light of the role of Rhodesian intelligence, several theories have been advanced to explain the assassination of ZANU's national chairman in Zambia, Herbert Chitepo. One school of thought argues that the assassination was done in such a way as to suggest that his death by a car bomb was due to factional fighting within ZANU. On the other hand, the assassination of Chitepo is blamed on ZANU for the sole reason that Chitepo had expressed reservations about the way the Nhari rebellion had been handled. Over and above, Rhodesian intelligence worked round the clock to guarantee the security of the country they adored so much.

Divisions in Nationalist Parties

In addition, the naked rivalry between ZAPU and ZANU since the ZANU-ZAPU split of 1963 raised questions as to whether the Zero Hour Operation was going to come to fruition. Arguments about tactics, ideology, and personality led to the split and the formation of ZANU under the leadership of Ndabaningi Sithole. Nkomo remained the head of ZAPU. Although Sithole had taken six from Nkomo's executive council of eleven, ZAPU was far from dead.[23] Nkomo kept control of Bulawayo and Matabeleland, while ZANU came to command undisputed support in Umtali and the eastern districts, Fort Victoria and the southern Mashonaland, and Gwelo and the Midlands. Nevertheless, the question over ideology falls out because Nkomo eventually accepted the argument that freedom could not come to Rhodesia by constitutional negotiations, as had happened in Zambia and Malawi, and that the nation must embrace the armed struggle or remain under the colonial boot. It then appeared to the outside world that the differences were based on the personalities of the leaders. Tribalism was in the background, although it was strenuously denied by both sides.[24] ZANU actions during the ZIPA period help us understand the kind of relationship that existed between the two guerrilla parties, always plotting to outdo each other. ZAPU's conventional plan also points in the same direction.

Evidence of inter-party rift was further revealed after Zimbabwe's independence in 1980 when the general of the ZAPU army, Lookout "Mafela" Masuku, died in prison despite being acquitted by Zimbabwe's Supreme Court.[25] Masuku's burial at the Lady Stanley Cemetery in Bulawayo was ignored by the ZANU PF government.[26] ZPRA and ZANLA were fighting for the same aim and objectives but they were traditional foes.[27] After independence, Mugabe made an effort to undermine ZAPU's role in the war of liberation. Addressing the ZANU PF Youth League in 1983, Mugabe relegated ZAPU's role to almost nothing: "Without the youth, there would never have been ZANLA, and without ZANLA, there would never have been a struggle by ZANU, and without a struggle by ZANU, freedom and independence would never have come as early as 1980."[28] The brutalities of the Rhodesian Security Forces on ZPRA camps were also ignored: "Most of the people lost, among these thousands, were young refugees brutally massacred by the callous enemy at such centres as Nyadzonia, Chimoio and Tembwe."[29] Mugabe's attitude towards ZAPU could be summed up by the Gukurahundi massacres which happened after independence. The massacres testify to ZANU's long-harbored wish to dump ZAPU into political oblivion. In the event of ZPRA scoring military success during its conventional aerial operations, there was likelihood, close to 100 percent, that ZANU PF was going to seize the opportunity by tenaciously fighting ZPRA, again giving leverage to Smith's forces or imposing themselves as the new rulers. It is thus imperative to focus on the strategic and tactical reasons why the Zero Hour Plan was going to face serious challenges in its execution. ZANU were not friends of the plan at all.

ZPRA's "Inaction" in the Face of Incessant Attacks

The preparedness of the "ZPRA Air Force" was seriously doubtful, especially considering that the RhAF could raid ZPRA bases outside the country almost at will. ZPRA planners were quoted as saying that 1979 was the year in which the air campaign would commence. Surprisingly, several raids on ZPRA camps and plots to assassinate Nkomo in Zambia went on unabated during the same period. In retaliation for the downed Viscounts and ZPRA's conventional plan, in February 1979 Canberra bombers and Hawker-Hunter fighters of the RhAF launched a raid at Luso in Angola. The raid killed 160 ZPRA insurgents and wounded 530.³⁰ The Angolan air force's advanced Soviet MiG-21 manned by Cuban pilots, and antiaircraft fire in the hands of some 20,000 Cuban troops in Angola, did not do anything to stop the invading RhAF. Added to that, the Angolans had a radar system supplied and operated by the Russians. The ZPRA base housed about 3,000 soldiers.³¹ Total surprise was achieved and this could be attributed to the offensive capabilities of air power. The attack took place in the morning. Rain had further confined the majority of the recruits to their huts, meaning they were easy targets.³² A Special Air Service mission in April 1979 in Lusaka destroyed Nkomo's headquarters.³³ Economic targets such as railways and bridges were also destroyed. The security forces launched pre-emptive raids by Special Air Service troops into the heart of Lusaka during April and June 1979 to disrupt ZPRA command and control structures. ZPRA central command and communication facilities were severely damaged by these operations.³⁴ The ZPRA airmen could have seized such opportunities to showcase the military abilities of their aircrew. The best that could be done by ZPRA was defending the bases and dividing major camps into numerous small ones spread over remote areas. The tendency before was to erect camps close to urban areas like Lusaka.³⁵ The SAS mission to assassinate Joshua Nkomo, codenamed *Operation Bastille*, failed to materialize because Nkomo had been apparently tipped off, thus he escaped death by a whisker.³⁶ Even if it was not strategic to engage the RhAF in foreign soil, ZPRA's air force could have demonstrated the credibility and capability of its plan by exchanging directions with the RhAF. It is important to highlight at this juncture that Angola was one of ZAPU's closest allies, as put forward by ZAPU cadre Callistus Ndlovu: "ZAPU had a very strong alliance with the MPLA in Angola and was close to all other liberation movements including FRELIMO…."³⁷ The Cubans were also heavily involved in training ZPRA fighters in Angola and Zambia.³⁸

What is even more baffling is the fact that the Zambian Air Force, which was equipped with up-to-date Soviet MIG-21 aircraft and other models, did not dare raise a finger against the RhAF, which was blatantly violating its airspace.³⁹ There were also Macchi 326 jet fighters and the British Aircraft Corporation ground-to-air missile system in Zambia.⁴⁰ This alone says a lot about the military capabilities of the RhAF as an instrument of conventional warfare. Although the armed forces of Mozambique and Zambia only actively intervened on a small scale on four occasions, adequate provision had been made for dealing with such an eventuality.⁴¹ The Zambian Air Force started as the Northern Rhodesian Air Wing, a mere branch of the Royal Rhodesian Air Force. The air unit started with two squadrons. With the dissolution of the Federation of Rhodesia and Nyasaland in 1963, four Dakotas from the Royal Rhodesian Air Force were transferred to Northern Rhodesia (not yet Zambia) together with the two Hunting Percival Pembroke, employed in supporting the army and police on internal security. The air wing was largely staffed by 15 RAF officers and 30 airmen, while Zambian personnel were recruited and trained.[42] Several countries such as the UK, Italy, Yugoslavia, China and Russia supported the development of the ZAF. In 1978, China presented Zambia with 12 SHENYANG F-6 (MiG-19) day fighters. These were to act as a deterrent to the Rhodesian Air Force, which regularly entered Zambian airspace.[43] Still, this did not help because the RhAF continued to raid Zambia. In the same year, the first major external raid took place into Zambia. From here, half-trained ZPRA insurgents were forwarded to Luso for a final four-month training period.[44] The air raids were humiliating and sad for Zambia as she was completely powerless to prevent them. The most compelling evidence shows that the RhAF would communicate with the airport at Lusaka as it was entering Zambian airspace to notify them that all planes should be kept on the ground. And when leaving, they would radio that their work was finished and their airport was free to open.[45] Although the ZAF was reasonably equipped, its airmen lacked the qualities needed to confront the RhAF. The confidence to fight in the air obviously lacked.

The RhAF was up to the task, as noted by Rhodesia's intelligence chief, Ken Flower, who argued that in the dying phase of the war the RhAF had developed into a well-organized weapon in counterinsurgency, otherwise the war could have been lost.[46] Guerrilla infiltration into Rhodesia continued unabated. It was thus strategic to bomb their staging bases. ZPRA started training regular forces in 1978.[47] It is clear that this regular force was the one mandated to spearhead the aerial strikes during the envisaged plan scheduled for 1979. Nonetheless, its preparedness was very doubtful in light of the unceasing and "successful" RhAF raids. ZPRA's regular forces were also expected to provide defense against airborne attack and greater firepower in mounting attacks against garrisons.[48] On the other hand, the RSF emphasized the importance of the need for Rhodesia to maintain a state of preparedness. This was echoed by the then MP for Salisbury City, Sutton-Pryce. The MP elucidated that readiness and a high level of efficiency were to be maintained at the highest peak.[49] In addition, the Rhodesians opted to sacrifice other basics provided the defense section was in a good state. This was clearly spelled out by the MP for Midlands South in 1954, Ian Smith, when he emphasized: "I think it would be very unwise if we were not to prepare ourselves, and I for one—it is the main point that I wish to make—would never shirk my responsibility even if it meant taxes had to be increased, so that the Federation could play a fair part in our contribution towards the defence of the Commonwealth."[50] Consequently, the Minister of Defence justified the defense spending of 10 percent compared to the United Kingdom's 40 percent and the United States' 60 percent.[51]

Justifying Low Mobilization?

It can also be argued that ZPRA popularized the Zero Hour Operation in order to justify its low mobilization in the country in the late 1970s. There are scholars who argue that ZAPU began to take a more active role in the war in 1978 after being stung by Mugabe's accusations that ZANLA was doing all the fighting.[52] In contrast to ZANU, which had committed all its forces to Rhodesia, consolidating its power base and even attempting to infringe on that of ZAPU, Nkomo's forces were training and waiting *en masse* in Zambia and Angola. Nonetheless, had the war reached the final stage of insurgency, that of mobile warfare, the outcome of the Lancaster House talks might have been quite different.[53] Although figures differ, what comes out clearly is that ZPRA did not deploy with the same intensity as ZANLA, especially during the dying phases of the war. Rhodesian intelligence estimated that there were 4,000 ZPRA and 10,000 ZANLA fighters in the country in 1979. An additional 16,000 ZPRA and 3,500 ZANLA guerrillas were situated across the border, while 2,900 ZPRA and 14,000 ZANLA were training externally. What this meant was that only 25 percent of ZPRA forces were in the field.[54] Figures given by other writers reveal that ZANLA deployed 9,000 guerrillas in 1979 while ZPRA soldiers were about 1,000.[55] ZAPU argued that they were preparing for the final battle. ZAPU leader Nkomo preferred a conventional, Cuban-assisted offensive into Matabeleland.[56] All the same, ZPRA became gradually aggressive as the war progressed.[57] Their soldiers were more thoroughly trained than ZANLA's and put up more resistance when attacked than ZANLA did.[58]

Deterrence Strategy?

It is also reasonable to argue that the Zero Hour Operation was a deterrence strategy to halt the RhAF cross-border operations which had become periodic. If so, the Rhodesians were even so not intimidated. Deterrence theory has been in existence since time immemorial. As a theory, it gained prominence during the Cold War conflict between the United States and the Union of Soviet Socialist Republics (USSR). Deterrence theory is hinged on second-strike capability or massive retaliation. The core of nuclear deterrence consists of convincing the opponent that the cost of an aggressive action exceeds the rewards.[59] Deterrence was widely employed by all forces during the Second Chimurenga. Due to the global nature of Zimbabwe's liberation war, the RSF were aware of possible Cuban intervention in support of guerrilla movements. To curb such an undertaking, Rhodesia responded by threats: "We are as well-equipped and prepared to deal with conventional invasion as we are for terrorists—in many cases better equipped and prepared, in fact. If the Cubans are fool-hardy enough to come—or any other foreign troops for that matter—they will find it is no Ogaden and no Angola.[60] On the Rhodesian side, deterrence effectively worked because it achieved its military objectives of curbing a foreign invasion. ZAPU was possibly scared to implement its plan because of the seemingly efficient RhAF, which had caused havoc to ZPRA and ZANLA camps inside and outside Rhodesia. ZPRA boasted of an army trained along conventional lines, but its plan did not live a single day. According to de Kock, the then Deputy Minister in the Department of the Prime Minister, the air force was a deterrent weapon to would-be aggressors in its own right, as evidenced by the free skies of Rhodesia.[61] The bombardments of the RhAF were also indiscriminate. Numerous attacks were carried out inside Rhodesia against the guerrilla forces and unarmed civilians. On April 19, 1974, a light aircraft attacked six African male juveniles who were in proximity to a "terrorist" group, leading to the death of two on the spot; one died a few days later at Bindura hospital, and others were hospitalized.[62]

The Role of South Africa

The Zero Hour Plan needs to be assessed within the global context of the Second Chimurenga. The Soviet Union was the major sponsor of the Zimbabwe African People's Union. The downing of the Viscount civilian aircraft in September 1978 and February 1979 by ZAPU, using new Soviet surface-to-air (SAM) missiles, revealed the active role of the USSR in the conflict.[63] Two ZAPU training areas were established, one at what was once the Zambian Army Barracks at Mulungushi, and the other at Boma camp in Luso, Angola. The Soviets were in charge of the training of ZAPU's conventional forces. The Soviet Union was spread all over the continent supporting groups which opposed the West. It was involved in the Ogaden War, which took place between mid–1977 and March 1978. However, the Soviet Union did nothing more than the provision of equipment and expertise. It is precisely in this context that the extent of the Soviet Union's commitment in the event of ZAPU using air power needs to be scrutinized. It should be highlighted that Russia played a critical role in influencing ZPRA's conventional strategy. One of the contributory factors why the Soviet Union supported ZAPU from the early 1960s was that ZANU had established close contacts with China.[64] The study thus fully acknowledges the role of Russia in oiling ZPRA's war machinery but analyzes it within the context of her generosity in sustaining the war option. An analysis of the fundamentals of Russian assistance to liberation movements in southern Africa would be mere repetition in the sense that writers like Vladimir Shubin, Dumiso Dabengwa, Joshua Nkomo, Eliakim Sibanda and Kimpton Ndlovu, to mention but a few, did that in varying degrees.

The Zero Hour Plan reveals that the Soviet Union and Cuba were supposed to play an important role, especially in the supply of aircraft, spare parts and experts. In the event of this happening, there were high chances that Pretoria was going to provide substantial war material and manpower resources across the Limpopo. In fact, this kind of support was even coming before the beginning of the war. The kith-and-kin relationship that existed between Salisbury and Pretoria cannot be taken for granted in the event of external interference. The Total National Strategy Document/1 (TNSD/1), signed between South Africa and Rhodesia in 1979, affirmed the commitment by both countries to guard their borders from what they called the communist menace. TNSD was, in fact, a reaffirmation of the already warm relations between South Africa and Rhodesia. South Africa played a very important role in the development and sustenance of the Rhodesian military system, especially during World War II and the Second Chimurenga. The SAAF boasted an early date of birth, having been formed on February 1, 1920, whereas an air unit of Southern Rhodesia was formed in 1935. Two D.H.9 aircraft of the Union of South Africa Defence Force, flown by Capt. Meredith and Lieut. Tasker, arrived in Bulawayo in July 1925 for the purpose of an air survey of the Okavango Swamp area.[65] The two governments kept each other posted about the military developments that were happening in their respective countries. On January 7, 1938, Prime Minister Huggins wrote to the Union: "I have the honour to inform you that this government have recently acquired 6 Hawker Hart single engine day Bombers with Rolls Royce Kestrel IB5 engines for use as service aircraft in this colony."[66] Southern Rhodesia wanted South Africa to help in major repairs to aircraft and engines by the South African Air Force Depot where it was not practicable to effect the repairs locally.[67] Added to that, the colony required supplies of perishable parts and other spares when urgently required from the South African Air Force Depot.[68]

Besides, South Africa was keen to play an influential role in assisting Southern Rhodesia during the Second World War. Both countries were seriously committed to imperial defense, and as such mutual cooperation was beneficial to the fulfillment of this single cause. On May 4, 1942, Brigadier-General Mitchell Baker of the Union of South Africa wrote to the Minister of Air, Colonel Ernest L. Guest, "If any little hitch should occur at any time and you think I can assist in clearing the matter up, I should be only too ready to help if you or Meredith will refer the matter to me."[69] The establishment of the RhAF itself reveals how much South Africa was determined to improve the military strength of her neighbor. South African aviation industry was very advanced compared to her neighbor Southern Rhodesia. More importantly, a good number of Rhodesian military personnel had a strong South African background. Lt. General K.R. Coster joined the South African Defence Force (SADF) in 1937 and after being commissioned in the South African Air Force (SAAF), he served in Second World War before returning to regimental and staff duties.[70] Coster joined the Southern Rhodesian Staff Corps in 1955, and on the dissolution of the Federal Army joined the Rhodesian Defence Forces in January 1964. He assumed command of the Rhodesian army in October 1968 and was promoted to lieutenant general in 1971. Coster was succeeded by Peter Walls after his death in 1972.[71]

South Africa's military presence in Rhodesia began in August 1967 when the regime was seriously threatened by the joint forces of the ZAPU and South African ANC. From the early 1960s, there were regular meetings at top level between the defense chiefs representing South Africa, Rhodesia and Portugal.[72] By 1969, South Africa had deployed some 2,700 ground troops and units of the South African Air Force in Rhodesia, and had sent over a thousand more into Mozambique.[73] The fact that various insurgent groups allied themselves with South Africa's African National Congress led the apartheid-era South African government to assist the Rhodesians with manpower, logistical support, and military equipment.[74] The importance of the alliance between South Africa and Rhodesia was expressed by Senator Brendon in 1975. He revealed that the result of the war in Rhodesia had a bearing on South Africa because if Rhodesia fell, South Africa would be overthrown in due course.[75] The same point was reiterated by Air Marshal Wilson when he argued that the pressure on South Africa would be unbearable if Rhodesia fell "under the communist yoke."[76] South Africa assisted Rhodesia in the spirit of avoiding majority rule in southern Africa.

Pretoria and Salisbury exhibited their cooperation in a number of ways. When ZANLA guerrillas set fire to Salisbury's fuel storage tanks, which blazed for almost a week in 1978, Pretoria's assistance was visible.[77] The Salisbury bulk fuel storage tank was set aflame at 9:20 p.m., and it took firemen from the Department of Civil Aviation; the team from Johannesburg, Pretoria, Alberton; SAAF and RhAF to extinguish the flames.[78] The resulting fire lasted six days and destroyed tens of million liters of precious fuel.[79] Airmen from the RhAF worked throughout the week, continually bringing up relief services, manhandling equipment, and sharing the risks experienced by the professional firefighters at the scene of the blaze.[80] When the Salisbury bulk fuel storage tank was set ablaze, the SAAF came to the rescue of their ally. David Smith, the Joint

Minister of Finance, cherished the aid when he said, "The assistance which was offered by our good friends in South Africa was warmly welcomed and was very useful."[81] The SAAF assistance was always available when needed. In a meeting held at New Sarum on August 17, 1978, the Rev. Ndabaningi Sithole stressed the importance of good relations with South Africa. He said that Rhodesia was dependent on that country in many ways.[82] In that regard, the RhAF was extremely appreciative to all sections of the public and the South Africa-Rhodesia Association for their generous contributions towards the welfare of the security forces. The facilities and comforts provided from these sources were significantly treasured, but more especially by those deployed on operational duties.[83]

The Rhodesians had a powerful air force and had the backing of the whites in neighboring South Africa. They were determined to resist world pressure and keep unchanged their own political system.[84] South Africa and Rhodesia were both determined to protect and maintain minority privileges in their own countries. The independence of Mozambique and Angola impacted negatively on the aspirations of these racist tendencies. The attainment of independence by Zimbabwe further endangered the security of South Africa. Besides, the South African Air Force was very pivotal in complementing the efforts of the RhAF during the war. It therefore becomes clear that the Zero Hour Plan faced many hurdles in its implementation. Besides enjoying the support given by South Africa, the Rhodesian Air Force was an experienced force capable of violating the airspace of its neighbors. Problems in guerrilla camps added to the woes facing ZPRA, while there was no formidable sign to prove the existence of the plan.

Conclusion

Without disputing the existence of the Zero Hour Plan, it is still questionable regarding ZPRA failed to prove its shape in the face of many tribulations. Giving the benefit of the doubt, it can be assumed that ZPRA was probably waiting for an opportune moment to launch aerial attacks against Rhodesia. Still, it is a mammouth task of trying to justify why the "air force" was not used a single day to defend bases outside the country, even for deterrence purposes. The Rhodesian Air Force violated the airspace of Angola, Zambia and Mozambique at will, but these countries did not move an inch to stop the barefaced aggression. The easiest interpretation is that these countries did not want to be drawn into a long war with Rhodesia. The development of the air force and army in Rhodesia progressed apace, mainly because of the need to ensure sufficient internal security against external and internal aggression. One thing for sure is that Rhodesia was well aware of the impact of her provocations against the countries that provided sanctuary and support to guerrilla armies. As a result, she was equally prepared to deal with such scenarios. Moreover, no matter how the Zero Hour Plan was closely guarded, Rhodesian intelligence was undoubtedly not going to be caught off guard. There is ample evidence to prove that the Central Intelligence Organisation kept abreast of what was happening in the whole region. Once the implementation details were sniffed at, it was going to be difficult for ZPRA. A lot of factors, predominantly the efficiency of Rhodesian intelligence and armed forces in conventional warfare, as well as the challenges inherent in the guerrilla armies, provided ZPRA with a herculean task in squaring off with the RhAF. South Africa was not even prepared to see Rhodesia falling apart.

9

The Effects of Civilian Bombing on Guerrilla Strategy

Introduction

The history of warfare has demonstrated that battles are not only fought between combatants' armed forces, but that civilians play a critical role in determining the outcome of wars, whether regular or irregular.[1] During the Second Chimurenga campaign, the civilians were made to play a "direct" role in the prosecution of the conflict through the provision of food, sanctuary, clothes, information and recruits. Civilians who served in the war revealed that at most, the RhAF did not attack civilian targets. They were particularly vulnerable during clashes between the belligerents or when spotted delivering supplies to the guerrillas during the day or when sold out for supporting the guerrillas. Still, this does not rule out the fact that the RhAF initiated indiscriminate attacks against the civilians. The operations of the RhAF had a crippling effect on the morale of the civilians, who failed to understand the ability of *vanamukoma* (guerrillas, as they were known) subjugating the militarily superior Rhodesian forces. The RhAF launched unselective attacks on individuals and villages suspected of collaborating with the guerrillas. Guerrilla forces approached the civilians in order to get support in all its forms. Resultantly, the Second Chimurenga saw civilians taking an active role (voluntary and involuntary) in complementing the war effort.[2] The people resented the racist nature of the regime, and as a result they joined the war largely from a point of discontentment rather than an act of force. It was the involvement of the black population in the war that made the war more complicated for the RSF. The Rhodesian Special Branch had, through their excellent network of ground agents, kept abreast of "terrorism" in the early days of the war, but it was an entirely different matter once the conflict was taken into the population.[3] This, then, explains why civilians were targets of the Smith regime during the war.

Civilians' Reasons for Participating in the War

Prior to examining the challenges that were experienced by the civilian population as a result of the RhAF operations during the Second Chimurenga, it is important to elucidate the reasons which led the civilians to join the war and why they were obvious targets.

THE POLICY OF SEPARATE DEVELOPMENT IN THE EDUCATION SYSTEM

The white population hated coexistence with blacks in all economic, social, religious and political spheres of life. Education for the European, colored, Asian and African populations had completely different standards. European education had the best facilities, whereas blacks were mainly taught practical subjects that would prepare them for the European industry. Native education, according to the government, was based on the premise that character training was most vital to "the development of the African in his emergence from barbarism."[4] On paper, the goal of the education system was noble, as articulated by the Select Committee on Education, which enunciated that all education was supposed to be directed toward developing the greatest potential of any pupil in order to be able to compete to the best advantage in the employment and economic fields.[5] The amount of money spent by the government on European education was $12 million for 60,000 pupils or $200 per pupil in 1965. In contrast to this, the regime spent $14 million on African education for 650,000 pupils or $20 per pupil.[6] In 1969, approximately two percent of the gross national product was spent on African education, which was £6,600,000 and slightly less than what was spent on European education.[7] The inequalities in the education system led to heated debate among parliamentarians in Rhodesia. On September 1, 1970, the MP for Manica, called Gandanzara, recommended that the education of Rhodesians be governed on an equal basis so that it would generate equal opportunities for every person. Money was supposed to be voted for equally and shared equally for the education of the people so that they could prepare themselves to take their place in commerce and government.[8] Gandanzara believed that equality was needed through implementing a single syllabus for all children, one ministry without divisions in that particular ministry, and the provision for the same quality of education so that the children would be equally competent after completing their studies.[9] In view of the education offered to Africans, Advocate S.K. Sibanda, in 1974, told a meeting of teachers in Vashee Hall, Bulawayo, that the system of education was aimed at producing a mass labor force able to understand the orders of European supervisors in the industry.[10] This goal of the education system was further revealed in President William J. Harper's speech: "My Government will continue to pursue a vigorous educational policy designed to meet the demands of society and the economy. In 1978, for the first time, African students who have completed Grade 11 would be accepted for teacher education courses. With their background in practical subjects, they will follow a new three year course of concurrent training from which they emerge better qualified teachers of home economics, brickwork, metal work and woodwork for secondary schools."[11]

African education was designed in such a way that the interests of the Europeans were best served. Africans were required to remain subordinate, according to the Select Committee on Education, which revealed that the entire subject of African education was determined by the amount of money which government could make available without affecting development in other fields.[12] From 1962 onwards, 70 percent of all Africans aged 16 years or above were illiterate. They were unable to read and write a letter, read a newspaper with some comprehension, add up an economic account, read a weight scale, or use numbers to about 1,000.[13] The growth of the African population exceeded the available educational facilities. Every year the number of illiterates grew.[14] When the war began, there were a lot of illiterate and semiliterate Africans who saw it as an opportunity to end white arrogance.

Domestication of African People in the Protected Villages

Conditions in the Tribal Trust Lands were terrible, but the whites underestimated the grievances of the local population. Despite the deplorable conditions in the protected villages (PVs), President John Wrathall held that good progress was being made in the program of consolidating the people into PVs, thereby saving the lives of many Africans.[15] Wrathall was not being realistic, considering that in the previous year an Internal Affairs Committee responsible for PVs had complained that they were losing the people physically, psychologically and emotionally due to the conditions in the PVs.[16] The treatment given to Africans led Wing Commander Simmonds to confess that they were fighting a war on three fronts: the economic, the military and the psychological.[17]

The concept of PVs or "Keeps" was developed by the British in Malaya and Kenya, and much later by the Americans in Vietnam. The story of PVs in Rhodesia began when a section of ZANLA guerrillas led by Solomon Mujuru (*nom de guerre* Rex Nhongo) attacked Altena farm near Centenary in December

1972. The farm belonged to Marc De-Borchgrave, commonly known as "Maka." This was the first occasion on which rocket launchers had been used within Rhodesia. The attack resulted in injury to an eight-year-old child.[18] In February 1973, the Chiweshe Tribal Trust Land was chosen as a testing ground for a new government policy.[19] The situation in the PVs was characterized by poor sanitation. Certainly, Africans were generally reduced to primitive levels of existence. The "Keeps" were hastily implemented under the pretext of saving the lives of civilians from "terrorist brutality," but it is known that the program was an attempt to alienate guerrillas from civilian support (food, intelligence and recruits). However, the strategy backfired. According to the MP for Mabvazuwa, Nyandoro, the Africans were perturbed by the fact that they had developed their homes, planted trees and made permanent contour ridges as required by the regime.[20] The people were forcibly removed from their traditional, and in some instances substantial, homes with no compensation and no aid towards buying materials to erect new homes. No timely and adequate water supply was installed. There was a general lack of sustained development projects to better the living conditions of the people. The Rhodesian PVs were health hazards and the high concentration of population in them tended to exacerbate malnutrition and disease.[21] Consequently, the people in PVs devised several strategies to escape from these camps. Some would bolt from the camps, running away from them because life was not normal and there was no freedom of movement.[22] Crops belonging to civilians were destroyed to deny their use by the guerrillas. The removal of people was regarded as beneficial to the war effort because they gave relief and help to the guerrillas.[23]

Aircraft played an important role in carrying out surveillance operations on protected villages and bombing fields after PVs had been established. In addition, the whites introduced collective fines on civilians who sympathized with the guerrillas on the basis that some guerrillas were being harbored in small villages in circumstances where everyone present had knowledge about their presence, but this information was concealed from the RSF.[24] From the beginning, life in the PVs was a nightmare. The conditions motivated the civilians either to intensify their support for the guerrillas or even join the war. The whites still continued to give themselves a false sense of security by claiming that they had enormous civilian support: "Having failed to subdue the fighting qualities of our rural population, the terrorists are turning increasingly to harassing our urban population, and for the next months we must be ready for any eventuality."[25]

As a result of their racist policies, the Rhodesians were never able to win the campaign for the "hearts and minds," a prerequisite in any guerrilla campaign. With a population ratio of 1:10 in favor of blacks, the campaign was critical.[26]

Although the Malayan campaign provided the Rhodesian soldiers with the elementary principles of counterinsurgency such as tracking and ambush,[27] the "hearts and minds" campaign dismally failed because the locals were badly treated in the so-called protected villages. While this system had worked well during insurgency problems in Malaya, it seemed in Rhodesia to be more a form of collective punishment than of protection and tended to alienate the local population.[28]

Repressive Legislation

Quite a number of laws were put in place in order to suppress Africans. The Industrial Conciliation Act of 1934 instituted a formal color bar against African workers. The shutters were put in place to prevent African competition, and further legislation protected the privileged position of the white elite, like the Maize Control Acts.[29] Although the white regimes were oppressive, the positives cannot be ignored. The government of Godfrey Huggins built Harare and Mpilo hospitals in the early fifties.[30] Most of the infrastructure in Zimbabwe was built by the Rhodesians. Rhodesia declared a state of emergency from UDI days in 1965. The Emergency Powers (Maintenance of Law and Order) Regulation of 1966 ensured that the regime assumed additional powers to control the people. In late 1972, the Identification Bill was passed so that Africans would carry a valid registration document on their person. The representative for Lowveld known as Makaya underscored that the Identification Bill made the Africans furious and terrified because it was among the list of a chain of repressive legislation passed by the regime. Before it there was the Pass Law. Makaya described the bill as the most insulting and most stupid piece of legislation ever put through the house.[31] The state of emergency declared in the colony from 1965 implied that the movement of people was extremely difficult because they were always stopped. Those traveling by buses were made to get off. When found without passes, Africans were made to pay sums of money. Many Africans were taken by the police, underwent vicious interrogation, and endured torture. After a detention of about 30 days or so the police would discover that many civilians were innocent. As a result, most people came out of detention with bitterness.[32] The state of emergency required all Africans to carry a piece of paper called *situpa/chitupa*. Anyone who failed to produce it, in spite of producing all other documents, was in trouble.[33]

The cornerstone of security legislation in Rhodesia was the Law and Order Maintenance Act (LOMA). The law enabled the government to prohibit meetings, publications, and demonstrations at will. It laid down mandatory prison sentences for certain political offenses, including the common one of "intimidation." The minister was given extra-judicial powers to restrict people to a designated area for up to five years. Mandatory death penalties were imposed on persons who used gasoline bombs, and on those who possessed arms with the intent to endanger the maintenance of law and order in Rhodesia or any neighboring territory. Five years' imprisonment was the minimum, with the death sentence being the maximum for an act of terrorism or sabotage.[34] Although death penalties for firebomb and possession of arms offenses were abolished in 1968, the judge retained the option of the death sentence. Detention without trial was very common. The civilians suffered heavy penalties for refusing to report "terrorists" to the authorities.[35] Despite its notoriety as an undemocratic piece of legislation, the Law and Order Maintenance Act remained on Zimbabwe's statute books for 22 years after independence. The law was invoked from time to time to prosecute political activists, demonstrators, and the media. Its successor legislation, the Public Order and Security Act (POSA) of 2002, has been castigated as equally draconian. The act restricts freedom of expression, movement and assembly, and makes it a punishable offense for anyone to undermine or make "any abusive, indecent, obscene or false statement about or concerning the President or an acting President, whether in respect of his person or his office."[36]

As a result of repressive colonial legislation, many Africans were punished and killed. Chief Maduna of the Filabusi District was arrested on June 13, 1976, for suspected involvement in subversive activities, in terms of Emergency Powers (Maintenance of Law and Order) Regulations, 1976.[37] Elias Nyamadzawo was sentenced to 21 years in jail for assisting guerrillas with food and blankets at Highlands Estate in August 1977.[38] In 1978, Mr. Gaza, a businessman in the Buhera District from Viriri Township, was hospitalized after allegations of not reporting the presence of guerrillas. This followed 44 days of incarceration and beatings.[39] On January 28, 1978, in the Charter District in Gwazurembaka, the security forces flew helicopters to Chirwa area, where 11 children were killed; and their parents were given permission to collect their corpses from the scene within three days for burial.[40] Simon Mututeku, a grade seven student, was killed on April 22, 1977, in the area of sub–Chief Chendambuya in Makoni TTL. The boy was taken away from his home by four security forces for interrogation between 4 p.m. and 5 p.m. but was brought back dead, and the report was that he had been killed for breaking a curfew.[41] On February 17, 1978, Leah Chipise from Umtali in the Zimunya TTL was shot by soldiers in a helicopter while working in a garden, but did not die. Her husband and a young lady called Eddie were also shot but were not seriously injured. The cause of the attacks was that they were all breaking curfew laws.[42] Curfew laws were so tough that they resulted in the death of many Africans.

Added to repressive legislation, the government was determined to uphold minority privileges as highlighted by the president's address to the Senate and the House of Assembly in 1977: "My government is continuing its efforts to achieve a constitutional settlement for Rhodesia which will not only bring peace to our land, but will safeguard the interests of minority groups and guarantee the rights and liberties of individuals."[43] Africans wanted privileges to vote, a right completely denied by the regime. The sentiments were publicly raised by the Africans when they said: "They think that the vote is a privilege for the white people only, they do not want to compromise with Africans on this issue which is vital if there is to be harmony in this country."[44] Racial segregation was rife, as evidenced in Section 86 of the Constitution, which stipulated that an African could not vote in an election for or be elected or appointed as a member of a local authority in a European area, and likewise that a European could not vote in an African area.[45] In 1961, the National Democratic Party (NDP) publicity chief, Robert Mugabe, addressed about 2,000 people at the Monomotapa Welfare Hall. He said that it was not a matter of being ruled well, but the Africans wanted to govern themselves. He also said that the laws in the country were not for ordinary criminals but were made to trap the NDP. It was therefore important for the NDP to eradicate the country's "one European vote" and replace it with "one man one vote."[46]

Land Seizures

The peasants took up arms because they were frustrated with the violent land seizures done by the whites since occupation in 1890. Various policies were enacted, much to the detriment of African agriculture. The cornerstone of Rhodesian segregation was the Land Apportionment Act of 1930.[47] The Land Tenure Act awarded half the land to the white minority, who constituted just five percent of the population.[48] Land segregation was initiated to protect white interests. Due to the overcrowding conditions in African areas, soil conservation methods became problematic. Forty-two thousand acres of land were reserved for 2,400,000 Africans, whereas 48,000 acres were reserved for 234,000 Europeans. The unfair land distribution pattern was justified for the following reasons[49]:

- contributions to the national income
- private capital established at upwards of £250,000,000 invested in European farms on water supplies, fences, conservation works and other capital expenditure
- the 1959 total gross output of £52,400,000 from European agriculture

in Southern Rhodesia compared with £14,700,000 from African farms. Tobacco alone provided £27,700,000 of vital exports
- European agriculture provision of 230,000 Africans with employment (40 percent of the total African labour force).[50]

It is therefore apparent that the whites believed that land deserved to remain in their hands because of the conviction that the Europeans were better farmers who were contributing to economic growth, had heavily invested in the land, and moreover provided employment to the African, who was "regrettably ungrateful." Overcrowding in the reserves inevitably led to land degradation. As early as 1948, the Africans were blamed for the deteriorating food production in the country on the basis that they were working the land merely to get sufficient food for themselves and their families without considering the country's need for increased food production.[51] African agriculture was neglected, yet various schemes were designed for European farmers. It is hence unsurprising that the land issue was at the heart of the African population from the day the whites set their foot on the territory between Zambezi and Limpopo.

The Europeans were primarily successful in exploiting African labor and devising strategies to empower European farmers. Still, Africans expressed their displeasure by deserting white farms. The environmental degradation in African areas reflected the pressure that existed on reserves allocated to them. The aerial photographs of various Tribal Trust Lands taken in 1963 exposed the pressure that existed in the reserves occupied by the Africans.[52] The Europeans still maintained that Africans had enough land: "We feel that there is sufficient now for the Africans to have and the Europeans are entitled because we have been giving, giving, giving all the time, there has been no response from the African, they have been taking, taking, taking. We have now decided you can get no more, that you have sufficient."[53] The Second Chimurenga was therefore inevitable in light of the attitude of the white population to the plight of black people. The policy of separate development meant the Africans were completely disenfranchised in everything that mattered to their survival. Prime land and the best education and health facilities belonged to the whites. Repressive legislation and humiliation added to the list of African grievances.

The Challenges Suffered by Civilians as a Result of the RhAF Activities

The civilians suffered during the Second Chimurenga as a result of the brutalities executed by the Rhodesian Security Forces and guerrilla armies.

The intensification of the war in 1977, with a growing tendency by both RSF and guerrilla armies to engage in unselective shooting, led to an increase in civilian casualties.[54] The Rhodesians found out that various regions of the country were now inoperable as a result of the assistance given to the guerrillas by the civilians. Consequently, the civilians who were suspected of aiding the guerrillas suffered various forms of torture and bombardments from the RSF. On April 19, 1974, an armed aircraft killed two children herding cattle in the northeast border area.[55] Likewise, Headman Velati's area under Chief Maduna had five kraals burned by members of the security forces on June 20, 1977, during the day because it was alleged that the inhabitants of that area had fed the "terrorists."[56] Hence, the civilians experienced a difficult time during the war. On one hand, they were supposed to feed the guerrillas, and on the other they were required to report the same guerrillas to the security forces. This wartime reality was not accepted by the ZANU PF–led government, which gave all the credit to men and women who were at the front. In fact, when the civilians said they no longer wanted to support the ZANU PF, the term "sellout" was invoked.

The civilians were targeted because they provided succor to the guerrillas. A Rhodesian parliamentarian for Mtoko admitted these challenges when he confessed: "I understand the difficulties that our security forces have in fighting an enemy that is not in uniform and hides behind the skirts of people in the country, and it is difficult for him to be located."[57] The civilians were expected by both sides to fully cooperate in the execution of the war. Any failure to do so resulted in reprisals. As told by the African MP for Mabvazuwa, Elijah Nyandoro, there was a European who was abducted by guerrillas and led through Chitora School in the African area in 1976. When the security forces came for investigations, some teachers and children were taken and badly treated and finally detained.[58] Consequently, the school was bombed because the children and the teachers were not able to give the direction where the white man went. More than 500 children were left stranded and more than 30 teachers were jobless after the demolition of the school.[59] In a similar incident, on January 30, 1979, a group of white soldiers raided the auxiliary forces (Pfumo reVanhu or Spear of the People) at Holy Cross School base in the Manyene TTL, killing seven auxiliaries and civilians, including one woman and two schoolchildren.[60] The attack left the school badly damaged. Samuel Noti Moyo of Tigere Kraal under Chief Chizungu in the Belingwe TTL was shot dead by the security forces on August 14, 1978, because he was suspected of collaborating with the guerrillas.[61]

In the Ndanga TTL, Dabwa Village in Fort Victoria (Masvingo), the people were gathered for a traditional ceremony when soldiers arrived and embarked on an indiscriminate shooting and bombing, claiming that the meeting had been organized by "terrorists." The operation led to the instant death of 35 men, women and children.[62] According to ZAPU leader Joshua Nkomo, details about the Dabwa villages indicated that the attack was led by a military aircraft that dropped a "few" bombs on the crowd.[63] Similarly, in Nyajena TTL, Chauya village was burnt by RSF on the basis that the villagers had harbored and assisted freedom fighters. In the process, about 20 people were killed.[64] On April 19, 1974, at about 10 o'clock in the morning at kraal head Kadona's village near Chawanda Township, seven African children who were herding cattle were bombed by a fighter plane. Two died on the spot and the other one died a few days later at Bindura hospital. Others were hospitalized at Mount Darwin and Karanda Hospitals with injuries to their arms and legs.[65]

Civilians were also vulnerable to the RhAF if spotted carrying food and other supplies to the guerrillas. It happened that people carried food to the guerrilla bases during the day. Once these people were located, the planes would be called by Smith's agents in the reserves. Many civilians were killed for assisting the guerrillas. It was mandatory for the civilians to supply food to the guerrillas and it was the peasants, especially girls, who always remained vulnerable under such circumstances. In Zaka District, at a place called Zibwowa, the *chimbwidos* (female aides) narrowly survived when a guerrilla base they were at was bombed by the RhAF.[66] The *chimbwidos* served a multi-purpose role. They performed laundry duties as well as engaging in sex with the guerrillas. In many incidences, the guerrillas, *mujibhas* and *chimbwidos* were killed during raids.[67] The guerrillas were, however, experts who had the skills to escape the RhAF, but normally at the expense of the *mujibhas*, *chimbwidos* and the civilians. When the RhAF bombed a base in the Chidziva-Makoho area (Chipinge South) at a *pungwe* organized by the guerrillas in 1977, a sizeable number of *mujibhas* were killed. Boy Chipadza was one of the victims. *Pungwes* were more dangerous to the untrained people because comrades knew how to escape and a few of them were affected, whilst most of the *mujibhas* who were not skilled in escaping danger lost their lives. Some were permanently crippled.[68] The RSF usually took out their anger on the civilians after failing to kill the guerrillas. The soldiers who dropped in at Ngwana Ranch during the bombing of Rupuwu Base in 1977 avenged the death of two soldiers on civilians on the premise that they had harbored the guerrillas. The soldiers intimidated and assaulted the civilians who resided in the area: "After the bombing the civilians in the area had no rest. The soldiers were now coming regularly torturing the local civilians by beating them up and four civilians were killed by gun fire. The victims were sons of Headman Rupuwu."[69]

Air power posed a psychological threat to the civilians during the Second

Chimurenga. Prior to the war it was uncommon to see planes flying in TTLs. The air force was used as a psychological weapon to deter the Africans from opposing the government. It was also a good example to demonstrate the consequences awaiting anyone who dared oppose the regime. The bodies of Sinoia victims (1966) were suspended in cargo nets from an Alouette and flown around as a warning for the Africans to heed.[70] The air force was not exclusively or even primarily used for operations against guerrilla units, but also as a crucial element in the regime's terror tactics of blanket bombing African villages, refugee camps and other civilian and economic targets in neighboring countries.[71] Besides serving a purpose in tactical maneuvers, the RhAF was a weapon of terror. All the same, the people did not take long to learn to live with this terrifying weapon. It therefore became common that the presence of a plane in the TTLs was associated with a specific target, especially the guerrillas. Over and above, the RhAF was supposed to be economical in fighting a war that did not seem to have an end. On the impact of the presence of airplanes in the TTLs, the civilians revealed that the airplanes were dreadful. People truthfully became unsettled.[72] The dropping of paratroopers was somehow mysterious: "We just heard that aeroplanes dropped people from the sky. People were surprised, saying: 'These children [guerrillas] are playing, they will not win.'"[73] The civilians were bewildered by the sight of airplanes, which for the bulk of them was the first time witnessing these flying machines in action.

As highlighted above, civilians suffered during clashes between the guerrillas and RSF. During the "Battle of Nyagombe" in the 1970s, the RhAF attacked the guerrillas who were camping in a mountain called Nyagombe in Zaka district. No guerrilla was killed, but a boy herding cattle was killed after being "mistaken" for a popular guerrilla called Musa. Jamukoko's cattle were also shot during the same incident for allegedly protecting the guerrillas.[74] Guerrillas, as trained people, were able to escape the RhAF raids. At the same time the peasants were left vulnerable. Jamukoko lost most of his possessions and suffered economically and psychologically just like the other peasants who throughout the war suffered from the brutalities of the Smith regime. Similarly, in May 1978, John Zoushe, in the Matswero kraal, Marimba area under Chief Makumbi, was killed together with 12 of his cattle.[75]

Bombing and rocket attacks against the civilian population became more frequent and indiscriminate from 1976.[76] The African villages that suffered from bombings were primarily the ones suspected of assisting guerrillas. According to Mabika, the MP for Highveld, on May 15, 1978, at about 12:30 p.m. in the Buhera TTL at Kandenga School, the security forces flew about four helicopters plus one spotter plane to the school, where schoolchildren and their teachers were conducting educational activities.[77] The security forces from one helicopter started firing at defenseless schoolchildren and teachers, resulting in the death of a deputy headmaster, aged 50, a child of four years, and Jane, a girl of 11 years, while schoolboys James and Isaiah Kaseti were hospitalized.[78] The crime was that they had failed to report the presence of "terrorists" on June 11 at about 8 p.m.[79] The RSF enjoyed air superiority because the guerrillas were poorly equipped. At the Battle of Manica Bridge in 1978, air power was employed by the RSF but the guerrillas did not shoot any because they were flying at a high altitude. The planes were successful in harassing people.[80] Overall, the civilians were terrorized by the RhAF and other RSF in the belief that they would cease to support the guerrillas, but this came at a huge casualty roaster on the part of the civilians. While these air strikes had devastating effects, the civilians did not entirely cease their support for guerrilla activities.

Conclusion

The Second Chimurenga reflects the true nature of war, in which violence is not only limited to the combatants. The civilians were made to taste the bullets. The war reflects the reality of the old adage which says: "When the bulls fight, it is the grass that suffers most." This chapter makes it clear that a lot of resentments made it possible for the civilians to join the war. It also provides an appreciation of the reasons why the peasants were air force targets. It is significant to note that the attack on civilian centers of population was part of the regime's psychological operations to intimidate the peasants against supporting the liberation war. The civilians who were suspected of supporting the guerrillas endured numerous forms of torture and suffered bombardments from the RhAF throughout the course of the war. Evidence reveals that African schools, villages and livestock were bombed. This was deliberately done after the realization that the civilians supported the guerrillas in different forms even when stopped from doing so. This, however, did not deter the civilians from supporting the war. Nevertheless, the guerrillas were neither polite nor friendly to the civilians.

10

The Significance of Air Power in Guerrilla Warfare: An Analysis

Introduction

In light of the operations of the Rhodesian Air Force in Zimbabwe's war of liberation and other guerrilla wars where air power was used, this chapter examines the efficacy of air power in irregular warfare. The adaptability of guerrilla warfare has proved that "poorly" equipped armies have the potential to upset technologically superior forces. Humanity has ever been innovative in order to evade domination, torture, harassment, poverty and even extermination. It is verifiable that air power, when synergized with land and maritime forces, is the offensive weapon par excellence in conventional warfare. Its use in guerrilla warfare, however, demands deeper scrutiny than it has yet received. Using examples drawn from different countries where air power was used in guerrilla warfare, this study argues that well-sustained guerrilla bands have the potential to frustrate reasonably equipped conventional armies. According to the late U.S. President John F. Kennedy, guerrilla warfare represents a type of war that is new in its intensity, ancient in origins and seeking victory by eroding and exhausting the enemy instead of engaging him.[1] Guerrillas mainly depend on hit-and-run tactics; thus, full confrontation with enemy forces is avoided. Although guerrilla strategy has come of age, the role of air power in modern warfare, both guerrilla and conventional, is indisputable. The mere sight of an enemy airplane flying overhead is unpleasant. Besides, it is "disgusting" to be enveloped from the air. The effects run from psychological intimidation to the infliction of casualties. The superior mobility offered by airplanes is an important tactical advantage in combat situations. The tactical ability of air power gives it an edge over other fighting instruments. Airplanes' reaction rate is also superior compared to ground forces. In July 2015, Turkish planes demonstrated what aircraft could do in situations considered critical to the security of the nation. A few days after a terror attack on the Turkish town of Suruc killed 32 people, Ankara launched air strikes against a Kurdish guerrilla group, the Kurdistan Workers Party (PKK), in northern Iraq, as well as Islamic State of Iraq and the Levant (ISIL) positions in Syria.[2] This was followed by another heavy air strike on PKK targets including shelters, depots and caves.[3] The coming in of drones has revolutionized air warfare. For over a decade, America's drone campaign was driven by short-term objectives: the degradation of al-Qaeda and militant groups like the Taliban through the use of targeted killings on a tactical scale.[4] Up to May 2015, there were 515 U.S. drone strikes in Pakistan, Yemen and Somalia since 2002, killing at least 2,887 people.[5] However, as observed by scholars, "Air power is a powerful tool, but technology is no panacea in the small-war arena."[6] The nature of guerrilla warfare sends shivers down the spines of regular armies. Moreover, irregular warfare has tremendously benefited from the ever-dynamic world of technology.

What Is Guerrilla Warfare?

In practice, guerrilla warfare has a very long history. It can be traced back to thousands of years ago. It was, however, synthesized into a coherent and logical concept by strategists such as Sun Tzu, Genghis Khan, Mao Tse-tung, and Che Guevara. The term "guerrilla" was originally applied to describe military operations carried out by men opposed to regular methods of conducting war. Typical guerrilla operations include harassing the enemy, fighting in small groups, evasion of decisive battles, sabotage tactics such as cutting lines of communication, surprise attacks, and gaining civilian support. The tactics are not homogeneous but vary from country to country depending on the terrain and strength of enemy forces. Nonetheless, as noted by Mao Zedong, the cardinal principle of guerrilla warfare is that the guerrilla must move amongst the people as a fish swims in the sea.

Irregular/guerrilla warfare is defined as the use of violence by sub-state actors or groups within states for political purposes of achieving power, control and legitimacy, using unorthodox or conventional approaches to warfare due to fundamental weakness in resources or capabilities.[7] Groups conducting irregular warfare are basically attempting to defeat or overcome adversaries that possess significantly more powerful and numerous resources. In order to have a reasonable chance of success in any type of irregular warfare, groups must keep their activities as hidden from their adversary for as long as possible, so as not to be detected, tracked or destroyed.[8] It is thus apparent that guerrilla warfare is the conflict of the weak against the strong. Small, lightly armed units of irregular troops conduct swift operations against an enemy mainly defending fixed positions, avoiding open conflict. In the more distant past such tactics were significant in eventually securing territory that could be used as a base for more conventional action. Since the second half of the 20th century, guerrilla tactics have become much more closely associated with progressing a program of political action, and have been designed not necessarily to result in outright military victory but to wear down those in power so as eventually to secure the political aims of the liberation movement. The prolonged nature of the conflict becomes an essential factor and at the same time it becomes much less of a purely military struggle.[9] The strategic defensive is only necessary when there is equipment worth dying for; otherwise, guerrillas depend on hit-and-run tactics. The essence of success in guerrilla warfare, as defined by Captain Callwell, is surprise followed by retreat before the opponent can recover. Operations are necessarily on a small scale because surprise is difficult to achieve with large forces.[10] Guerrilla warfare in its modern form was first waged not by the armies of the French Revolution but against them, in the Vendee, and later on against Napoleon, in Spain, Tyrol and Russia. It was a system of warfare chosen instinctively, without the benefit of any preconceived doctrine. The guerrilla detachments in the Vendee, in Spain and in Tyrol were no longer operating in the framework of a regular army and subject to its command, but most of the time acted altogether independently. Their war was insurrectionist and chaotic, revolutionary and subversive, not in its aims but in its implications for the future, and it was therefore highly suspected by the European monarchies. The Russian partisan units were dissolved the moment the French invaders had been defeated. The Vendee and Spain, Tyrol and partisan activities in Russia remained isolated episodes and the doctrine of conventional war continued to prevail. The emphasis remained on big armies and battles; fighting between small detachments was regarded as the exception.[11] Guerrilla war became an integral part of national wars, mainly against colonial powers or other foreign occupants on the part of nations (or tribes) which had no regular armies.[12]

The ultimate objective of the guerrilla force is to inflict maximum damage on the enemy while avoiding the same. Analysts and scholars of guerrilla warfare generally agree that in order to survive, the weak guerrilla force must avoid decisive engagements in which it may be destroyed by a stronger force. For prolonged harassment, the tactic found most appealing by guerrilla theorists is the hit-and-run.[13] The guerrillas avoid destruction by shunning the tactical defensive; they abandon their position rather than defend it where there is no need. The most effective means for guerrillas to avoid the destructive strength of the adversary is to operate from a sanctuary, where guerrilla forces would be beyond the reach of the superior foe.[14] ZPRA's tactical defensive during the attack of Mulungushi camp northeast of Lusaka in 1979 for two days proved the ineffectiveness of air power when attacking well-organized guerrilla bands. The Rhodesian Air Force had in their possession 12 Canberra and 18 Hunter sorties. ZPRA forces remained dug in throughout the attack, sustaining only seven deaths with 30 to 40 wounded, despite the resources worth thousands of dollars used in the operation. This was the second attack on Mulungushi. It was first bombed on December 22, 1978, and only 35 died. At the time it contained 270 conventionally trained soldiers.[15] According to Chairman Mao, guerrilla strategy must be based primarily on vigilance, mobility, and attack. It must also be suited to the enemy situation, terrain, the existing lines of communication, weather and the situation of the people.[16] Asymmetric warfare survives on the exploitation of low-technology principles, whereas technologically advanced forces base their strategy on technological superiority.[17]

Guerrilla warfare is influenced by factors such as geographical conditions, social and political processes and technological innovation.[18] Guerrilla warfare distinctly differs from conventional warfare in that it operates in "bands" rather than in armies. Its philosophy stipulates that "bands" avoid direct confrontation with the government forces. The use of small, armed bands of irregulars is meant to create terror and anarchy throughout the general population and also avoid massacres on their part.[19] The Communist guerrillas in Greece lost because they refused to work in strict guerrilla bands and lacked the backing of the population. Added to that, they lacked privileged sanctuary into which to retreat.[20] Civilian support remains a key ingredient of guerrilla warfare. The masses provide essentials such as food, shelter, clothes and information, among others. Once alienated from popular support, guerrilla operations will be difficult if not impossible to execute. Sabotage is a crucial tactic of guerrilla warfare. According to the *African Communist* (the official organ of the South African Communist Party), Spear of the Nation/*Umkonto We Sizwe* organized a series of planned attacks with explosives against government buildings. In Algeria, the rebels made effective use of neighboring nations as sanctuaries. Algerians operated from Morocco, Tunisia and Egypt.[21]

The center of gravity, as espoused by Carl von Clausewitz, is that element that gives the enemy the strength and will to fight. Put differently, the U.S. Army sees the enemy's center of gravity as his "source of strength." Once destroyed, the enemy finds it difficult to sustain the campaign. The center of gravity for counterinsurgency operations centers on the "hearts and minds" campaign. Without popular support, the insurgents become isolated and unable to achieve their political goals. The insurgency war is widely acknowledged to be a "hearts and minds'" campaign. The concept was articulated by Lieutenant

General Sir Gerald Templar when conducting the successful Malayan counterinsurgency: "The shooting side of the business is only twenty-five percent of the trouble. The other seventy-five percent is getting the people of this country behind us."[22] The Malayan protected villages program, for example, formed the cornerstone of the British government's "hearts and minds" campaign to wean popular support from the communist guerrillas. The success of the program was hinged on the premise that only when the people felt secure and protected from the guerrillas would they cooperate fully with the government. In addition, the British recognized that the program had to be aggressively and effectively "sold" to persons who were being forced to leave their traditional homes and resettle in new government-built villages. To achieve this, the government embraced a two-pronged approach involving actual physical measures to improve the relocated villagers' standard of living by providing electricity, indoor plumbing, and other essentials, alongside a sophisticated psychological warfare campaign directed by an information department that the government created specifically for this purpose.[23] It thus becomes simple to understand why guerrilla wars in Africa and other terrains were successful. Civilian support was simply overwhelming, although the guerrillas were ruthless to the hands that fed them.

For a long time, Britain's center of gravity was her navy. She was the sea mistress for many decades if not centuries. Britain confirmed her mastery of the sea at the Battle of Trafalgar on October 21, 1805. Admiral Nelson obliterated the combined French and Spanish fleets.[24] The victory was so complete that the British public demanded the same at the Battle of Jutland in 1916. Instead, Jellicoe of Scapa managed to score "only" a strategic victory against the German High Seas Fleet (Hochseeflotte). The result at Jutland forced the High Seas Fleet never again to engage in direct naval engagement with the British Grand Fleet. Instead, the Germans resorted to unrestricted submarine warfare, which then gave the Americans an excuse to join the war in 1917.

On the other hand, Napoleon Bonaparte's center of gravity was his army. Napoleon's victories depended on the concentration of the army. On October 15, 1805, he imposed a crushing defeat on the Austrians at Ulm, from where proceeded to occupy Vienna. In an attempt to cut Napoleon off from Vienna, the Russian army was led into an ambush at Austerlitz on December 2, 1805. The battle resulted in 9,000 French soldiers dying out of an army of 73,000; as against 27,000 Russians and Austrians in an army of 87,000. The victories made Napoleon the king of Europe, effectively ending the 1,000 years of the Holy Roman Empire for the German people.[25] When it became clear that Napoleon's army was invincible, the Spanish guerrillas in 1811 ravaged the French lines of communication, overwhelmed isolated detachments, and seized convoys with arms and supplies. In June 1812, the Grand Army, with a troop strength of 611,000 men, prepared to invaded Russia. There were only 300,000 Frenchmen in this army. Every satellite state and ally was also represented. Realizing that Napoleon's center of gravity was his army, the Russians avoided contact and began to fall back across the endless plains without offering resistance. Eager to exchange bullets with the enemy, Napoleon entered ever more deeply into an area in which the Russians had burnt all the food supplies. Thousands of soldiers fell by the wayside due to heat, exhaustion and hunger, and many were killed by the local population. Napoleon then decided to march on Moscow. In an attempt to halt Napoleon's advance on Moscow, Field Marshal Kutuzov waited for him at Borodino, a battle which cost Napoleon 30,000 men, while Kutuzov lost nearly 50,000. When Napoleon entered Moscow, the city was deserted, and reduced to three-quarters ruins by fire. When Tsar Alexander rejected the offer of a truce, Napoleon retreated in mid–October with only 100,000 men left. Setbacks including heavy snowfalls, temperatures of 30 degrees below freezing, typhus and pneumonia, and the merciless attacks of the Russians, devastated the French army. Under those circumstances, only a force of about 20,000 to 30,000 survived.[26] It did not take long before Napoleon surrendered at the Battle of Waterloo in 1815. His soldiers were war-weary and the people back home were also tired of war. It is therefore important in warfare to know the enemy's center of gravity in order to have realistic chances of winning a war. Guerrilla tactics played an indispensable role in subjugating Napoleon's army. In Zimbabwe, the guerrillas realized that their center of gravity was the civilian population. This then explains why the civilians were subjected to constant harassment and bombardment.

The Communist notion of guerrilla warfare believed in basing operations in the countryside. This was meant to provide the guerrillas with a safe haven. Privileged sanctuary is a prerequisite for a successful guerrilla campaign. The campaign must also be conducted on an international basis in order to gain support. The Cuban experience demonstrated for Communists three important principles about revolutionary guerrilla warfare: "They are: popular forces can win a war against the army, it is not necessary to wait until all conditions for making revolution exist; the insurrection can create them, in underdeveloped America the countryside is the basic area for armed fighting."[27] One aspect that makes guerrilla warfare a unique military strategy is its ability to adapt to any terrain. A suitable example is that of a British operative called Thomas Edward Lawrence (Lawrence of Arabia), who extensively used armored cars to assist in his ambushes on Turkish trains during the First World War.[28] Lawrence played a huge part in leading an Arab revolt against Turkey, an ally of Germany. He was an outstanding tactician and a highly influential theoretician of guerrilla warfare. His small but effective irregular forces attacked Turkish communications and supply routes, tying down thousands of Turkish troops and preventing them from fighting against regular Allied forces under the command of British General Edward Allenby.[29] Irregular warfare over the years has managed to defy the odds by challenging and subjugating enemies with superior air power. The major strength lies in simple maneuvering guerrilla tactics: "Traditionally, weak forces on the ground have been able to survive and overcome stronger adversaries because they have found relatively simple means by which to fulfil the essential elements of guerrilla warfare. Likewise, a weak force in the air power environment must seek correspondingly simple measures to achieve the essential elements of superior intelligence, security, mobility advantage, surprise, and sustainment in the face of a superior foe."[30]

Lessons from Military History

Regular armies have since ancient times studied guerrilla warfare, but the results have revealed the hurdles of dealing with this kind of warfare. Conventional forces worldwide are failing to come to terms with guerrilla bands that have immensely benefited from the robust technological innovations. As previously alluded, air power is an effective weapon of warfare considering the important role it played in the Second World War. Adolf Hitler's blitzkrieg machinery, supported by the Luftwaffe, blitzed across Europe in the name of creating Lebensraum for the so-called Aryan race. Contemporary wars like the Gulf War (1990–91) and the Libyan conflict (2011–) are crucial in exemplifying how air power can annihilate a seemingly strong opponent within a short duration. Although airplanes have impressively performed in conventional warfare, the opposite is true in guerrilla warfare, where technologically advanced forces have struggled to assert their dominance. The major strength of guerrilla fighters lies in the flexibility of their operations and the ability to melt into their surroundings. Air-power theories of strategic bombing and the shattering of civilian morale have not yielded the desired results, particularly due to the nature of guerrilla warfare, which disobeys these well-developed theories.

Guerrilla strategy had a bearing on the conduct of most, if not all, revolutionary wars in Africa. The Cold War contest played an influential role in determining the source of aid for the liberation movements. The era of the Cold War saw the United States Department of Defence (DoD) and the Soviet Union sponsoring proxy wars in order to gain influence, especially in sub–Saharan Africa. The Central Intelligence Agency (CIA) masterminded concealed operations aimed at undermining pro–Soviet regimes in Africa.[31] The

Zimbabwe African National Liberation Army was mentored by the Chinese Communist Party (CCP), whereas the Zimbabwe People's Revolutionary Army was under the tutelage of the Soviet Union. The Ian Smith regime was sponsored by the West, despite the sanctions imposed when the country unilaterally declared independence from the British government in 1965. As a result of Chinese orientation, ZANU waged the Maoist strategy in the countryside. The then Chairman of ZANU, Herbert Chitepo, revealed in 1972 that his party believed that open confrontation in outlying areas should be abandoned in favor of other tactics: "It is useless to engage in conventional warfare with well-equipped Rhodesian and South African troops along the Zambezi."[32] China first became a major player in the African continent in the 1960s and 1970s when African countries were fighting for their independence. As a result of the Sino-Soviet split from 1960 to 1989, China supported militarily and ideologically those national liberation movements in the continent which opposed Soviet aid. These included the National Union for the Total Independence of Angola (UNITA) and ZANU in Zimbabwe.[33] China herself had employed the people's war to depose imperialistic Japan. The Chinese civil war resulted in the defeat of Chiang Kai-shek in 1949. The result was a triumph of the Chinese Revolution and the birth of the People's Republic of China (PRC), which had popular support during the revolution. Still in the 21st century, China's People's Liberation Army (PLA) refers to their strongest doctrinal traditions when confronting an opponent that is superior in arms and technology.[34] It must, however, be noted that China is now one of the world's powers, with superior military technology.

Afghanistan

Lessons from the Afghanistan War (1979–1989) awakened strategists and policy makers to the fact that irregular warfare has enormous potential to give serious strategic puzzles to a large conventional force.[35] The operations of the insurgents in Afghanistan against the Soviet Union were swift and targeted strategic centers such as road convoys and military posts. The guerrillas usually dispersed before Soviet and Afghan forces could strike back.[36] Population support was also immense. The Mujahedeen guerrillas had also the advantages of familiarity with the terrain, tactical mobility, ability to achieve surprise, ability to operate at night, rugged and highly motivated fighters, and sanctuaries in Pakistan and Iran.[37]

The September 9/11 attacks that happened in 2001 prompted the U.S. and allies to invade Afghanistan and Iraq in 2003 in order to "cleanse" the countries of terrorists believed to be multiplying in their thousands. On March 19, 2003, a U.S.-led coalition invaded Iraq under the pretext that Saddam Hussein possessed weapons of mass destruction (WMDs) and had connections to the terrorist group al-Qaeda.[38] In the case of Afghanistan, the official mission was to curb the country from once again becoming a haven for terrorists, to help provide security, and to contribute to a better future for the Afghan people.[39] From 2003, the U.S.–NATO led forces faced some serious strategic challenges as a result of the sophistication of the Taliban guerrilla tactics in Afghanistan. The Taliban insurgents, through the use of guerrilla tactics, resisted the American war machine incorporating drones. The Taliban guerrillas employed several stratagems such as deception. They pretended to join the security forces and then attacked from within. The North Atlantic Treaty Organization (NATO) and International Security Assistance Force (ISAF) admitted that their experiences in Afghanistan revealed that guerrilla warfare has survived the test of time and military technology has enhanced the activities of irregular armies the world over. In view of the exploits achieved by the Taliban, it is clear that the Americans have no solution to guerrilla warfare wherever they go.

Vietnam

The Vietnam War (1954–1975) provides useful insights into the challenges of an air power fighting guerrilla warfare. France's ninety-year-old rule in Indochina ended after their comprehensive defeat in 1954 after a 55-day siege at Dien Bien Phu. At the Geneva Accords held after the famous victory, peace was lost because the country was divided at the 17th parallel into Communist north and U.S.-backed south.[40] At the Battle of Dien Bien Phu, Giap's guerrillas were well concealed by dense foliage. This aspect demonstrates the importance of terrain in sustaining guerrilla operations. During the Second Chimurenga, the Rhodesian Security Forces explicitly complained about the tactical hitches that were brought by the rainy season because the guerrillas had more cover and water. The entire Vietminh force at Dien Bien Phu of 40,000 guerrillas were invisible to both the ground force and French reconnaissance aircraft.[41] Prior to the battle, the French had concentrated twelve battalions, six fighter bombers and ten light tanks flown in by aircraft. Six more paratroop battalions were flown in during the course of the battle.[42] This is exactly the importance of air power at the tactical level. Guerrillas also cover up for their military inferiority by relying on numerical superiority. The French soldiers were less than half the size of the besieging army although the casualties were high on the side of Vietminh. The operations of aircraft were hampered by morning fogs and afternoon rains. According to Prussian philosopher Carl von Clausewitz, such unforeseen circumstances in war are known as friction. Vietminh guns put the airstrip out of operation while porters brought in enough ammunition to sustain the operation.[43]

The defeat of the French exposed Vietnam to the Cold War confrontation between the United States and the Soviet Union. The United States government was clearly against a takeover by Communist North Vietnam.[44] The Americans took part in the struggle in Vietnam because they viewed it as part of a new global conflict against Communism. At the same time, the Vietnamese saw the war against the U.S. as the latest phase of a long war for independence.[45] The Vietnam War (1965–1973), code named Operation Rolling Thunder, is important because it demonstrates the dynamics of guerrilla strategy where irregular warfare transforms itself into highly mobile warfare through the acquisition of modern technology. The Soviets provided MiG fighters, antiaircraft guns and surface-to-air missiles (SAM) to the north. By the end of 1967, North Vietnam had gunned down over 700 U.S. aircraft. On the other hand, sporadic ground fire drove enemy planes off course, making the bombing less accurate.[46] The North Vietnamese intercept controllers were able to direct their MiG fighters against the U.S. aircraft.[47] Despite these heroics, the war also sheds light into the destruction that was precipitated by the U.S. air bombardments. The north suffered as a result of saturation or carpet bombing carried out by the U.S. and South Vietnamese aircraft. Through the use of the doctrine of strategic bombing, roads, port facilities and industry were crippled.[48]

The U.S., a world-class military power, failed to come to terms with the partisans in Vietnam. The United States dropped eight million tons of bombs in Vietnam, which was twice the amount dropped in World War II by all the belligerent nations combined. The ingredients of guerrilla warfare enabled the Vietnamese guerrillas to frustrate the U.S. efforts in Vietnam. Military technology added an extra dimension to their already fruitful tactics. The North Vietnamese air defenses included 1,400 AAA guns, 22 acquisition radars, and 4 fire control radars in 1964. Early 1965 saw an increase from 22 to 31 radars, 9 fire control radars, and 30 MiG-15 and MiG-17 fighters. In addition, by mid–1965 North Vietnam had acquired an SA-2 surface-to-air missile.[49] Although air power is very efficient, modern air vehicles are vulnerable to enemy air defenses. As air power technology has advanced, so has the technology of air defenses, particularly surface-to-air missiles. According to General Vo Nguyen Giap, the then military commander of North Vietnam, guerrilla warfare wears out the enemy by causing many difficulties and losses. Giap stated that guerrilla warfare was not meant to be static, but should gravitate towards mobile warfare.[50] Vietnam is a superb example in history where the massive use of air power failed to bring Viet Cong down to its knees and ultimately could not stop the retreat of U.S. forces from this theatre.[51] The involvement of the Soviet Union saw the U.S. leaving Vietnam with its tail firmly tucked between its legs. The war in the then Yugoslavia also exemplifies the limitations of air power in guerrilla warfare. Yugoslavian guerrillas or the partisans resisting Axis invasions got air support from the Allied forces. Tito's partisans sometimes enjoyed allied air support during major offensive operations.[52]

Syria

The Syrian conflict, which began in March 2011 between the Bashar al-Assad government and the opposition groups, shed light into the role of air power in guerrilla warfare in the 21st century. What began as peaceful protest in Syria quickly turned violent after the government's bloody crackdown.[53] In Cold War fashion, the revolution was hijacked by the superpowers for regional hegemony. Following the first spark in Tunisia, which toppled its regime, Arabs began to believe that popular will could lead to change in their part of the world.[54] The Syrian conflict itself was inspired by the successful Tunisian and Egyptian revolutions of 2011.[55] The apparent victories of the Tunisian and Egyptian revolutions in ousting dictators convinced the Syrian youth to ooze with the confidence of seeing change in their lifetime.[56] In Egypt, Mubarak's "three decades of iron rule," characterized by murder, torture and indefinite detention for dissidents, were ended by the Egyptian revolution.[57] Driven by frustration, the Egyptians marched to Tahrir Square in February 2011 to demonstrate against repression. As expected in any revolution, there were losses. About 846 demonstrators were killed during the 2011 revolt.[58] Having gained inspiration from the Arab Spring protests that had erupted in Tunisia, Egypt and elsewhere, Syrians marched peacefully and cautiously, fully aware that they lived in a place where such actions were not tolerated.[59]

Nevertheless, the gains of the Egyptian revolution were subsequently reversed. In 2013, Mubarak's successor, Mohamed Morsi of the Muslim Brotherhood party, was ousted by the military. The chief of the armed forces, General Abdel-Fatah al-Sisi, took over.[60] Although the Obama administration advised Egypt's military to hand back control to a democratic, civilian government without delay, it refused to call Morsi's ouster a coup.[61] Human rights groups revealed that the army's crackdown on the supporters of Morsi by end of March 2015 had led to the deaths of over 1,400 people and the arrest of 22,000 others, including some 200 people sentenced to death in mass trials.[62] Mubarak himself was cleared by the Egyptian court of conspiring to murder protesters during the 2011 Egyptian revolution due to a "technicality and lack of jurisdiction."[63] His sons and former Mubarak-era interior minister and six senior security commanders were also acquitted. As concluded by Al Jazeera political analyst Marwan Bishara, the trial was highly politicized and the verdict was stunning: "This is an arrogant attempt to make people sorry for coming out to the streets. This is trying to retrieve the old Egypt and basically clear three decades of dictatorship. Basically we have everyone that has been in charge of the violence and corruption cleared of all charges, while in prison we have thousands of peaceful civil rights activists."[64]

Air power played an enormous part in maintaining the grip of the Assad government onto power by controlling the skies and striking opposition targets, including civilians.[65] There is no doubt about what air power can do in conflict considering the destruction caused by air strikes in Syria and Libya. The Syrian Air Force managed to terrorize the civilians and slow down the rebel advance.[66] The rebels used antiaircraft guns to bring down some aircraft. Despite the air strikes launched by the Assad regime, there were no clear gains strategically except killing the rebels and civilians and obliterating infrastructure. The Syrian conflict demonstrated the challenges of air power in urban guerrilla warfare. The Assad regime was never able to sweep away the rebels, who continued to hold onto their strongholds. The situation of the Assad regime was further aggravated by the rise of a radical Sunni Islamic group called the Islamic State of Iraq and Levant (ISIL) in 2014.[67] Born as a result of the Iraqi and Syrian civil wars, ISIL further deteriorated the security situation, particularly in Iraq and Syria and the Middle East in general.[68] ISIL terrorists were initially trained by the CIA in Jordan in 2012 to destabilize the Syrian government in the midst of the Arab Spring. The situation was further heightened by the fact that other armed groups trained to fight ISIL defected, thus making it difficult to impose a crushing defeat on the group. Accordingly, that is the "confusion" of the U.S. foreign policy in the Middle East. Many people joined the group not entirely because they believed in the ideology of ISIL. It is, in fact, a lucrative business decision to be one of them. Oil alone generates about $1 million to $2 million per day for ISIL. Besides oil smuggling, ISIL obtains its revenue from robbing banks, stores and civilian homes, and even loots areas for priceless antiques and artifacts; it also engages in human trafficking and obtains funding from local businesses and civilians in cities or territories it has claimed.[69] In August 2014, the U.S.-led coalition initiated air strikes against ISIL, which by then controlled large swaths of territory in both Syria and Iraq.[70] Although the air strikes destroyed ISIL war material, they could not deal with the bigger problem of terrorism. The point was articulated by Syrian President al-Assad when he said that terrorism could not be defeated by aerial strikes. Assad emphasized the importance of ground troops in complementing the efforts of men in air.[71]

Although the U.S., France and Russia were determined to launch countless air strikes against the Islamic State, there was no end to terrorism in sight. The Islamist group employed refined tactics such as disarming opponents, seizing weapons and infiltration into hostile countries. On November 13, 2015, ISIL attacks in Paris at an international soccer match between Germany and France led to the deaths of 129 people and wounded more than 350. ISIL carried out attacks on bars, restaurants, a concert hall and a stadium. France's immediate reaction was to send aircraft to bomb Raqqa, the Islamist terror group's stronghold in Syria. French jets dropped guided bombs targeting sites including a command center, a recruitment center for jihadists, a munitions depot and a training camp. ISIL laughed off such attacks by claiming that the raid targeted empty locations and that there were no casualties. Prior to that, ISIL had gunned down a Russian airliner in Egypt's Sinai Peninsula on October 13, 2015, killing all 224 people on board. In November 2015, ISIL released a photo of the bomb it said was used to bring down Russia's passenger plane carrying mainly Russian tourists. ISIL used its powerful affiliate in the Sinai to carry out the attack. ISIL said both attacks were in retaliation for French and Russian air raids in Iraq and Syria. Guerrilla strategy is the backbone of the insurgent group. The challenge of fighting insurgents is that they are the ones who usually take the initiative through the use of hit-and-run tactics. So it means the adversary can react only after the damage is already done. The unpredictability of their operations perturb conventional security details. ISIL attacks in France jangled nerves across Europe. People were arrested and released; a Germany-Netherlands soccer match in Hanover was canceled. Belgium's match against Spain on November 17, 2015, was also canceled because of security concerns. The United Kingdom banned flights to Sharm el-Sheikh International Airport in Egypt on November 4, 2015, and a day later Russia banned all flights to Egypt. Egypt's national carrier was also banned from flying to Russia. This dealt a major blow to Egypt's vital tourism industry. In addition, the irony of counterstrikes carried out by both Russia and France is that they cost millions of dollars, whereas the insurgents used very few resources to hurt these countries. That is guerrilla warfare for beginners. It is all about using low-technology principles until the enemy is exhausted.

America and its coalition partners, including Britain, mounted air strikes against ISIL, but they had to rely on local forces like the Kurds, the Iraqi military and others to fight on the ground. Nonetheless, the ground forces struggled to match the strength of the well-funded and heavily armed extremists.[72] On the other hand, the beleaguered Bashar al-Assad government heavily relied on air strikes in order to contain the operations of the insurgents. On August 16, 2015, the government attacked the rebel-held town of Douma, killing 82 people, the bulk being civilians. About 250 people were also injured. The Syrian conflict demonstrates the strengths and restrictions of air power in modern guerrilla warfare. Despite the unending U.S. strikes, the city of Mosul was seized by the Islamic State in June 2014. ISIL combines religious fanaticism and military prowess to wreak havoc that cannot even be contained by air strikes. The U.S. weakened Iraq as a result of her invasion in 2003. This in turn led ISIL to find an easy route into Iraq. It is apparent that the occupation of Iraq was motivated by the selfish interests of the United States rather than a genuine security concern. The truth is that from 2001 the West has been struggling to deal with terrorism once and for all. An anti–ISIL strategy rooted in air strikes is the least of the terrorists' worries. If the West continues to despise the Assad-led government and Putin and ignore Muslim groups that are anti–ISIL, then there is a long way to go.

Libya

The Libyan civil war, which erupted in 2011 in the wake of the Arab Spring, resulted in the ouster of Muammar Gaddafi. Since the ouster of the Libyan dictator the country has not known peace. In fact, conditions in Libya created fertile recruitment ground for the Islamic State and other warring militias. The security situation during Gaddafi's era was not as pathetic as it eventually became after his brutal murder by the West. The war further exemplifies the strategic and tactical significance of air power in modern warfare. As enunciated by Giulio Douhet, airplanes possess the advantages of speed and flexibility. These tactical advantages put air power in an enviable position. Air power was decisive in the Libyan conflict because by the time no-fly zones were declared, Gaddafi was in a difficult position militarily. The West crippled any form of resistance by seizing command of the air from Gaddafi. The United Nations Security Council (UNSC) resolution 1973, passed on March 17, 2011, authorized member states "to take all necessary measures ... to protect civilians and civilian populated areas under threat of attack in the Libyan Arab Jamahiriya" and introduce a "no fly zone" above Libya.[73] This therefore meant that the NATO had gained for themselves command of the air. Libya's Air Force was completely put out of action. NATO air strikes on Libya revealed the true nature of war, in which civilians are not spared. This was also evident during the Second Chimurenga. Civilians suffered as a result of the indiscriminate attacks mainly spearheaded by the Rhodesian Air Force. Dozens of Libyan civilians were killed in NATO air strikes. Residential areas, both urban and rural, were attacked. Observers found no evidence of military objectives at the bombed locations despite claims by NATO that they wanted to protect civilians.[74]

Way Forward

Evidence reveals that air power's use in campaigns is important but should not be overestimated. At the tactical level, airplanes can be used to transport soldiers, ammunition, food and clothing, to name a few. They could also be used to launch limited air strikes, evacuate casualties and carry out reconnaissance. However, combatant duties are very limited, and where forced, the end result is huge expenditure, strained manpower and over-packed mortuaries. Guerrilla warfare demands response from a strong ground force. Airplanes alone cannot do the job, as military history has testified. There is need for a strong ground force in guerrilla warfare to carry out mopping-up operations around the areas where the battle took place. Group Captain Tony Forestier correctly noted that offensive air power has many strengths in modern warfare, but its utility in counterinsurgency warfare is not well understood. He further added that many of air power's traditional strengths, such as strategic strike, have limited use in a counterinsurgency warfare environment. In fact, employing offensive air power in a traditional manner may even undermine the effects being sought. War fighters and planners need to appreciate the fundamentals of counterinsurgency warfare in order to employ offensive air power effectively within its context. To ignore these fundamentals is to place at risk the broader outcome of the campaign.[75] During Operation Iraqi Freedom, air power delivered devastating battlefield effects, leading to the swift defeat of Iraq's conventional forces. When, however, the enemy transitioned to insurgent warfare, there was a limited understanding of how air power could best contribute. This primarily emanated from the fact that most western militaries are structured to fight conventional wars.

Conclusion

Overall, Zimbabwe's liberation war cannot be studied in isolation. The war can be understood by examining what happened in other guerrilla wars where air power was used. The study shows that air power plays an important role in guerrilla warfare. It is best suited to performing tactical duties such as transporting troops and supplies, tactical deployment, reconnaissance, limited air strikes, air search and casualty evacuation. It cannot ever be decisive because guerrillas do not stick to conventional methods of war. Guerrilla warfare demands a strong presence of men and women on the ground. The tendency, however, is that conventional armies are reluctant to commit as many foot soldiers as possible because of the obviously imminent losses. Resultantly, guerrilla forces maintain an upper hand. Infantry remains best suited to guerrilla warfare, whilst air power plays supportive roles. It is arguably in conventional warfare that airplanes can determine the outcome of wars. But the truth remains that guerrilla warfare has come of age if one takes a closer look at the exploits made by guerrilla fighters in Afghanistan, Yugoslavia, Vietnam, Zimbabwe, Angola, Namibia, Mozambique, South Africa and Cuba, to name but a few. In the Arab Spring that commenced in 2011, the Islamic State captured enemy soldiers, spread terror through cruel executions, and seized military hardware and oil fields belonging to the Syrian and Iraqi governments. The American and French air strikes resembled madmen chasing at the wind. The strikes could not stop ISIL from raping women, beheading civilians and soldiers, pumping oil, massacring Parisians and capturing cities. The same applies to Russian air strikes meant to support the Assad regime. It is best that the utilization of aircraft in guerrilla warfare be done at tactical level than strategic bombing.

Conclusion

This study makes it apparent from the outset that the story of the establishment of the Rhodesian Air Force would be incomplete if the role of Britain in the formation of the air force was not properly documented. From 1923, Southern Rhodesia's settler government showed great interest in aviation and contributed to the air campaigns of the Second World War and Cold War operations such as in Aden during the 1950s and early 1960s. As early as 1935, there were bold signs that Southern Rhodesia wanted to modernize her fighting forces, and this was cemented in 1936, when a crew of six boys was sent to Halton for apprentice training. It was, however, the outbreak of World War II which completely altered the shape of the air force. It should, nevertheless, be noted that the most compelling factor leading to the establishment of the British Empire Air Training Scheme was imperial defense, although there were strategic and tactical factors considered by both the colony and the Air Ministry for the project to take off. It therefore follows that the establishment and development of the RhAF was mainly due to the establishment of the Rhodesia Air Training Group in 1940. The lifetime opportunity of the RhAF emerged in 1940 as a result of the outbreak of the Second World War in 1939. The Air Ministry hunted for colonies and dominions where the training of pilots could be conducted without serious security and economic hindrances. The theatres of war during the Second World War were wide and demanding to the extent that the Air Ministry was in serious need of air training bases outside Great Britain. The Southern Rhodesian political and military leadership exploited the "God-given" opportunity offered by the Air Ministry to establish the foundation of their own air force. The era when the army and the police used to be the first lines of defense was over. Overall, the establishment of the RhAF was a by-product of the strategic and tactical considerations conceived by both the Air Ministry and the government of Southern Rhodesia. Although historical ties naturally bonded Southern Rhodesia and Great Britain, national security played a pivotal role in stimulating the interests of both countries in the air training scheme.

The cessation of hostilities in 1945 threatened the future of air power development in the colony, but this was averted when Britain agreed to continue air training in April 1947. Evidence reveals that it became less burdensome for Southern Rhodesia to resume the air training program because of the availability of airfields, buildings and hangars. In fact, it became a matter of policy to extend the lifespan of the project for internal security and other duties related to imperial defense. Although imperial defense continued to be a priority, the RhAF focused more on the internal security of the colony and federal partners Nyasaland (Malawi) and Northern Rhodesia (Zambia). White members of the Federation appreciated the advantages offered by aircraft in case of emergency, as had happened in 1959, when the Royal Rhodesian Air Force went into action to suppress the uprising in Malawi. The RRAF was deployed for the first time in internal security duties. The air force was active in throwing tear gas bombs and leaflets, and in carrying out reconnaissance. Southern Rhodesia felt compelled to meet its internal security requirements as a result of the winds of change which were sweeping across the continent. Added to that, the cordial relationship between the United Kingdom and the colony saw members of the Staff Corps being ferried to the UK, where they received courses on offensive support at the School of Land Air Warfare and flying instructors' refresher courses at the Empire Flying School.

The interwar period witnessed a notable transformation of the RhAF as a viable weapon of war because of the tremendous benefits ushered in by the Federation of Rhodesia and Nyasaland between 1953 and 1963. Before the Federation, the army and the air force were a composite force, but this changed in 1954 when the force rebranded to Royal Rhodesian Air Force. The divisions in command were effected due to the differences in the operational techniques and approach. The air force was freed from army structures. The entire Federation became reliant on the RRAF, and subsequently there was a swift mobilization of resources to make the unit a modern and effective instrument of war. The federal armed forces were primarily responsible for defending the Federation. The two squadrons which existed prior to the Federation were increased by five to make them seven, plus a parachute training school. Equally important, the interwar period divulged the hypocrisy which existed in the Rhodesian Security Forces. The Africans who had loyally served in imperial defense during World War II were relegated to jobs and ranks snubbed by the white population despite the blatant lie that all security forces were held in high esteem. The neglect of African soldiers in the RSF revealed the racial discrimination which existed in all the security forces' structures. There was, in fact, a deliberate policy to sideline Africans in all spheres of life. Under those circumstances, it did not come as a surprise when the Africans took up arms in the 1960s. When the Second Chimurenga broke out, the RhAF mobilized in full force to meet the guerrilla threat, but the war resulted in a stalemate that favored ZANU. ZANU did not take long to forget its mandate of nation building. Mugabe used violence and egotism to extend his rule to an extent that he even shouted "Pasi neZANU PF" (down with ZANU PF),[1] while doing the same was a cardinal sin for opposition supporters. His reign was characterized by dictatorship and economic meltdown. The fame he had in the 1980s swiftly vanished as people helplessly watched their beloved country being ruined by a few gluttonous chiefs.

This study reveals fundamental aspects which shed light on the military history of Zimbabwe. Accounts of the war as explicated by historians and journalists concentrated on various aspects of the fighting process. It was an appreciation of these works which inspired this study after realizing that the history of the Second Chimurenga lacks detail on some critical aspects of the war. Nevertheless, there are still more areas for further research. There is need to critically investigate how violence within liberation parties derailed the struggle for independence, and the role of Frontline states in these atrocities. The murder of civilians by the belligerents, especially African armies, should also be thoroughly researched. For those researchers passionate about air power studies, they are encouraged to zero in on specific case studies in order to advance research on the impact of the RhAF on guerrillas and civilians. It is also important to investigate the responses of the aforementioned to the RhAF air strikes. This entails a comparison of the ways in which ZANLA and ZPRA responded to the RhAF threat as distinct fighting units. The history of the Air Force of Zimbabwe since 1980 is also not covered in any great detail.

An examination of air power during the Second Chimurenga leads one to arrive at the conclusion that the Rhodesian Air Force was a pivotal component of the Rhodesian Security Forces. Its absence or inefficiency could have resulted in dire consequences for the Rhodesians. Evidence emerging from this research divulges that guerrillas suffered serious setbacks as a result of the air strikes carried out by the RhAF. It is important to highlight that although the guerrillas for the most part grew up in the reserves and were used to the terrain, they were certainly not supermen. The guerrillas failed to defeat the all-important element of surprise, which was facilitated by swift fireforce and hot-pursuit operations. The firepower released by the helicopters was too powerful to be contained by ill-equipped guerrilla fighters. New recruits especially were dealt a heavy psychological blow because the sight of an airplane created pandemonium. Resultantly, some were not able to grasp the stratagems of the RhAF and ended up being ensnared, resulting in huge massacres.

Under Peter Walls, the Rhodesian forces accepted their inability to control the terrain and the civilian population. As a result, they directed their operational planning toward limiting and reducing the growth of the insurgent forces within Rhodesia. The tactics developed to accomplish this mission were based upon an accurate evaluation and the dissemination of intelligence, ambushes, ground and aerial reconnaissance, the rapid deployment of forces in order to gain and maintain contact with confirmed enemy movements, and the development and use of a unique military organization known as the "pseudo-gang" to disrupt enemy forces in a particular area.

It was also the intention of this study to analyze the reasons why the RhAF, despite the raids it executed, failed to paralyze the guerrilla war machinery. Evidence shows that the reasons were twofold, that is, the strategies devised by the guerrillas and the inherent weaknesses of the RhAF as an instrument of war. The guerrillas employed a variety of strategies such as changing bases after an attack or deserting bases during the day and returning at night, studying the behavior of wild animals, or even relying on the guidance of spirit mediums, and taking the advantage of the terrain to get maximum cover, especially during the rainy season. The aim was to prolong the war, which is the essence of guerrilla warfare. The Frontline states ensured that the guerrillas maintained their grip. The international community became hostile and enraged by the number of noncombatant blacks who were killed and wounded during these raids. And the role of the RhAF in this regard largely negated the success of air power in a purely military sense.

Although guerrillas died in their thousands, their tactics dealt a heavy blow to the regime because air strikes were limited in containing their activities. It should be made clear that the RhAF was not a super-weapon as depicted by former RhAF personnel like Cowderoy and Nesbit. Furthermore, the RhAF suffered from the shortage of aircraft and manpower. Qualified personnel moved to civil aviation, where remuneration was higher compared to what was offered in the RhAF. The financial rewards for men in civil aviation far outweighed the benefits of pilots and technicians in the air force. These disparities inevitably forced the RhAF experts to join civil aviation at the expense of the already understaffed air force. There also lacked an air force reserve to reinforce and relieve the regular personnel. The state of affairs overstretched the capabilities of the available manpower. The RhAF had to frequently rely on retired pilots and civil aviation for the transportation of troops and supplies. Compared to the rate at which the guerrillas were deployed into the country, the RSF had a mammoth task at hand. In order to address the persistent problem of manpower shortage, the regime resorted to forced enlistment and engaged "fragile" men in their 50s and 60s. In addition, the efficiency of the RhAF was hampered by accidents which were attributed to inexperienced pilots. Added to this, there were technical challenges, especially the shortage of spare parts. Smith's declaration of UDI made it difficult for Rhodesia to purchase equipment and spares from its traditional markets. Efforts were made to obtain replacements through smuggling and homemade substitutions, but this could not match the huge demand created by massive guerrilla infiltrations. Moreover, the aircraft were old, much to the detriment of the RhAF, which was finding it difficult to contain and defeat the guerrillas. This was worsened by low morale in the security forces, partly as a result of the unequal racial treatment, which prevailed despite attempts by subsequent military details to foster a nonexistent spirit of harmony and togetherness.

It would be incomplete to give an account of the Second Chimurenga without explicating the experiences of civilians as a result of the attacks on guerrilla camps, raids during *pungwes*, and indiscriminate bombardments of villages by the Rhodesian Air Force. Civilians were attacked directly or indirectly in order to warn them of the consequences of supporting the guerrillas. The truth about modern warfare is that it makes very little, if any, distinction between combatants and noncombatants. The civilians were hit while taking supplies to the guerrillas, and in most cases the regime resorted to blanket bombing as part of terror tactics to deter civilians from joining and supporting the war. Many Africans lost their lives and livestock as the regime tried to cut off any form of support to the guerrillas. Terrorized by guerrillas at night and intimidated by RSF during the daylight hours, civilians hoped to survive until one side or the other won. Inside the country, the guerrillas' constant nemesis during the war was not the RhAF, but rather the Rhodesian police force. Supporters of the Smith government attributed this efficiency to the loyalty of black Rhodesians and their desire to compromise the murderous "terrorists." The leadership of ZAPU and ZANU, conversely, charged Rhodesian security forces (military, paramilitary, and police) with brutality, intimidation, and torture of the populace. There was truth to both charges. The bottom line, however, is that the civilians suffered as a result of the operations of both the RSF and the guerrillas.

Although fully acknowledging the inherent weaknesses of the RhAF as an instrument of war marked by periodic lack of spare parts, flying personnel and technical staff, it is evident that viable measures were put in place to keep the air force operational in the midst of very difficult circumstances. The shortage of spare parts had devastating effects on the operations of the RhAF, but this does not sufficiently explain why ZPRA's envisaged conventional aerial warfare was expected to be an imminent success. With all the experience gained by the RhAF from the Second World War up to the liberation war, ZPRA's strategic and tactical dilemmas are hitherto unthinkable. The argument sounds like it sympathizes with the Rhodesian Air Force, thereby falling deep in the already exhausted scholarship that unreservedly praises the Rhodesian Security Forces "where unnecessary." Our evaluation of ZPRA's plan should look at both sides, that is, from the point of the effectiveness of the RhAF as a military instrument in conventional operations, and the chances of ZPRA to wrestle that command of the air. The nature of domestic politics during that period cannot also be ignored.

This study argues that air power is an indispensable instrument of war but not purely decisive. Its effort needs to be synergized with the other forces such as land and maritime because independent action is inadequate. The Second World War demonstrated the effectiveness of combined operations, while the American, French, Syrian and Russian air strikes against the Islamic State fighters from 2014 revealed the wastefulness of independent air action. Air raids were not supported by ground forces except the inadequate Syrian, Kurdish and Iraqi soldiers. An important observation is that although air strikes are important in guerrilla warfare, guerrilla tactics naturally inhibit the efficiency of air operations, thereby giving guerrillas "enough" space and freedom. This is why air power performs best when used at tactical level in guerrilla warfare.

The RSF infantry units such as the Rhodesian Light Infantry and Rhodesian African Rifles were not adequate to reinforce the air strikes; thus, the air force did most of the fighting. It is therefore the argument of this study that the RhAF failed to achieve its objectives because the type of war it was fighting naturally restricted its operations; otherwise Peter Walls would remain for centuries an example of a man who knew how to deal with insurgency. The outcome was inevitable, especially given the fact that, in the aftermath of World War II, the structure of society and government in Rhodesia was obsolete in an era of decolonization and national self-determination. The use of guerrilla strategy implied that the Rhodesian Defence Forces, including the Rhodesian Air Force, could only contain the insurgency, not defeat it. In short, the counterinsurgency effort simply could not be won militarily, especially with Rhodesia hemorrhaging its white population as the black population grew, thereby intensifying the insurgency. Air power in guerrilla warfare is mainly important at tactical level than strategic bombing because guerrillas do not own valuable infrastructure worth dying for. Air power can do anything from tactical deployment to troop transportation, casualty evacuation, air strikes, reconnaissance and air search, but not winning guerrilla war. Its use should therefore be rationalized.

The war in Rhodesia was prolonged and history attests to the fact that prolonged wars exact heavy material and human costs. After counting their losses, the Rhodesians saw a political settlement as the only solution.

Chapter Notes

Introduction

1. The words were uttered by Stanley Baldwin in 1932, in the speech "A Fear for the Future." The argument was based on the premise that regardless of air defense, the bombers would always get through to destroy cities. At that time Baldwin was Lord President of the Council, a Cabinet-level post with no major duties attached to it. The occasion for the speech was a debate in the House of Commons about disarmament, held on November 10, 1932. Baldwin was essentially arguing that disarmament would not stop war. See B. Holman, "The bomber will always get through," http://airminded.org/2007/11/10/the-bomber-will-always-get-through/ (Accessed December 2014). The speech plays an important part in appreciating the influence of Douhet's theory of air power.
2. http://info.uwe.ac.uk/news/UWENews/news.aspx?id=917 (Accessed September 2015).
3. P. McLaughlin, Essay Review: "The Thin White Line: Rhodesia's Armed Forces since the Second World War," *Zambezia* 6, No. 2 (1978).
4. R. Red Daily and P. Stiff, *Selous Scouts: Top Secret War* (Alberton: Galago, 1982); K. Flower, *Serving Secretly: An Intelligence Chief on Record* (London: Murray, 1987); O. Cowderoy and R.C. Nesbit, *War in the Air: Rhodesian Air Force 1935–1980* (Alberton: Galago, 1987); W. Beverly, *A Pride of Eagles: The Story of Rhodesia's Air Force* (Salisbury: Graham, 1976); Peter J.H. Petter-Bowyer, *Winds of Destruction: The Autobiography of a Rhodesian Combat Pilot* (Johannesburg: 30° South, 2005); Beryl Salt, *A Pride of Eagles: The Definitive History of the Rhodesian Air Force, 1920–1980* (Durban: 30° South, 2015).
5. The war is known to the English-speaking world as the Rhodesian Bush War or the Zimbabwe War of Independence.
6. See N. Kriger, *Zimbabwe's Guerrilla War: Peasant Voices* (Cambridge: Cambridge University Press, 1992); K.D. Manungo, "The Role Peasants Played in Zimbabwe's War of Liberation, with Special Emphasis on Chiweshe District," Ph.D. thesis, Ohio University, 1991; P. McLaughlin and P. Moorcraft, *Chimurenga: The War in Rhodesia 1965–1980* (Marshaltown: Sygma Books, 1982); D. Lan, *Guns and Rain: Sprit Mediums in Zimbabwe* (London: James Currey, 1985).
7. Cowderoy and Nesbit, *War in the Air*; Beverly, *A Pride of Eagles*; H. Trealor, ed., *Fighting Forces of Zimbabwe Rhodesia*, No. 6 (Rhodesia: Amalgamated Publications).
8. N. Bhebe and T.O. Ranger, eds., *Soldiers in Zimbabwe's Liberation War*, vol. 1 (Harare: University of Zimbabwe Publications, 1995), p. 2.
9. D. MacIsaacs, "Voices from the Central Blue: The Air Power Theorists." in P. Paret, ed., *Makers of Modern Strategy: From Machiavelli to the Nuclear Age* (New Jersey: Princeton University Press, 1986), pp. 625–640.
10. L.M. Wortzel, "U.S.–Chinese Military Relations in the 21st Century," in L M. Wortzel, ed., *The Chinese Armed Forces in the 21st Century* (U.S. Army War College: Strategic Studies Institute, 1999), p. 194.
11. O. Bräuner, M. Bromley, and M. Duchâtel, "Western arms exports to China," Solna: Stockholm International Peace Research Institute Policy Paper 43, 2015, p. 18.
12. http://www.au.af.mil/au/awc/awcgate/au/faber.htm (Accessed 15 December 2011).
13. Initially called Southern Rhodesia, the colony later changed its name to Rhodesia.
14. The interwar period refers to the period of cessation of hostilities. By 1946, the Second World War was over and Southern Rhodesia returned home although still remotely engaged in other imperial commitments. No major war Southern Rhodesia was engaged in until 1966.

Chapter 1

1. S. Ndlovu-Gatsheni, "Mapping Cultural and Colonial Encounters, 1880s–1930s," in B. Raftopoulos and A. Mlambo, eds., *Becoming Zimbabwe: A History from the Pre-colonial Period to 2008* (Harare: Weaver Press, 2009), p. 46.
2. http://www.compassionatejustice.com/projects/zimbabwe.html (Accessed November 2015).
3. http://www.war-memorial.net/Maji-Maji-revolt-3.12 (Accessed November 2015).
4. T. Ranger, *Writing Revolt: An Engagement with African Nationalism* (Harare: Weaver Press, 2013), p. 8.
5. Zimbabwe Press Statement 589/80/SFS.
6. B. Moore-King, *White Man: Black War* (Harare: Baobab Books, 1988), p. 77.
7. Rhodesia Parliamentary Debates, The Senate, Vol. 7, Second Session-Thirteenth Parliament, 22 August 1975, p. 705.
8. Debates of the Federal Assembly, Vol. 17, Fourth Session-Second Parliament, 12 February 1962, p. 27.
9. S.M. Lanigan O'Keeffe, "Southern Rhodesia's War Effort," *Journal of the Royal African Society* 39, No. 156 (1940): p. 211.
10. T.A. Chimuka, "Ethics among the Shona," *Zambezia* 28, No. 1 (2001).
11. Rhodesia Parliamentary Debates, Vol. 99, Second Session-Fourteenth Parliament, 1 September 1978, p. 998. The words were said by Eastwood, M.P. for Mtoko.
12. Rhodesia Parliamentary Debates, Vol. 97, First Session-Fourteenth Parliament, 19 September 1977, p. 14.
13. P. Godwin, *Mukiwa: A White Boy in Africa*, p. 14. Godwin was a former police officer with the Police Anti-Terrorist Unit (PATU).
14. Report of the Commission on the siting of the capital of Southern Rhodesia 1955, p. 1.
15. *Ibid*.
16. B. Cole, *The Elite: The Story of the Special Air Service* (Transkei: Three Knights Publishing, 1984), p. 14.
17. Northern Rhodesia Legislative Council Debates, 3rd Session-3rd Council, 18 November 1930, p. 50.
18. *Ibid*.
19. Federation of Rhodesia and Nyasaland Economic Report, 1959, p. 13.
20. Debates of the Federal Assembly, Vol. 2, First Session-First Parliament, 22 July 1954, p. 1648.
21. T. Ranger, *Writing Revolt*, p. 9.
22. *Ibid*., pp. 9–10.
23. B. Hoffman, J.M. Taw, D. Arnold, *Lessons for Contemporary Counterinsurgencies* (Santa Monica: RAND, 1991), p. 6.
24. *Ibid*., pp. 6–7.
25. Rhodesia Parliamentary Debates, 5th Session-11th Parliament, Vol. 75, 27 August 1969, p. 3180.
26. Rhodesia Parliamentary Debates, 1st Session-12th Parliament, Vol. 78, 6 April 1971, p. 2226.
27. *Ibid*.
28. Beverly, *A Pride*, p. 95.
29. *Ibid*.
30. Rhodesia Parliamentary Debates, 1st Session-12th Parliament, Vol. 77, 11 June 1970, p. 440.
31. F. Chung, *Re-living the Second Chimurenga: Memories from Zimbabwe's Liberation Struggle* (Harare: Weaver Press, 2007), p. 90. Ndangana died in a car accident on June 27, 1989, near Nyazura in unclear circumstances.
32. Zimbabwe Press Statement 208/89/CB/SK/SG.
33. J. Moyo, "Zim: The clock is ticking for The Crocodile," *Mail and Guardian*, 19 December 2014.
34. B. Hungwe, "Zimbabwe's Emmerson Mnangagwa—Mugabe's heir apparent," BBC News, 11 December 2014, http://www.bbc.com/news/world-africa-30421768 (Accessed September 2015).
35. H. Moyo, "Zimbabwe's liberation struggle history remains untold," *Zimbabwe Independent*, 6 September 2013.
36. A.R. Wilkinson, "Political violence, counter-insurgency and change in Rhodesia," C.R. Hill and P. Warwick, eds., Collected Papers 1, Centre for Southern African Studies, University of York, 1974, p. 122.
37. D. Martin and P. Johnson, *The Chitepo Assassination* (Harare: Zimbabwe Publishing House, 1985), p. 7.
38. http://www.zbc.co.zw/index.php?option=com_content&view=article&id=624:zim-celebrates-44th-anniversary-of-chinhoyi-battle&catid=41:top-stories&Itemid=86 (Accessed 17 December 2011).
39. P. Godwin and I. Hancock, *"Rhodesians Never Die": The Impact of War and Political Change on White Rhodesia c. 1970–1980* (Harare: Baobab, 1995), p. 89.
40. D. Cowderoy and R.C. Nesbit, *War in the Air*, pp. 47–48.
41. P. Godwin and I. Hancock, *"Rhodesians Never Die,"* p. 90.
42. *Ibid*.
43. A.R. Wilkinson, "Political violence,

counter-insurgency and change in Rhodesia," p. 122.
44. B. Cole, *The Elite*, p. 36.
45. Hoffman, Taw, and Arnold, *Lessons*, p. 14.
46. Zimbabwe Press Statement 507/83/SK/JM.
47. L. Gumbo, "VP Mujuru stole my picture," *Herald*, 2 December 2014, http://www.herald.co.zw/vp-mujuru-stole-my-picture-war-veteran/ (Accessed November 2015).
48. Tino Chinyoka, "When we revise everything," Nehanda Radio, 12 October 2015, http://nehandaradio.com/2015/10/12/when-we-revise-everything/ (Accessed November 2015).
49. L. Sachikonye, *Zimbabwe's Lost Decade: Politics, Development and Society* (Harare: Weaver Press), p. 3.
50. Zimbabwe Press Statement 507/83/SK/JM.
51. *Ibid.*
52. J.K. Cilliers, *Counter-insurgency in Rhodesia* (Sydney: Croom Helm Ltd., 1985), p. 5.
53. Zimbabwe Press Statement 507/83/SK/JM.
54. *Ibid.*
55. M. Preston, *Ending Civil War: Rhodesia and Lebanon in Perspective* (New York: Tauris Academic Studies, 2004), p. 126.
56. Fungi Kwaramba, "Gumbo, Tongo helped Mugabe," *Daily News*, 2 December 2014.
57. V. Sithole, *My Life with an Unsung Hero* (Bloomington, IN: AuthorHouse, 2006), p. 60.
58. Zimbabwe Press Statement 784/80/SFS.
59. Zimbabwe Press Statement 394/80/SFS.
60. F. Chung, *Re-living*, p. 89.
61. *Ibid.*
62. *Ibid.*, pp. 91–92.
63. *Ibid.*, pp. 92–93
64. V. Sithole, *My Life*, p. 80.
65. C. Sanyanga, "Chitepo case: Key witness speaks out," *Sunday Mail*, 26 May–1 June 2013, p. 11.
66. V. Sithole, *My Life*, p. 80.
67. See F. Chung, *Re-living*.
68. C. Sanyanga, "Chitepo case: Key witness speaks out," p. 11.
69. Hoffman, Taw, and Arnold, *Lessons*, p. 35.
70. J.K. Cilliers, *Counter-insurgency*, p. 34.
71. N. Kriger, *Guerrilla Veterans in Post-war Zimbabwe: Symbolic and Violent Politics, 1980–1987* (Cambridge: Cambridge University Press, 2003), p. 25.
72. *Daily News*, 15 August 2012, p. 6. The newspaper article was a serialization of Joshua Nkomo's book, *The Story of My Life*.
73. J. Mtisi, M. Nyakudya and T. Barnes, "War in Rhodesia, 1965–1980," in B. Raftopoulos and A. Mlambo, eds., *Becoming Zimbabwe*, p. 147.
74. Zimbabwe Press Statement 75/83/AC.
75. Zimbabwe Press Statement 589/80/SFS.
76. L. Sachikonye, *Zimbabwe's Lost Decade*, p. 9.
77. I. Martinez, "The History of the Use of Bacteriological and Chemical Agents during Zimbabwe's Liberation War of 1965–80 by Rhodesian Forces," *Third World Quarterly* 23, No. 6, 2002, pp. 1162–64.
78. *Ibid.*, p. 1163.
79. *Ibid.*
80. P. Sturges, "Information in the national liberation struggle: developing a model," *Journal of Documentation* 60, No. 4 (2004): p. 433.

Chapter 2

1. K.P. Mueller, "Air Power," Project Air Force, Rand Corporation, p. 1.
2. B. Renz, "Airpower in the 21st Century," 2014. http://nottspolitics.org/2014/03/24/airpower-in-the-21st-century/ (Accessed September 2015).
3. N. Tangye, *Britain in the Air* (London: William Collins, 1944), p. 10. The poem is particularly celebrated in Britain as the "Battle of Britain Prophecy."
4. *Ibid.*
5. *Ibid.*
6. C.H. Gibbs-Smith, *The Invention of the Aeroplane 1799–1909* (London: Faber and Faber, 1996), p. 1.
7. N. Tangye, *Britain in the Air*, pp. 18–19.
8. P.B. Walker, *The Early Aviation at Farnborough: The History of the Royal Aircraft Establishment* (London: McDonald, 1971), p. 10.
9. J.A. Brendon, *Britain and her Neighbours: The Twentieth Century* (London: Black and Sun, 1923), p. 122.
10. C.H. Gibbs-Smith, *The Invention of the Aeroplane*, p. 210. According to Percy Walker in *The Early Aviation at Farnborough*, the whole British people were stunned and forced an apathetic government to take some action.
11. *Ibid.*, pp. 210–211. The overall cost was £2,500.
12. *Ibid.*, p. 213.
13. http://www.thosemagnificentmen.co.uk/rheims/ (Accessed July 2015).
14. J.A. Brendon, *Britain*, p. 192.

15. F.C. Kelly, *The Wright Brothers* (London: George G. Harrap, 1994), p. 121.
16. *Ibid.*, p. 122.
17. N. Tangye, *Britain in the Air*, p. 24.
18. *Ibid.*, pp. 25–26.
19. G. Lyall, "Marshal of the Royal Air Force: The Viscount Trenchard," in M. Carver, ed., *The War Lords* (London: Weidenfeld and Nicolson, 1976), pp. 185–186.
20. *Ibid.*
21. W. March, "Air Power, Doctrine and the Anglo-American Approach, Different Shades of Blue: Interwar Air Power Doctrine Development, Part 1," *The Canadian Air Force Journal* 2, No. 1 (2009): p. 20.
22. T. Biddle, "Learning in Real Time: The Development and Implementation of Air Power in the First World War," in S. Cox and P. Gray, eds., *Air Power History: Turning Points from Kitty Hawk to Kosovo* (London: Frank Cass, 2002), pp. 9–10.
23. *Ibid.*, p. 12.
24. W. March, "Air Power, Doctrine and the Anglo-American Approach," p. 18.
25. D. Jordan, "Air and Space Warfare," in *Understanding Modern Warfare* (Cambridge: Cambridge University Press, 2008), pp. 206–207.
26. T. Biddle, "Learning in Real Time," p. 3.
27. *Ibid.*, p. 4.
28. D. MacIsaacs, "Voices from the Central Blue," p. 628.
29. *Ibid.*
30. W. March, "Air Power, Doctrine and the Anglo-American Approach," p. 17.
31. G. Lyall, "Marshal of the Royal Air Force," pp. 185–186.
32. *Ibid.*, p. 4.
33. *Ibid.*
34. *Ibid.*, p. 44.
35. J.R. Jones, "William 'Billy' Mitchell's Air Power," Air Power Research Institute, Maxwell Air Force Base, Alabama, 1997, p. xii, http://www.au.af.mil/au/awc/awcgate/mitchell/front.pdf (Accessed December 2014).
36. R.G. Miller, *Billy Mitchell—Stormy Petrel of the Air* (Washington, D.C.: Office of Air Force History, 2004), p. 9.
37. *Ibid.*, p. 6.
38. D. MacIsaacs, "Voices from the Central Blue," p. 631.
39. J.B. Morris, ed., *Encyclopedia of American History*, 6th ed. (New York: Harper and Row, 1982), p. 396.
40. *Ibid.*
41. R.G. Miller, *Billy Mitchell—Stormy Petrel of the Air*, p. 24.
42. *Ibid.*
43. *Ibid.*, p. 1.
44. *Ibid.*
45. N.F. Rasmussen, "For years, military has tested the waters on the bay," 2005. http://articles.baltimoresun.com/2005-03-12/features/0503120090_1_billy-mitchell-battleship-chesapeake-bay (Accessed December 2014).
46. R.G. Miller, *Billy Mitchell*, p. 1. The military leadership and civilian politicians were angry because at that time a nation's military might was measured by its battleships.
47. G. Carruth, *The Encyclopedia of American Facts and Dates*, 8th ed. (New York: Harper and Row, 1987), p. 468.
48. R. Robbins, "Fighting Billy Mitchell founded our modern Air Force," *Weekly World News* 2, No. 29 (26 April 1961): p. 32.
49. http://www.historynet.com/william-billy-mitchell-an-air-power-visionary.htm (Accessed September 2015).
50. B. Brodie, "The Heritage of Douhet," U.S. Air Force Project Rand Research Memorandum, 1952. www.rand.org/pubs/research_memoranda/2009/RM1013.pdf (Accessed 15 March 2012).
51. *Ibid.*
52. G. Douhet, *The Command of the Air*, translated by Dino Ferrari (New York: Coward-McCann, 1942), p. 3.
53. *Ibid.*
54. *Ibid.*, p. 15.
55. N.A. Schwartz, "Air power in Counterinsurgency and Stability Operations," *Prism* 2, No. 2, NDU Press, http://www.ndu.edu/press/airpower-in-counterinsurgency-stability-operations (Accessed 15 April 2012).
56. *Ibid.*
57. W. March, "Air Power, Doctrine and the Anglo-American Approach," p. 17.
58. S.E. Gilson, "A Study on Contrasts Similarities and Differences between Development of Airpower and Space Power," Air Command and Staff College, Air University, Alabama, 1998, pp. 5–6.
59. T. Biddle, "Learning in Real Time," p. 5.
60. D. MacIsaacs, "Voices from the Central Blue," pp. 630–631.
61. J.F.C. Fuller, *The Conduct of War*, p. 240.
62. *Ibid.*
63. B. Brodie, "The Heritage of Douhet."
64. *Ibid.*
65. *Ibid.*
66. *Ibid.*
67. G. Douhet, *The Command*, p. 25. This

point also brings out Douhet's theory of bombing civilian centers of population.
68. Ibid., p. 28.
69. Ibid., pp. 31–32. Douhet advocated an independent air force because airplanes were under the command of the army and the navy, thus limiting their roles to assisting land and naval forces.
70. T. McGrath, "Drone footage reveals what little now remains of Gaza" (2008). http://timeli.info/item/2462834/Salon_Politics/Drone_footage_reveals_what_little_remains_of_Gaza_right_now___Salon_com (Accessed September 2014).
71. AFP, "Israeli strike on Syrian town kills 5 pro-regime forces: monitor," http://news.yahoo.com/israeli-strike-syrian-town-kills-five-pro-regime-100637132.html (Accessed July 2015).
72. P. Salisbury, "Yemen has turned from a local conflict into a regional Cold War," *Global Post*, 26 March 2015. http://www.globalpost.com/article/6502603/2015/03/26/yemen-has-turned-local-conflict-regional-cold-war (Accessed March 2015).
73. Ibid.
74. D.W. Allvin, "Air power Strategy in the Interwar Years: Not Ready for Prime Time," www.dtic.mil/cgi-bin/GetTRDoc?AD=ADA441608 (Accessed April 2012).
75. D. MacIsaacs, "Voices from the Central Blue," p. 630.
76. S. Conway-Lanz, "The Ethics of Bombing Civilians after World War II: The Persistence of Norms against Targeting Civilians in the Korean War," *Online Encyclopedia of Mass Violence*, p. 3, http://www.massviolence.org/The-Ethics-of-Bombing-Civilians (Accessed August 2015).
77. C.C. Harmon, "Are we beasts?": Churchill and the moral question of World War II 'Area Bombing,'" The Newport Papers, Newport Paper #1, Naval War College, Newport, 1991, p. 10.
78. M. Walzer, *Just and Unjust Wars: A Moral Argument with Historical Illustrations* (New York: Basic Books, 1977), p. 256.
79. Ibid.
80. S. Conway-Lanz, "The Ethics of Bombing Civilians after World War II," p. 3.
81. J.M. Spaight, *The Battle of Britain* (London: Geoffrey Bles, 1941), pp. 225–6.
82. P. Mavriks, ed., *History of World War II* (Marshal Cavendish Corporation, 2005), p. 527.
83. Ibid., 539.
84. D. Thompson, *England*, p. 192.
85. Ibid.
86. W. March, "Air Power, Doctrine and the Anglo-American Approach," p. 17.
87. M.J. Armitage et al., *Air Power in the Nuclear Age 1945–82: Theory and Practice* (London: Macmillan, 1983), p. 1.
88. D. MacIsaacs, "Voices from the Central Blue," p. 629.
89. K.P. Mueller, "Air Power," p. 2.
90. M.L. Powell, "Army Co-Operation Command and Tactical Air Power Development in Britain, 1940–1943: The Role of Army Co-operation Command in Army Air Support," Ph.D. dissertation, University of Birmingham, 2013, p. 1.
91. K.P. Mueller, "Air Power," p. 3.
92. D. Jordan, "Air and Space Warfare," p. 185.
93. Ibid., p. 207.
94. K.R. Whiting, *Soviet Air Power* (London: Westview Press, 1986), p. 15.
95. K.P. Mueller, "Air Power," p. 4.

Chapter 3

1. See D. MacIsaacs, "Voices from the Central Blue," p. 633.
2. Southern Rhodesia Central African Statistical Office, Official Year Book of Southern Rhodesia, No. 4, 1952, p. 352.
3. Rhodesia Parliamentary Debates, Vol. 83, Third Session-Twelfth Parliament, 29 March 1973, p. 1104.
4. Southern Rhodesia Central African Statistical Office, Official Year Book of Southern Rhodesia, No. 4, 1952, p. 355.
5. *Sunday Mail*, 2 June 1974, p. 1.
6. Southern Rhodesia Legislative Assembly Debates, Vol. 5, 26 November 1926, p. 101.
7. Ibid., pp. 111–112.
8. Ibid., p. 112.
9. Southern Rhodesia Report on Defence for the Year 1926, p. 1.
10. Ibid.
11. Southern Rhodesia Central African Statistical Office, Official Year Book of Southern Rhodesia, No. 4, 1952, p. 359.
12. Southern Rhodesia Report on Defence for the Year 1927, p. 1.
13. Ibid.
14. Ibid.
15. Southern Rhodesia Report on Defence for the Year 1926, p. 1.
16. Ibid., p. 2.
17. Ibid.
18. Ibid.
19. Rhodesia-Nyasaland Royal Commission Report, March 1939, pp. 23–24.

20. Northern Rhodesia Legislative Council Debates, 3rd Session-3rd Council, 25 November 1930, p. 107.
21. J. McAdam, "The Flying Mapmakers: Some Notes on Early Development of Air Survey in Central and Southern Africa." *Rhodesiana*, No. 30 (June 1974): p. 44.
22. *Ibid.*
23. *Ndege*, May 1970, p. 29.
24. J. McAdam, "Pat Judson: First Rhodesian Born Airman," *Rhodesiana*, No. 16 (July 1967): p. 2.
25. Southern Rhodesia Report on Defence for the Year 1928, pp. 2–3.
26. J. McAdam, "The Flying," p. 51.
27. J. McAdam, "Pat Judson," p. 3.
28. *Ibid.*
29. NAZ S482/471/39 Southern Rhodesian Air Force.
30. Southern Rhodesia Report on Defence for the Year 1929, p. 7.
31. Southern Rhodesia: The Economic Outlook 1946–1951, Salisbury.
32. J. McAdam, "Pat Judson," p. 7.
33. A.S. Mlambo, "Civil Aviation in Colonial Zimbabwe," *Zambezia* 19, No. 2 (1992): p. 103.
34. Southern Rhodesia Report of the Surveyor General 1939, p. 3.
35. J. McAdam, "Pat Judson," p. 15.
36. NAZ S759/4 Southern Rhodesia Defence Scheme.
37. *Ibid.*
38. Annual Report Defence and Aviation 1932, p. 1.
39. *Ibid.*
40. Annual Report Defence and Aviation 1933, pp. 1–2.
41. Annual Report Defence and Aviation 1934, p. 4.
42. Annual Report Defence and Aviation 1933, pp. 2–3.
43. *Ibid.*
44. Annual Report Defence and Aviation 1934, p. 6.
45. *Ibid.*, p. 12.
46. *Ibid.*, p. 1.
47. NAZ S482/88/43 Emergency landing grounds.
48. Annual Report Defence and Aviation 1932, p. 4.
49. *Ibid.*, pp. 4–7.
50. Southern Rhodesia Report on Department of Defence 1947, p. 7.
51. Annual Report Defence and Aviation 1933, p. 2.
52. *Ibid.*
53. NAZ S482/471/39 Southern Rhodesian Air Force.
54. *Ibid.*
55. Annual Report Defence and Aviation 1934, p. 6.
56. *Ibid.*
57. *Ibid.*
58. *Ibid.*
59. NAZ S482/471/39 Southern Rhodesian Air Force.
60. *Ibid.*
61. Debates of the Federal Assembly, Vol. 3, First Session-First Parliament, 18 August 1954, p. 2981.
62. *Encyclopedia Rhodesia* (Salisbury: The College Press, 1933), p. 19.
63. Southern Rhodesia Report on the Department of Defence 1947, p. 6. The pilots received their wings in 1938. The official year for the formation of the Air Unit is 1935.
64. C. Meredith, "The Rhodesian Air Training Group 1940–45," *Rhodesiana*, No. 28 (1973): pp. 16–17.
65. *Encyclopedia Rhodesia*, p. 19.
66. Rhodesia-Nyasaland Royal Commission Report 1939, Presented to Parliament by Command of His Majesty, March 1939, p. 24.
67. NAZ S817 Orders 1947–1954.
68. NAZ S1962/1 RATG Statistics.
69. Estimates of Expenditure from Revenue Funds 1937–38, p. 38.
70. *The Walrus* 1, No. 20 (1 January 1945): p. 6. The few officers there held army ranks.
71. *Ibid.*
72. K.R. Coster, "The Training of Rhodesian officers at the Royal Military Academy," *Scientia Militaria: South African Journal of Military Studies* 9, No. 3 (1979): p. 53.
73. *War Effort* 1, No. 2 (1 July 1940): p. 7. *War Effort* was a newspaper published in Southern Rhodesia to further the cause of imperial defense and the National War Fund.
74. *Rhodesia Herald*, 8 March 1940.
75. H. Beadle, "Sir Ernest Lucas Guest: A Tribute," *Rhodesiana*, No. 30 (June 1974): p. 77.
76. NAZ S1801 Rhodesia's war efforts.
77. S.M. Lanigan O'Keeffe, "Southern Rhodesia's War Effort," p. 213.
78. NAZ S1801 Rhodesia's war efforts.
79. M. Rupiya, "The Development of the Southern Rhodesia Armed Forces from the 1926 Defence Act to the Dissolution of the Federation in 1963," Ph.D. dissertation, University of Zimbabwe, Harare, 2000, p. 94.
80. Southern Rhodesia Central African Statistical Office, Official Year Book of Southern Rhodesia, No. 4, 1952, p. 359.

81. *The Walrus* 1, No. 20 (1 January 1945): p. 5.
82. NAZ S1801 Rhodesia's war efforts.
83. *War Effort* 1, No. 2 (1 July 1940): p. 3.
84. *Ibid.*
85. NAZ S3292/56/9/1 War Expenditure general: 1939.
86. NAZ S3292/56/9/19 War expenditure: Government Stationery office: 1939.
87. NAZ S1952 RATG Memoranda.
88. *Ibid.*
89. NAZ S1953/3 Munitions Production Board-Minutes of meetings.
90. Southern Rhodesia Department of Supply Report for the Year ended 31 December 1944, p. 16.
91. NAZ S1801 Rhodesia.
92. NAZ S1949/2/4 Supply of information for publication.
93. *Ibid.*
94. K.R. Coster, "The Training," p. 53.
95. *The Walrus* 1, No. 20 (1 January 1945): p. 5.
96. D. Thomson, *England in the Twentieth Century, 1914–1963* (Middlesex: Penguin Books, 1965), p. 177.
97. Meredith, "The Rhodesian Air Training Group," p. 19.
98. *Ibid.*
99. NAZ S1801 Rhodesia.
100. *Ibid.*
101. NAZ S801/1 RATG 1943–1953.
102. *Ibid.*
103. NAZ S817 Orders 1947–1954.
104. W. Beverley, *A Pride of Eagles*, p. 25.
105. NAZ S1801 Rhodesia's war efforts.
106. *War Effort* 1, No. 2 (5 July 1940): p. 3.
107. *The Walrus* 1, No. 20 (1 January 1945): p. 5.
108. *War Effort* 1, No. 1 (14 June 1940): p. 16.
109. *War Effort* 1, No. 2 (1 July 1940): p. 20.
110. NAZ S1801 Rhodesia's war efforts.
111. *Ibid.*
112. *Ibid.*
113. *The Walrus* 1, No. 20 (1 January 1945): p. 5.
114. *War Effort* 1, No. 2 (1 July 1940): p. 20.
115. C. Meredith, "The Rhodesian Air Training Group," p. 16.
116. NAZ S1801 Rhodesia's war efforts.
117. NAZ S1949/2/4 Supply.
118. *The Walrus* 1, No. 20 (1 January 1945): p. 5.
119. NAZ S759/4 Southern Rhodesia Defence Scheme.
120. NAZ S1959 Air Ministry.
121. NAZ S1801 Rhodesia.
122. *Ibid.*
123. Southern Rhodesian Department of Statistics, Statistical Year Book of Southern Rhodesia 1947, p. 210. The costs do not reflect the total expenditure incurred yearly as a result of the air training scheme.
124. S1948/1 Financial Statements Minister's Copy.
125. *Ibid.*
126. C. Meredith, "The Rhodesian Air Training Group," p. 26.
127. NAZ S3309/28 RATG: Transport Establishment and Control: 1942–44.
128. *Ibid.*
129. *Ibid.*
130. Southern Rhodesia Legislative Assembly Debates, Vol. 21, Third Session-Fifth Parliament, 21 May 1941, p. 515.
131. NAZ S1953/1 RATG Minutes: General 1940 Sep.–1945 Nov.
132. *Ibid.*
133. NAZ A312/695 Air Force Headquarters-Old stables 1931–1948.
134. *Ibid.*
135. NAZ S1949/2/1 Promotions: SRAF and RAAC. Airmen policy RAAC.
136. *Ibid.*
137. *Ibid.*
138. *Ibid.*
139. NAZ S235/398 Labour.
140. Southern Rhodesia Central African Statistical Office, Official Year Book of Southern Rhodesia, No.4, 1952. p. 360.
141. Southern Rhodesia Legislative Assembly Debates, Fourth Session-Fifth Parliament, 27 April 1942, Vol. 22, pp. 4–5.
142. *Ibid.*
143. Southern Rhodesia Central African Statistical Office, Official Year Book of Southern Rhodesia, No. 4, 1952, p. 3.
144. NAZ S235/398 Labour.
145. NAZ S3311/3 RATG Financial section standing instructions 1944–45. The letter "d" stands for "pence"; e.g., 2/8d was read as 2 shillings 8 pence.
146. *Ibid.*
147. NAZ S745/12 RATG Unit Orders.
148. NAZ S2921/1–3 RAAC Record of service cards.
149. NAZ S745/12 RATG Unit Orders.
150. NAZ S1949/2/1 Promotions: SRAF and RAAC-airmen policy RAAC.
151. Southern Rhodesia Central African Statistical Office, Official Year Book of Southern Rhodesia, No. 4, 1952, p. 360.
152. NAZ S2919/1 RAAC Discharges

1939–45.
153. NAZ S1949/2/3 Rhodesian Air Askari Corps: Employment of natives on skilled labor. The policy restricted Africans in the RAAC to laborers.
154. Ibid.
155. Ibid.
156. NAZ S131/40 Medical Attention for Air Forces in Southern Rhodesia.
157. Ibid.
158. NAZ S1959 Air Ministry and RATG Publications.
159. C. Meredith, "The Rhodesian Air Training Group," p. 24.
160. Debates of the Federal Assembly, Vol. 6, Third Session-First Parliament, 1 August 1956, p. 874.
161. P. McLaughlin, "The Thin White Line: Rhodesia's Armed Forces since the Second World War," *Essay Review in Zambezia* 6, No. 2 (1978).
162. NAZ S3302/28 Reinforcing Line: Finance 1942.
163. NAZ S1959 Air Ministry.
164. Southern Rhodesia Legislative Assembly Debates, Fourth Session, Fifth Parliament, Vol. 22, 27 April 1942, p. 3.
165. C. Meredith, "The Rhodesian Air Training Group," p. 17.
166. Ibid., p. 27.
167. *The Walrus* 1, No. 20 (1 January 1945): p. 4.
168. C. Meredith, "The Rhodesian Air Training Group," p. 25.
169. NAZ S1949/1/2 RATG General Correspondence.

Chapter 4

1. Debates of the Federal Assembly, Vol. 2, First Session-First Parliament, 22 July 1954, p. 1646.
2. Debates of the Federal Assembly, Vol. 3, First Session-First Parliament, 18 August 1954, p. 2971.
3. Southern Rhodesia Report on the Department of Defence for the Years 1945 and 1946, pp. 6–7.
4. Ibid.
5. Rhodesia Nyasaland Annual Report of the General Officer Commanding Central Africa Command for the Year Ending 31 December 1954, p. 6.
6. Ibid.
7. D. Cowderoy and R.C. Nesbit, *War in the Air*, p. 17.
8. NAZ S1953/1 RATG Minutes.
9. Southern Rhodesia Report on Department of Defence 1947, pp. 6–7.
10. Southern Rhodesia Report on Department of Defence, 1948, p. 7.
11. NAZ S2786/1 Visit of Air Ministry Mission to Southern Rhodesia in May 1946.
12. Ibid.
13. Ibid.
14. NAZ S748 Post war Air Training Scheme 1945.
15. Ibid.
16. http://www.rhodesianforces.org/RhodesianAirForceHistory.htm (Accessed 10 April 2012).
17. Southern Rhodesia Central African Statistical Office, Official Year Book of Southern Rhodesia, No.4, 1952, p. 360.
18. NAZ S1949/2/8 Aircraft-state owned Southern Rhodesian Government.
19. NAZ S3132 Agreement UK/Southern Rhodesia Government postwar air training.
20. NAZ S2786/1 Visit of Air Ministry.
21. Southern Rhodesia Report on the Department of Defence for the Years 1945 and 1946, pp. 9–11.
22. NAZ S748 Post War Air Training Scheme 1945.
23. Southern Rhodesia Report on the Department of Defence for the Years 1945 and 1946, p. 9.
24. NAZ S3292/56/7/4 War Assets: Disposal of RATG Workshop Equipment to Messrs. Crowther and Perry 1945–46.
25. Ibid.
26. NAZ S1949/2/12 Letters of appreciation.
27. C. Meredith, "The Rhodesian Air Training Group," p. 17.
28. NAZ S2785/18 CMF: Southern Rhodesia war book 1949 July 16–1950 November 6.
29. Southern Rhodesia Report on Department of Defence 1948, p. 12.
30. Ibid., p. 8.
31. Southern Rhodesia Annual Report of the Commander of the Military Forces for the year ending 31 December 1949, p. 4.
32. Ibid.
33. Southern Rhodesia Annual Report of the Commander of the Military Forces for the year ending 31 December 1950, p. 4.
34. Southern Rhodesia Annual Report of the Commander of the Military Forces for the year ending 31 December 1951, p. 5.
35. Ibid.
36. Ibid.
37. Southern Rhodesia Report on Department of Defence 1948, p. 7.

38. *Ibid.*
39. Southern Rhodesia Central African Statistical Office, Official Year Book of Southern Rhodesia, No.4, 1952, p. 360.
40. *Ibid.*
41. *Ibid.*
42. Southern Rhodesia Annual Report of the Commander of the Military Forces for the year ended 31 December 1952, p. 8.
43. Southern Rhodesia Annual Report of the Commander of the Military Forces for the year ended 31 December 1951, p. 5. See also Annual Report of the Commander of the Military Forces for the year ended 31 December 1952, p. 8.
44. *Ibid.*
45. Debates of the Federal Assembly, Vol. 2, First Session-First Parliament, 22 July 1954, p. 1647.
46. Southern Rhodesia Annual Report of the Commander of the Military Forces for the year ended 31 December 1951, p. 18.
47. Rhodesia Nyasaland Annual Report of the General Officer Commanding Central Africa Command for the Year Ending 31 December 1954, p. 1.
48. *Ibid.*
49. Debates of the Federal Assembly, Vol. 3, First Session-First Parliament, 18 August 1954, p. 2956.
50. Debates of the Federal Assembly, Vol. 3, First Session-First Parliament, 18 August 1954, p. 2954.
51. Annual Reports of the Secretary for Defence, the Chief of General Staff and Chief of Air Staff, Year 1964, pp. 2–9.
52. *Ibid.*
53. P. Godwin and I. Hancock, *"Rhodesians Never Die,"* p. 89.
54. Debates of the Federal Assembly, Vol. 9, Fifth Session-First Parliament, 21 July 1958, p. 517.
55. Debates of the Federal Assembly, Vol. 6, Third Session-First Parliament, 31 July 1956, p. 874.
56. Appendices I, II and III to the Report of the Apportionment Commission containing lists of assets and liabilities of the S. Rhodesian Government designated for transfer to the Federal Government, pp. 23–24.
57. Advisory Commission on the Review of the Constitution of the Federation of Rhodesia and Nyasaland, Survey of Developments since 1953, London, 1959, p. 127 (Report by Committee of Officials).
58. *Ibid.*
59. Southern Rhodesia Annual Report of the Commander Military Forces for the Year Ending 31 December 1953.
60. *Ibid.*, p. 128.
61. NAZ S1949/2/2 Amalgamation of air and defence.
62. http://www.ipmsstockholm.org/magazine/2006/09/stuff_eng_photo_rhodesian_af.htm (Accessed 23 Nov. 2012).
63. Advisory Commission on the Review of the Constitution of the Federation of Rhodesia and Nyasaland, Survey of Developments since 1953, London, 1959, p. 129 (Report by Committee of Officials).
64. Peter-Bowyer, *Winds of Destruction*, p. 17.
65. W. Beverly, *A Pride*, p. 15.
66. B. Cole, *The Elite*, p. 22.
67. S. Monick, "The Rhodesian Air Force: A history from inception to the bush war," in S.J. McIntosh, *Armed Forces* (Booysens, 1982), p. 21.
68. http://www.scramble.nl/zw.htm (Accessed 18 November 2012).
69. S. Monick, "The Rhodesian Air Force," p. 20.
70. *Ibid.*
71. Annual Reports of the Secretary for Defence, The Chief of General Staff and Chief of Air Staff, 1970, p. 8.
72. *Ndege*, May 1970, p. 10.
73. *Ibid.*
74. Rhodesia Nyasaland Annual Report of the General Officer Commanding Central Africa Command for the Year Ending 31 December 1954, p. 22.
75. Debates of the Federal Assembly, Vol. 2, First Session-First Parliament, 22 July 1954, p. 1653.
76. *Ibid.*
77. Southern Rhodesia Central African Statistical Office, Official Year Book of Southern Rhodesia, No. 4, 1952, p. 130.
78. Debates of the Federal Assembly, Vol. 10, First Session-Second Parliament, 21 July 1959, p. 1646.
79. Rhodesia Nyasaland Annual Report of the General Officer Commanding Central Africa Command for the Year Ending 31 December 1954, p. 1.
80. *Ibid.*
81. Debates of the Federal Assembly, Vol. 10, First Session-Second Parliament, 21 July 1959, p. 1641.
82. *Ibid.*
83. Debates of the Federal Assembly, Vol. 15, Third Session-Second Parliament, 29 June 1961, p. 231.

84. *Ibid.*
85. *Ibid.*, p. 232.
86. Debates of the Federal Assembly, Vol. 9, First Session-First Parliament, 21 July 1958, p. 515. Joseph was member of the Federal Assembly and Member of Parliament for Mrewa.
87. W. Beverly, *A Pride*, p. 21.
88. *Ibid.*
89. NAZ S817 Orders 1947–1954.
90. NAZ S2786/1 Visit of Air Ministry.
91. W. Beverly, *A Pride*, p. 15.
92. *Ibid.*
93. D. Cowderoy and R.C. Nesbit, *War in the Air*, p. 29.
94. Debates of the Federal Assembly, Vol. 10, First Session-Second Parliament, 9 April 1959, p. 109.
95. D. Cowderoy and R.C. Nesbit, *War in the Air*, p. 29.
96. http://www.rhodesianforces.org/RhodesianAir ForceHistory.htm (Accessed 25 November 2012).
97. http://www.rhodesianforces.org/No3Squadron.htm (Accessed 25 November 2012).
98. I. Mandiza, "Civil-military relations in Malawi: An historical perspective," in R. Williams, G. Cawthra and D. Abrahams, eds., *Ourselves to Know: Civil-Military Relations and Defence Transformation in Southern Africa*, Institute for Security Studies (Pretoria, July 1999), p. 115.
99. Debates of the Federal Assembly, Vol. 10, First Session-Second Parliament, 21 July 1959, pp. 1651–1652.
100. *Ibid.*, p. 1646.
101. Debates of the Federal Assembly, Vol. 10, First Session-Second Parliament, 29 June 1959, p. 986.
102. Debates of the Federal Assembly, Vol. 10, First Session-Second Parliament, 2 July 1959, p. 1220.
103. *Ibid.*
104. Debates of the Federal Assembly, Vol. 10, First Session-Second Parliament, 14 April 1959, p. 249.
105. Debates of the Federal Assembly, Vol. 18, First Session-Third Parliament, 18 July 1962, p. 754.
106. *Ibid.*
107. *Ibid.*, p. 757.
108. Debates of the Federal Assembly, Vol. 2, First Session-First Parliament, 22 July 1954, p. 1656.
109. Debates of the Federal Assembly, Vol. 8, Fourth Session-First Parliament, 1 August 1957, p. 786.
110. Debates of the Federal Assembly, Vol. 14, Second Session-Second Parliament, 27 February 1961, p. 4202.
111. Debates of the Federal Assembly, Vol. 16, Third Session-Second Parliament, 13 September 1961, pp. 2356–7.
112. Debates of the Federal Assembly, Vol. 12, Second Session-Second Parliament, 19 July 1960, p. 1443.
113. Debates of the Federal Assembly, Vol. 18, First Session-Third Parliament, 18 July 1962, p. 753.
114. Debates of the Federal Assembly, Vol. 11, First Session-Second Parliament,19 November 1959, p. 3817.
115. *Ibid.*
116. Debates of the Federal Assembly, Vol. 16, Third Session-Second Parliament, 4 September 1961, p. 1938.
117. http://www.rhodesianforces.org/RhodesianAirForceHistory.htm (Accessed 25 November 2012).
118. *Ibid.*
119. *Ibid.*
120. Debates of the Federal Assembly, Vol. 13, Second Session-Second Parliament, 26 July 1960, pp. 1825–1832.
121. *Ibid.*
122. Debates of the Federal Assembly, Vol. 3, First Session-First Parliament, 18 August 1954, p. 2971.
123. Debates of the Federal Assembly, Vol. 16, Third Session-Second Parliament, 11 September 1961, pp. 2305–6.
124. *Ibid.*, p. 2306.
125. W. Beverly, *A Pride*, p. 21.
126. Debates of the Federal Assembly, Vol. 2, First Session-First Parliament, 22 July 1954, p. 1646.
127. *Ibid.*, p. 1647.
128. NAZ S2785/4 CMF/1 Possible RAF assistance to the SRAF 1949–1951.
129. W. Beverly, *A Pride*, p. 15.
130. Southern Rhodesia Central African Statistical Office, No. 4, p. 360.
131. *Ibid.*
132. Debates of the Federal Assembly, Vol. 5, Second Session-First Parliament, 28 February 1956, p. 2203.
133. Debates of the Federal Assembly, Vol. 8, Fourth Session-First Parliament, 1 August 1957, pp. 786–7.
134. Debates of the Federal Assembly, Vol. 5, Second Session-First Parliament, 21 March 1956, p. 2710.
135. *Ibid.*
136. Advisory Commission on the Review of the Constitution of the Federation of Rhodesia

and Nyasaland, Survey of Developments since 1953, London, 1959, p. 127 (Report by Committee of Officials).

137. http://www.radfanhunters.co.uk/mec.htm (Accessed 28 November 2012).

138. Debates of the Federal Assembly, Vol. 9, First Session-First Parliament, 21 July 1958, p. 515.

139. http://www.rhodesianforces.org/RhodesianAirForceHistory.htm (Accessed 25 November 2012).

140. NAZ S2786/1 Visit of Air Ministry.

141. *Ibid.*

142. Debates of the Federal Assembly, Vol. 12, Second Session-Second Parliament, 19 July 1960, p. 1443.

143. *Rhodesia Herald*, 18 May 1974, p. 1.

144. http://www.rhodesianforces.org/No2Squadron.htm (Accessed 8 August 2012).

145. Annual Reports of the Secretary for Defence, the Chief of General Staff and Chief of Air Staff, 1964, p. 9.

146. http://www.rhodesianforces.org/No3Squadron.htm (Accessed 18 August 2012).

147. Debates of the Federal Assembly, Vol. 2, First Session-First Parliament, 22 July 1954, p. 1647.

148. Annual Reports of the Secretary for Defence, the Chief of General Staff and Chief of Air Staff, Year 1964, p. 9.

149. Anti-Apartheid Movement, *Fireforce Exposed: The Rhodesian Security Forces and Their Role in Defending White Supremacy* (London: 1979), p. 28.

150. http://www.rhodesianforces.org/No4Squadron.htm (accessed 18 August 2012).

151. Annual Reports of the Secretary for Defence, the Chief of General Staff and Chief of Air Staff, Year 1964, p. 9.

152. *Ibid.*, p. 10.

153. *Ibid.*

154. http://www.rhodesianforces.org/No6Sqn.htm (Accessed 18 August 2012).

155. Annual Reports of the Secretary for Defence, the Chief of General Staff and Chief of Air Staff, 1967, p. 9.

156. Annual Reports of the Secretary for Defence, the Chief of General Staff and Chief of Air Staff, 1969, p. 9.

157. *Ibid.*

158. Annual Reports of the Secretary for Defence, the Chief of General Staff and Chief of Air Staff, 1964, p. 9.

159. *Ibid.*

160. W. Beverly, *A Pride*, p. 53.

161. *Ibid.*

162. H. Trealor, ed., *Fighting Forces*, p. 49.

163. *Ibid.*

164. Annual Reports of the Secretary for Defence, the Chief of General Staff and Chief of Air Staff, Year 1964, p. 10. Details for Squadron No. 6 are in Annual Report for Year 1967.

165. NAZ S1801 Rhodesia's war efforts.

166. R. Howman, "Orlando Baragwanath: A Centenarian pioneer of Rhodesia," *Rhodesiana*, No. 28 (1973): p. 31.

167. I. Smith, *The Great Betrayal: The Memoirs of Ian Douglas Smith* (London: Blake Publishing Ltd., 1997), p. 223.

168. Debates of the Federal Assembly, Vol. 6, Third Session-First Parliament, 31 July 1956, p. 745.

169. Career Opportunities in the Rhodesian Air Force: Pilot Training Scheme, p. 3.

170. Debates of the Federal Assembly, Vol. 9, First Session-First Parliament, 21 July 1958, pp. 518–19.

171. *Ibid.*

172. NAZ S802 Certificates.

173. *Ibid.*

174. Debates of the Federal Assembly, Vol. 6, Third Session-First Parliament, 31 July 1956, p. 745.

175. Debates of the Federal Assembly, Vol. 8, Fourth Session-First Parliament, 29 July 1957, p. 516.

176. Debates of the Federal Assembly, Vol. 10, First Session-Second Parliament, 21 July 1959, p. 1641.

177. Report of the Secretary for Law and Order for the Year Ended 31 December 1965, p. 2. The comments were made on the basis that Africans believed what Radio Zambia told them, commonly viewed as propaganda by the Rhodesians.

178. E.I. Mandiza, "Civil-military relations…," p. 114.

179. T.J. Stapleton, *No Insignificant Past: The Rhodesia Native Regiment and the East African Campaign of the First World War* (Waterloo, Canada: Wilfrid Laurier University Press, 2006), p. 5.

180. C. Owen, *The Rhodesian African Rifles* (London: Leo Cooper Ltd., 1970), p. 2.

181. *Ibid.*, p. 38.

182. C. Meredith, "The Rhodesian Air Training Group," p. 23.

183. *Ibid.*

184. Survey of Federal developments from 1953–1958, p. 131.

185. Federation of Rhodesia and Nyasaland Economic Report 1959, p. 13.

186. Rhodesia Parliamentary Debates, Vol. 76, 14 November 1969, p. 1367.

187. NAZ F128/L135 Race affairs: Discrimination in military training.
188. Federation of Rhodesia and Nyasaland Economic Report 1961, p. 25.
189. C. Owen, *The Rhodesian*, p. 3.

Chapter 5

1. J.F.C. Fuller, *The Conduct of War 1789–1961: A Study of the Impact of the French, Industrial and Russian Revolutions on War and its Conduct* (London: Eyre and Spottiswoode, 1961), p. 241. The comment was made by Giulio Douhet during the interwar period to convince the military and political leadership of the day about the potential of air power to win battles.
2. Rhodesia Parliamentary Debates, Vol. 81, Third Session-Twelfth Parliament, 8 June 1972, p. 243.
3. Annual Reports of the Secretary for Defence, the Chief of General Staff and Chief of Air Staff, Year 1970, p. 9.
4. *Ibid.*
5. *Ibid.*
6. Rhodesia Parliamentary Debates, Vol. 97, First Session-Fourteenth Parliament, 21 September 1977, pp. 60–61.
7. W. Beverly, *A Pride*, p. 53.
8. *Ibid.*
9. The Joint Air Power Competence Centre, "Air Power in Countering Irregular Warfare," June 2008, p. 8. www.japcc.de (Accessed 17 June 2012).
10. *Ibid.*
11. J.M. Norton, "The French-Algerian War and FM 3-24, Counterinsurgency: A Comparison," Master's thesis, University of Maryland, 1992, p. 98. www.dtic.mil/cgi-bin/GetTRDoc?AD=ADA475521 (Accessed 23 September 2012).
12. *Bateleur*, The newspaper of the Air Force, Salisbury, December 1977, p. 4.
13. *Sunday Mail*, 23 June 1974, p. 1.
14. Interview with Easygo Mamboininga, war veteran, 55 years, 5 February 2013, Harare.
15. *Ibid.*
16. *Ibid.*
17. Debates of the Federal Assembly, Vol. 17, Fourth Session-Second Parliament, 12 February 1962, p. 15.
18. Rhodesia Parliamentary Debates, Vol. 81, Third Session-Twelfth Parliament, 6 June 1972, p. 108. A total of 426 miners lost their lives. It was originally believed that 468 miners were trapped, but the figure dropped after the owners found a number of people had not shown up for work. See http://familysurvival-protocol.com/tag/puerto-rico/page/11/ for more details.
19. *Ibid.*
20. I. Martinez, "The History of the Use of Bacteriological and Chemical Agents during Zimbabwe's Liberation War," p. 1162.
21. J.K. Bruton, "Counter Insurgency in Rhodesia," *Military Review* 59, No. 3 (March 1979): p. 35.
22. *Sydney Morning Herald*, 1 June 1977, p. 4.
23. F. Chung, *Re-living*, p. 144.
24. *Ibid.*
25. Interview with Peter Mhizha, war veteran, approx. 50 years, 17 May 2012, Masvingo Urban.
26. *Sunday Mail*, May 26–June 1, 2013, p. 7. The information was provided by war veteran Wereki Sandiani, whose *nom de guerre* was Philip Gabella.
27. F. Chung, *Re-living*, p. 143.
28. Interview with Easygo Mamboininga, war veteran, 55 years, 5 February 2013, Harare.
29. Interview with Chrispen Nyanga, war veteran, 57 years, 9 February 2013, Harare.
30. H. Ellert, "The Rhodesian security and intelligence community 1960 to 1980: A brief overview of the structure and operational role of military, civilian and police security and intelligence organisation which served in Rhodesia government during the Zimbabwean liberation war," in N. Bhebe and T.O. Ranger, eds., *Soldiers in Zimbabwe's Liberation War*, vol. 1, p. 101.
31. *Ibid.*
32. K. Flower, *Serving Secretly*, p. 191.
33. I. Martinez, "The History of the Use of Bacteriological and Chemical Agents during Zimbabwe's Liberation War," p. 1161.
34. *The Herald*, 7 July 2011.
35. Rhodesia Parliamentary Debates, Vol. 99, 20 December 1978, p. 1893.
36. J. F. C. Fuller, The Conduct of War, p. 69.
37. http://www.raf.mod.uk/role/air power.cfm (Accessed 10 April 2012).
38. *Herald*, 23 November 2011.
39. Interview with Titos Mtombeni, 55 years, 9 August 2012, Chisuma Business Centre.
40. http://www.zbc.co.zw/news-categories/top-stories/4459-survivors-recall-chimoio-massacre.html (Accessed 10 April 2012).
41. Interview with Benz Chavhundura, war veteran, 55 years, 6 February 2013, Harare.
42. *Ibid.*
43. *Ibid.*

44. Conversation with Lovert Makunike, 21 years, 22 April 2012, Harare. At the time of the discussion Lovert was a University of Zimbabwe student who visited Chimoio on 18 April 2012 (Zimbabwe's Independence Day). The story of the air raids was narrated to them by the survivors of the Chimoio attack.

45. *Ibid.* See also the *Herald*, 7 July 2011.

46. *Ibid.*

47. K. Flower, *Serving Secretly*, p. 192. There are sharp differences over the number of casualties suffered at Chimoio. According to F. Chung, *Re-living*, p. 144, 85 people died, 55 of whom were children, about 500 were injured by napalm and gunfire, and 200 were seriously injured. The *Herald*, 7 July 2011, puts them at plus or minus 5,000, whereas ZANLA estimated a total of 1,350. On the contrary, Ken Flower puts them at more than 2,000 killed and the same number incapacitated. See also Cowderoy and Nesbit, *War in the Air*, p. 77.

48. B. Cole, *The Elite*, p. 180.

49. For more information related to the execution of the plan, see http://rhodesian.tripod.com/rrd.html (Accessed 18 February 2013).

50. *Rhodesia Herald*, 30 November 1977, p. 1.

51. Interview with Margret Makomva, war veteran, 54 years, 5 February 2013, Harare.

52. Interview with Titos Mtombeni, 55 years, 9 August 2012, Chisuma Business Centre.

53. D. Cowderoy and R.C. Nesbit, *War in the Air*, p. 76.

54. *Ibid.*, p. 153.

55. *Sunday Mail*, 18–24 November 2012.

56. Interview with Chrispen Nyanga, war veteran, 57 years, 9 February 2013, Harare.

57. http://www.rhodesianforces.org/OperationUric.htm (Accessed 15 February 2013). Together with Pafuri, the Rhodesians failed to seize Mapai, thus the bases remained in the hands of the guerrilla forces.

58. *Sydney Morning Herald*, 1 June 1977, p. 1. Mapai was 75 kilometers from the border.

59. Institute for Security Studies, "External operations," p. 182, www.iss.co.za/pubs/Books/rhodesia/s101-120.pdf (Accessed 21 December 2012).

60. K. Flower, *Serving Secretly*, p. 213.

61. Rhodesia Parliamentary Debates, Vol. 99, Second Session-Fourteenth Parliament, 21 February 1979, p. 2896.

62. Rhodesia Parliamentary Debates, Vol. 99, Second Session-Fourteenth Parliament, 7 September 1978, p. 1169.

63. *Ibid.*

64. http://www.viscountdown.com/ (Accessed 21 December 2012). See also P. Stiff, *See You in November* (Alberton: Galago, 1985), p. 215.

65. *Ibid.*

66. Rhodesia Parliamentary Debates, Vol. 99, Second Session-Fourteenth Parliament, 21 February 1979, p. 2895.

67. Hoffman, Taw, and Arnold, *Lessons*, p. 9.

68. J. Nkomo, *The Story of My Life* (Harare: Sapes Books, 1984), p. 172.

69. *Ibid.*

70. E.M. Sibanda, *The Zimbabwe African People's Union 1961–1987: A Political History of Insurgency in Southern Rhodesia* (Asmara: Africa World Press, 2005).

71. K. Flower, *Serving Secretly*, p. 214. Joshua Nkomo criticized the attack on Freedom Camp on the basis that it was not a military camp, but a genuine refugee camp. See Nkomo, *The Story*, p. 173.

72. *Ibid.*

73. P. Stiff, *See You in November*, p. 216.

74. *Ibid.*, pp. 220–221.

75. http://www.zapu.org/index.php/2012-10-30-08-02-05/news-and-info/latest-zapu-news/item/74-mkushi-camp-survivors-tour-ZPRA-camp (Accessed 20 December 2012). Mkushi was exclusively for ZPRA women refugees.

76. *Ibid.*

77. B. Cole, *The Elite*, p. 180.

78. J. Alexander and J. McGregor, "War Stories: Guerrilla Narratives of Zimbabwe's Liberation War," *History Workshop Journal*, No. 57, 2004, p. 91.

79. K. Flower, *Serving Secretly*, p. 213.

80. P.L. Moorcraft and P. McLaughlin, *Chimurenga!*, p. 78.

81. *Ibid.*, p. 52.

82. Institute for Security Studies, "External operations," p. 182.

83. *Ibid.*

84. Interview with Lt. Col. Kingstone Kazambara, war veteran, 56 years, 14 February 2013, Harare.

85. *Ibid.*

86. *Sunday Mail*, 18–24 October 2012.

87. Interview with Peter Mhizha, war veteran, approx. 50 years, 17 May 2012, Masvingo Urban.

88. Interview with Zimbabwe Mutsikapasi (pseudonym), war veteran, 72 years, 11 May 2012, Masvingo Urban.

89. Interview with Margret Makomva, war veteran, 54 years, 5 February 2013, Harare.

90. *Sunday Mail*, May 26–June 1, 2013, p. 7.

91. *Rhodesia Herald*, 6 July 1978.
92. *Bush Telegraph* 1, No. 6 (7 December 1976).
93. *Rhodesia Herald*, 6 July 1978.
94. H. Ellert, *The Rhodesian Front War*, 1989, p. vi.
95. Southern Rhodesia Department of Supply Report for the Year Ended 31 December 1944, p. 16.
96. Interview with Easygo Mamboininga, war veteran, 55 years, 5 February 2013, Harare.
97. *Ibid.*
98. Interview with Lt. Col. Kingstone Kazambara, war veteran, 56 years, 14 February 2013, Harare.
99. Interview with Chrispen Nyanga, war veteran, 57 years, 9 February 2013, Harare.
100. *Ibid.*
101. http://www.rhodesia.nl/briefhi1.htm (Accessed October 2015).
102. Annual Reports of the Secretary for Defence, the Chief of General Staff and Chief of Air Staff, 1970, p. 9.
103. *Ibid.*
104. Hoffman, Taw, and Arnold, *Lessons*, pp. 21–22.
105. *Ibid.*, p. 22.
106. D. Cowderoy and R.C. Nesbit, *War in the Air*, p. 67.
107. J.K. Bruton, "Counter Insurgency,..." p. 32.
108. Rhodesia Parliamentary Debates, Vol. 94, Third Session-Thirteenth Parliament, 24 August 1976, pp. 1254–55.
109. B. Cole, *The Elite*, p. 85.
110. Hoffman, Taw, and Arnold, *Lessons*, p. 22.
111. Annual Reports of the Secretary for Defence, the Chief of General Staff and Chief of Air Staff, Year 1968, p. 8.
112. *Bateleur*, The newspaper of the Air Force, Salisbury, November 1976, p. 1.
113. *Bateleur*, The newspaper of the Air Force, Salisbury, October 1977, p. 2.
114. Rhodesia Parliamentary Debates, The Senate, Vol. 7, Second Session-Thirteenth Parliament, 25 June 1975, p. 42.
115. *Ibid.*
116. *Bateleur*, The newspaper of the Air Force, Salisbury, April 1977, p. 1.
117. Rhodesia Parliamentary Debates, Vol. 94, Third Session-Thirteenth Parliament, 24 August 1976, p. 1254.
118. *Bateleur*, The newspaper of the Air Force, Salisbury, April 1977, p. 1.
119. *Ibid.*
120. Rhodesia Parliamentary Debates, 3rd Session-13th Parliament, Vol. 94, 24 August 1976, 1254.
121. *Bateleur*, The newspaper of the Air Force, Salisbury, September 1978, p. 4.
122. *Ibid.*
123. W. Beverly, *A Pride*, p. 53.
124. J. Brickhill, "Daring to storm the heavens: The military strategy of ZAPU 1976 to 1979," in N. Bhebe and T.O. Ranger, eds., *Soldiers in Zimbabwe's Liberation War*, vol. 1, p. 53.
125. Interview with Chrispen Nyanga, war veteran, 57 years, 9 February 2013, Harare.
126. Interview with Lt. Col. Kingstone Kazambara, war veteran, 56 years, 14 February 2013, Harare.
127. *Ibid.*
128. *Sunday Mail*, May 26–June 1, 2013, p. 7.
129. *Ibid.*
130. Interview with Lt. Col. Kingstone Kazambara, war veteran, 56 years, 14 February 2013, Harare.
131. Debates of the Federal Assembly, Vol. 18, First Session-Third Parliament, 18 July 1962, p. 753.
132. Interview with Margret Makomva, war veteran, 54 years, 5 February 2013, Harare.
133. *Bateleur*, The newspaper of the Air Force, Salisbury, April 1979, p. 2.
134. *Ibid.*
135. Interview with Peter Mhizha (war veteran), approx. 50 years, 17 May 2012, Masvingo Urban.

Chapter 6

1. NAZ S/AS72 *Assegai: The Magazine of the Rhodesian Arm* 5, No. 1, May 15, 1965, p. 22.
2. *Ibid.*
3. Interview with Peter Dhliwayo, war veteran, 57 years, 1 July 2012, Chisuma Business Centre.
4. Interview with Margret Makomva, war veteran, 54 years, 5 February 2013, Harare.
5. Interview with Livison Makamu, 57 years, 25 June 2012, Chisuma Business Centre.
6. W. Beverly, *A Pride*, p. 53.
7. *Ibid.*
8. *Bateleur*, The newspaper of the Air Force, Salisbury, April 1977, p. 2.
9. http://www.rhodesianforces.org/No2 Squadron.htm (Accessed 21 December 2012).
10. H. Ellert, *The Rhodesian Front War*, p. 115.
11. S/ZIM 0897 Zimbabwe Chimurenga, Official Organ of ZANU Office in Scandinavia, Stockholm, Vol. 1, No. 1, 14 August 1974, p. 11.
12. *Ibid.*

13. *Bateleur*, The newspaper of the Air Force, Salisbury, January 1977, p. 2.
14. *Ibid.*
15. *Ibid.*
16. *Ibid.*
17. Rhodesia Parliamentary Debates, Vol. 99, Second Session-Fourteenth Parliament, 20 December 1978, p. 1885.
18. Interview with Easygo Mamboininga, war veteran, 55 years, 5 February 2013, Harare.
19. *Ibid.*
20. Interview with Livison Makamu, 57 years, 25 June 2012, Chisuma Business Centre.
21. Interview with Amon Dhliwayo, 68 years, 1 July 2012, Chisuma Business Centre.
22. *Ibid.*
23. Interview with Themba Nyati, 69 years, 2 July 2012, Chisuma Business Centre.
24. *Ibid.*
25. Interview with Titos Mtombeni, 55 years, 9 August 2012, Chisuma Business Centre.
26. *Ibid.*
27. *Ibid.*
28. *Sunday Mail*, 18–24 November 2012.
29. T. Musakuro, "The military role of FRELIMO in the liberation war of Zimbabwe from 1968 to 1980," B.A. honors thesis, University of Zimbabwe, Harare, 2008, p. 28.
30. *Ibid.*, p. 29.
31. Interview with Edmore Zvenyika, war veteran, 56 years, 8 February 2013, Harare.
32. *Ibid.*
33. Interview with Lt. Col. Kingstone Kazambara, war veteran, 56 years, 14 February 2013, Harare.
34. *Ibid.*
35. P. Doyle and M. Bennett, "Military Geography: The Influence of Terrain in the Outcome of the Gallipoli Campaign, 1915," *The Geographical Journal* 165, No. 1 (March 1999): p. 17.
36. B. Cole, *The Elite*, pp. 9–12.
37. *Ibid.*, p. 85.
38. Catholic Commission for Justice and Peace in Rhodesia and the Catholic Institute for International Affairs, *The Man in The Middle: Torture, Resettlement and Eviction and Civil War in Rhodesia* (CCJP Zimbabwe, 1975), p. 10.
39. Rhodesia Parliamentary Debates, Vol. 86, Fourth Session-Twelfth Parliament, 20 June 1974, p. 117.
40. NAZ RG 3/AIR 61 RhAF Flight Safety Bulletin, January 1979–June 1979.
41. Interview with Dick Chinovava (*nom de guerre*), war veteran, 66 years, 10 April 2012, Jerera Growth Point.

42. Interview with Jonah Jegede, 80 years, 9 April 2012, Zaka District.
43. A. K. Chordia, "Effect of Weather and Terrain on Airlift Operations," www.aerospaceindia.org/.../Winter%202011/Chapter%203.pdf (Accessed 23 September 2012).
44. T. Moyo, "Airborne Operations in the Mozambican Campaign 1982–1992: An analysis of the Zimbabwe Defence Forces Campaign Strategy," Master's thesis, University of Zimbabwe, November 2007, p. 93.
45. *Ibid.*
46. Interview with Themba Nyati, 69 years, 2 July 2012, Chisuma Business Centre.
47. *Sunday Mail*, 18–24 November 2012.
48. Interview with Peter Dhliwayo (war veteran), 57 years, 1 July 2012, Chisuma Business Centre.
49. Interview with Maphosa, war veteran, approx. 56 years, 5 February 2013, Harare.
50. G. Muzari, "When a luck-bringing bird falters," *The Standard*, 24 February 2013.
51. Interview with Maphosa, war veteran, approx. 56 years, 5 February 2013, Harare.
52. Interview with Margret Makomva, war veteran, 54 years, 5 February 2013, Harare.
53. *Ibid.*
54. *Ibid.*
55. *Sunday Mail*, 26 May–1 June 2013, p. 7.
56. Rhodesia Parliamentary Debates, Vol. 83, Third Session-Twelfth Parliament, 29 March 1973, p. 1072.
57. Interview with Mai Mataruse, 48 years, 10 September 2015, Harare.
58. Interview with Chrispen Nyanga, war veteran, 57 years, 9 February 2013, Harare.
59. *Ibid.*

Chapter 7

1. D. Cowderoy and R.C. Nesbit, *War in the Air*, p. 194.
2. W. Beverly, *A Pride*, p. 53.
3. P.L. Moorcraft and P. McLaughlin, *Chimurenga!*, pp. 69–70.
4. Rhodesia Parliamentary Debates, Vol. 73, No. 17, 16 April 1969, pp. 1062–3.
5. Rhodesia Parliamentary Debates, Vol. 77, First Session-Twelfth Parliament, 11 June 1970, pp. 438–39.
6. *Ibid.*
7. Rhodesia Parliamentary Debates, Vol. 99, 20 December 1978, p. 1874.
8. Report of the Secretary for Law and Order for the Year Ended 31 December 1964, p. 3. The name PCC was adopted after ZAPU had been banned by the Smith regime.

9. Rhodesia Parliamentary Debates, Vol. 97, First Session-Fourteenth Parliament, 19 September 1977, pp. 13–14.
10. Rhodesia Parliamentary Debates, Vol. 81, Third Session-Twelfth Parliament, 9 June 1972, p. 302.
11. Rhodesia Parliamentary Debates, Vol. 99, Second Session-Fourteenth Parliament, 20 December 1978, p. 1892. See also *The Herald*, 19 December 1978.
12. *Ibid.*, p. 1893.
13. *Ibid.*
14. *Ibid.*, p. 1894.
15. *Ibid.*
16. A. Astrow, *Zimbabwe: A Revolution That Lost Its Way?* (London: Zed Press, 1983), p. 75.
17. P.L. Moorcraft, P.L. Moorcraft, *A Short Thousand Years: The End of Rhodesia's Rebellion* (Salisbury: Galaxie Press, 1979), p. 164.
18. Rhodesia Parliamentary Debates, Vol. 73, No. 17, 16 April 1969, p. 1061.
19. *Ibid.*, p. 1062.
20. Report of the Secretary for Law and Order for the Year Ended 31 December 1968, p. 1.
21. Rhodesia Parliamentary Debates, Vol. 81, Third Session-Twelfth Parliament, 2 June 1972, pp. 3–4.
22. Rhodesia Parliamentary Debates, Vol. 81, Third Session-Twelfth Parliament, 16 June 1972, p. 670.
23. *Ibid.*, p. 671.
24. Rhodesia Parliamentary Debates, Vol. 73, No. 17, 16 April 1969, p. 1086.
25. *Sunday Mail*, 26 May 1974, p. 1.
26. Rhodesia Parliamentary Debates, Vol. 94, Third Session-Thirteenth Parliament, 24 August 1976, p. 1252.
27. Rhodesia Parliamentary Debates, Vol. 81, Third Session-Twelfth Parliament, 8 June 1972, p. 273.
28. Zambia Parliamentary Debates, Fourth Session-Third National Assembly, 8 February 1977, p. 1509.
29. R.M. Citino, *The Path to Blitzkrieg: Doctrine and Training in the German Army, 1920–1939* (Boulder, CO: Lynne Rienner Publishers, 1999), p. 1.
30. D. Thomson, *England in the Twentieth Century*, pp. 195–197.
31. *Ibid.*
32. S. Monick, "The Rhodesian Air Force," p. 25.
33. *Ibid.*
34. *Ibid.*
35. http://www.rhodesianforces.org/AntiTerroristOps.htm (Accessed 20 December 2012).
36. *Ibid.*
37. *Ibid.*
38. Hoffman, Taw, Arnold, *Lessons*, p. 22.
39. W. Beverly, *A Pride*, p. 53.
40. *Sunday Mail*, 26 May 1974, p. 2.
41. P. Stiff, *See You in November*, p. 215.
42. K. Flower, *Serving Secretly*, p. 213.
43. *Ibid.*
44. W. Beverly, *A Pride*, p. 5.
45. *Ibid.*
46. *Ibid.*, p. 61.
47. Annual Reports of the Secretary for Defence, The Chief of General Staff and Chief of Air Staff, 1967, p. 8.
48. Annual Reports of the Secretary for Defence, The Chief of General Staff and Chief of Air Staff, 1968, p. 8.
49. Rhodesia Parliamentary Debates, Vol. 76, Fifth Session-Eleventh Parliament, 14 November 1969, p. 1371.
50. *Ibid.*
51. Debates of the Federal Assembly, Vol. 18, First Session-Third Parliament, 5 July 1962, p. 441.
52. *Ibid.*
53. Debates of the Federal Assembly, Vol. 13, Second Session-Second Parliament, 26 July 1960, p. 1825.
54. Annual Reports of the Secretary for Defence, The Chief of General Staff and Chief of Air Staff, 1968, p. 8.
55. Annual Reports of the Secretary of Defence, the Commander of the Army and the Commander of the Air Force for the year ended 31 December 1972, p. 8. The shortage was attributed to high standards in the force and it remained imperative to retain that essential cadre of a high level of professional skill on which an effective Air Force could be built. See page 8.
56. *Bateleur*, The newspaper of the Air Force, Salisbury, April 1977, p. 1.
57. Debates of the Federal Assembly, Vol. 10, First Session-Second Parliament, 14 April 1959, p. 249.
58. Federation of Rhodesia and Nyasaland, Debates of the Federal Assembly, Vol. 10, 20 July 1959, p. 1635.
59. *Ibid.*
60. Rhodesia Parliamentary Debates, Vol. 84, Fourth Session-Twelfth Parliament, 25 July 1973, p. 810.
61. NAZ RG 3/AIR 61 RhAF Flight.
62. M. Evans, "The Wretched of the Empire: Politics, Ideology and Counterinsurgency in Rhodesia, 1965–80," in *Small Wars and Insurgencies* (London: Routledge, 2007), p. 179–180.

63. P. Godwin and I. Hancock, "*Rhodesians Never Die*," p. 6.
64. *Bateleur*, The Newspaper of the Air Force, Salisbury, August 1979, p. 2.
65. *Ibid*.
66. Rhodesia Parliamentary Debates, Vol. 97, First Session-Fourteenth Parliament, 5 October 1977, p. 644.
67. Rhodesia Parliamentary Debates, Vol. 97, First Session-Fourteenth Parliament, 12 October 1977, p. 979.
68. *Bush Telegraph* 1, No. 7, 24 December 1976, p. 1.
69. Southern Rhodesia Report on Department of Defence 1948, p. 8. It also needs to be highlighted that the color bar immensely applied to the recruitment process in the RSF.
70. *Ibid*.
71. Rhodesia Parliamentary Debates, Vol. 77, First Session-Twelfth Parliament, 11 June 1970, p. 438.
72. P. Godwin and I. Hancock, "*Rhodesians Never Die*," p. 88. Territorials were civilians who had completed military training but remained liable for call-up.
73. W. Beverly, *A Pride*, p. 99.
74. *Bush Telegraph* 2, No. 8, 24 April 1977, p. 1.
75. Rhodesia Parliamentary Debates, Vol. 94, Third Session-Thirteenth Parliament, 24 August 1976, p. 1253.
76. Rhodesia Parliamentary Debates, Vol. 77, 11 August 1970, p. 1497.
77. *Ibid*., p. 1498.
78. *Ibid*.
79. *Umtali Post*, 7 October 1977, p. 6.
80. *Ibid*.
81. *Ibid*.
82. *Ibid*.
83. Rhodesia Parliamentary Debates, Vol. 85, Fourth Session-Twelfth Parliament, 4 December 1973, pp. 1950–51.
84. *Ibid*., pp. 1951–52.
85. *Ibid*., p. 1953.
86. Rhodesia Parliamentary Debates, Vol. 94, Third Session-Thirteenth Parliament, 6 August 1976, p. 355.
87. *Ibid*., p. 356.
88. *Bateleur*, The newspaper of the Air Force, Salisbury, December 1979.
89. Zimbabwe Rhodesia Parliamentary Debates, Vol. 101, First Session-Fifteenth Parliament, 29 November 1979, p. 371.
90. Rhodesia Parliamentary Debates, Vol. 97, First Session-Fourteenth Parliament, 14 March 1978, pp. 2040–42.
91. *Ibid*., p. 2042.
92. J.K. Cilliers, *Counter-insurgency in Rhodesia*, p. 94.
93. Rhodesia Parliamentary Debates, Vol. 84, Fourth Session-Twelfth Parliament, 26 June 1973, p. 361.
94. *Rhodesia Herald*, 24 June 1974, p. 5.
95. J.K. Cilliers, *Counter-insurgency in Rhodesia*, p. 20.
96. Hoffman, Taw, and Arnold, *Lessons*, p. 25.
97. Parliamentary Debates, First Session, Fifteenth Parliament, Volume 100, 28 June 1979, pp. 97–98.
98. Rhodesia Parliamentary Debates, Vol. 83, Third Session-Twelfth Parliament, 29 March 1973, p. 1105.
99. NAZ S1949/2/5 Court of Inquiry: Accident to Harvard 163 NR.
100. *Ibid*.
101. *Ibid*.
102. NAZ F244/19/2/CAV: Accidents to aircraft reports.
103. *Ibid*.
104. Southern Rhodesia Report of the Commander Military Forces for the Year Ended 31 December 1951, p. 5.
105. NAZ S801/1 RATG 1943–1953.
106. *Ibid*.
107. Annual Reports of the Secretary for Defence, The Chief of General Staff and Chief of Air Staff, 1964, p. 11.
108. *Ibid*., p. 9.
109. NAZ RG 3/AIR 61 RhAF Flight.
110. Rhodesia Parliamentary Debates, Vol. 99, Second Session-Fourteenth Parliament, 1 September 1978, p. 978.
111. P. Godwin and I. Hancock, "*Rhodesians Never Die*," pp. 7–9.
112. D. Cowderoy and R.C. Nesbit, *War in the Air*, p. 220.
113. http://www.rhodesianforces.org/OperationUric.htm (Accessed 15 February 2013).
114. Rhodesia Parliamentary Debates, Vol. 81, Third Session-Twelfth Parliament, 8 June 1972, p. 269.
115. *Ibid*.
116. *Ibid*., p. 278.
117. Cowderoy and Nesbit argue that the RhAF was a remarkable fighting unit which at the height of the guerrilla war was probably the most skilled and experienced Air Force in the world in counterinsurgency operations. See page 194.
118. Southern Rhodesia Report on Department of Defence 1948, p. 8.
119. Rhodesia Nyasaland Annual Report of

the General Officer Commanding Central Africa Command for the Year Ending 31 December 1954, p. 8.
120. Southern Rhodesia Annual Report of the Commander of the Military Forces for the year ended 31 December 1949, p. 4.
121. Southern Rhodesia Annual Report of the Commander of the Military Forces for the year ended 31 December 1951, p. 6.
122. Debates of the Federal Assembly, Vol. 12, Second Session-Second Parliament, 19 July 1960, p. 1450.
123. W. Beverly, *A Pride of Eagles*, p. 15.
124. *Bateleur*, The newspaper of the Air Force, Salisbury, October 1977, p. 5.
125. *Ibid.*
126. Federation of Rhodesia and Nyasaland, Debates of the Federal Assembly, Vol. 10, 20 July 1959, p. 1634.
127. Annual Reports of the Secretary of Defence, the Commander of the Army and the Commander of the Air Force for the year ended 31 December 1972, p. 9.
128. *Ibid.*, p. 8.
129. *Ibid.*, p. 9.
130. *Ibid.*
131. *Ibid.*
132. *Bateleur*, The newspaper of the Air Force, Salisbury, December 1976, p. 2.
133. Rhodesia Parliamentary Debates, Vol. 99, Second Session-Fourteenth Parliament, 1 September 1978, p. 998.
134. K. Flower, *Serving Secretly*, p. 186. Of course it was a loss in the sense that the RSF failed to achieve their political and military objectives.
135. *Bateleur*, The Newspaper of the Air Force, Salisbury, December 1976, p. 2. No. 7 Squadron was equipped with Allouette III aircraft. It was responsible for troop transport, casualty evacuation (casevac) and battlefield support including fireforce.
136. *Ibid.*
137. *Ibid.*, p. 4.
138. Rhodesia Parliamentary Debates, Vol. 82, Third Session-Twelfth Parliament, 1 September 1972, p. 1079.
139. *Ibid.*
140. *Ibid.*, pp. 1079–1080.
141. NAZ F128/L135 Race affairs: Discrimination in military training.
142. *Sunday Mail*, March 31, 1974, p. 2.
143. *Ibid.*
144. *Ibid.*
145. Rhodesia Parliamentary Debates, Vol. 93, Third Session-Thirteenth Parliament, 20 July 1976, p. 1148.
146. *Ibid.*, p. 1147–48.
147. Rhodesia Parliamentary Debates, Vol. 93, Third Session-Thirteenth Parliament, 25 June 1976, p. 228.
148. Rhodesia Parliamentary Debates, Vol. 75, Fifth Session-Eleventh Parliament, 22 October 1969, p. 1751.
149. *Ibid.*
150. J.A. Ulio, "Military morale," *American Journal of Sociology* 47, No. 3 (1941): p. 321.
151. A.U. Pope, "The Importance of Morale," *Journal of Educational Sociology* 15, No. 4 (1941): p. 195.
152. *Ibid.*
153. E. Robson, "The Armed Forces and the Art of War," in *The New Cambridge Modern History: The Old Regime*, vol. 7 (Cambridge: Cambridge University Press, 1957), p. 178.
154. Rhodesia Parliamentary Debates, Vol. 99, Second Session-Fourteenth Parliament, 1 September 1978, p. 1011.
155. *Ndege*, May 1970, p. 4.
156. Annual Reports of the Secretary for Defence, the Chief of General Staff and Chief of Air Staff, Year 1969, p. 11.
157. P. Godwin and I. Hancock, *"Rhodesians Never Die,"* pp. 7–9.
158. P.L. Moorcraft, *A Short*, p. 4.

Chapter 8

1. P.L. Moorcraft, *A Short*, p. 165.
2. J. Nkomo, *The Story*, p. 173.
3. J. Brickhill, "Daring to storm the heavens," p. 59. Brickhill himself has attempted to give a brief outline of the Zero Hour Plan and this chapter will not repeat the same.
4. Hoffman, Taw, and Arnold, *Lessons*, p. 9.
5. E.M. Sibanda, *The Zimbabwe African People's Union, 1961–87*, p. 197.
6. *Ibid.*
7. *Ibid.*, p. 198.
8. Hoffman, Taw, and Arnold, *Lessons*, p. 9.
9. J. Brickhill, "Daring to storm the heavens," p. 59.
10. J. Brickhill, "Daring to storm the heavens," p. 60.
11. *Ibid.*, p. 59.
12. J. Cilliers, *Counter-Insurgency in Rhodesia*, p. 191.
13. J. Cilliers, *Counter-insurgency in Rhodesia*, p. 190.
14. P.L. Moorcraft, *A Short*, p. 164.
15. D. Thompson, *England in the 20th Century 1914–1963* (Middlesex: Penguin Books, 1965), p. 192.
16. I. Martinez, "The History of the Use of

Bacteriological and Chemical Agents during Zimbabwe's Liberation War," p. 1161.
17. Hoffman, Taw, and Arnold, *Lessons*, p. 33.
18. *Ibid.*, pp. 33–34.
19. *Ibid.*, p. 9.
20. *Ibid.*, p. 24.
21. I. Martinez, "The History of the Use of Bacteriological and Chemical Agents during Zimbabwe's Liberation War," pp. 1161–62.
22. *Ibid.*, p. 1162.
23. S. Mubako, "The Quest for Unity in the Zimbabwe Liberation Movement," *Issue: A Journal of Opinion* 5, No. 1 (1975): p. 8.
24. *Ibid.*, pp. 8–9.
25. I. D. Smith, *The Great Betrayal*, p. 383. See also J. Brickhill, "Making peace with the past: War victims and the work of the Mafela Trust," in N. Bhebe and T.O. Ranger, eds., *Soldiers in Zimbabwe's Liberation War*, vol. 1, pp. 164–165.
26. J. Brickhill, "Making peace," p. 165.
27. P. Godwin, *Mukiwa*, p. 20.
28. Zimbabwe Press Statement 507/83/SK/JM.
29. *Ibid.*
30. A. Clayton, *Frontiersmen: Warfare in Africa since 1950* (London: University College Press, 1998), p. 67.
31. B. Salt, *A Pride of Eagles: A History of the Rhodesian Air Force* (Solihull: Helion, 2012), p. 670.
32. J. Cilliers, *Counter-Insurgency in Rhodesia*, p. 196.
33. P. Godwin and I. Hancock, *"Rhodesians Never Die,"* p. 245.
34. J. Cilliers, *Counter-Insurgency in Rhodesia*, p. 190.
35. *Ibid.* p. 188.
36. M. Thomson, "Did UK warn Mugabe and Nkomo about assassination attempts?," 1 August 2011. http://www.bbc.co.uk/news/world-africa-14311834 (Accessed January 2013).
37. Callistus Ndlovu, interviewed by Mary Ndlovu on behalf of South African History Archive on 6 July 2011, Bulawayo.
38. *Ibid.*
39. P. Stiff, *See You in November*, p. 222.
40. Rhodesia Parliamentary Debates, Vol. 81, Third Session-Twelfth Parliament, 8 June 1972, p. 273.
41. J. Cilliers, *Counter-Insurgency in Rhodesia*, p. 198.
42. Flight International, Service Aviation: Air Force, Naval and Army Flying News, 4 June 1964, p. 945.
43. www.air-britain.com/zambia.pdf (Accessed August 2015).

44. J. Cilliers, *Counter-Insurgency in Rhodesia*, p. 188.
45. U. Nacciarone, SJ, *Accidental African Blessings: A Memoir* (Bloomington, IN: Xlibris Corporation, 2012).
46. K. Flower, *Serving Secretly*, p. 186.
47. D. Dabengwa, "ZIPRA in the Zimbabwe War of National Liberation," in N. Bhebe and T.O. Ranger, eds., *Soldiers in Zimbabwe's Liberation War*, vol. 1, p. 35.
48. J. Brickhill, "Daring to storm the heavens," p. 53.
49. Rhodesia Parliamentary Debates, 3rd Session-12th Parliament, Vol. 82, 1 September 1972, p. 1080.
50. Debates of the Federal Assembly, 1st Session-1st Parliament, Vol. 3, 18 August 1954, p. 2975.
51. *Ibid.*, p. 2981.
52. P. Abbott and P. Botham, *Modern African Wars (1): Rhodesia 1965–80* (Oxford: Osprey Publishing, 1986), p. 13.
53. J. Cilliers, *Counter-insurgency in Rhodesia*, p. 37.
54. A. Clayton, *Frontiersmen*, p. 67.
55. P.L. Moorcraft, *A Short*, p. 164.
56. P. Abbott and P. Botham, *Modern African Wars (1)*, p. 13.
57. J. Cilliers, *Counter-Insurgency in Rhodesia*, p. 199.
58. *Ibid.*, p. 188.
59. T. Kulkarni and A. Sinha, "India's Credible Minimum Deterrence: A Decade Later," Nuclear Security Programme, IPCS Issue Brief 179, New Delhi 2011, p. 1.
60. *Ibid.*
61. *Rhodesia Herald*, May 18, 1974, p. 1.
62. *Rhodesia Herald*, June 15, 1974, p. 6.
63. http://www.wilsoncenter.org/publication/robert-mugabe-and-todor-zhivkov (Accessed November 2013).
64. Vladimir Shubin, *The Hot "Cold War": The USSR in Southern Africa* (London: Pluto Press, 2008). Review by Lt. Col. (Prof.) Deon Visser, Department of Military History, Faculty of Military Science, Stellenbosch University.
65. J. McAdam, "The Flying," p. 44.
66. NAZ S482/471/39 Southern Rhodesian Air Force.
67. *Ibid.*
68. *Ibid.*
69. S1949/3/44 Provision of supplies from the Union.
70. Rhodesia Parliamentary Debates, Vol. 81, Third Session-Twelfth Parliament, 21 June 1972, p. 884.
71. *Ibid.*

72. J. Sprack, *Rhodesia: South Africa's Sixth Province, An analysis of the links between South Africa* (London: International Defence and Aid Fund, 1974), p. 62.
73. *Ibid.*, p. 63.
74. S. Pettis, "The Role of Air Power in the Rhodesian Bush War, 1965–1980." http://www.air power.maxwell.af.mil/airchronicles/cc/pettis.html (Accessed May 2012).
75. Rhodesia Parliamentary Debates, The Senate, Vol. 7, Second Session-Thirteenth Parliament, 22 August 1975, p. 709.
76. Rhodesia Parliamentary Debates, Vol. 94, Third Session-Thirteenth Parliament, 24 August 1976, p. 1251.
77. R. Weiss and J.L. Parpart, *Sir Garfield Todd and the Making of Zimbabwe* (London: British Academic Press, 1999), p. 195. There are arguments between the former guerrilla armies over who set alight the Salisbury fuel tanks. ZPRA claims to be the architects of the plan.
78. Rhodesia Parliamentary Debates, Vol. 99, 20 December 1978, pp. 1834–1835.
79. J. Cilliers, *Counter-Insurgency in Rhodesia*, p. 49.
80. *Bateleur*, The newspaper of the Air Force, Salisbury, April 1979, p. 3.
81. Southern Rhodesia Parliamentary Debates, Vol. 99, 19 December 1978, Second Session-Fourteenth Parliament, p. 1839.
82. *Bateleur*, The newspaper of the Air Force, Salisbury, September 1978, p. 4.
83. Annual Reports of the Secretary for Defence, the Chief of General Staff and Chief of Air Staff, 1970, p. 14.
84. D. Cowderoy and R.C. Nesbit, *War in the Air*, p. 37.

Chapter 9

1. See K.D. Manungo, "The Role Peasants Played in the Zimbabwe's War of Liberation, with Special Emphasis on Chiweshe District," Ph.D. dissertation, Ohio University, 1991.
2. M. Hove, "War legacy: A reflection on the effects of the Rhodesian Security Forces (RSF) in southeastern Zimbabwe during Zimbabwe's war of liberation 1976–1980," *Journal of African Studies and Development* 4, No. 8 (2012): p. 194. Hove's research in southeastern Zimbabwe reached the conclusion that civilians joined the war through voluntary and involuntary means. The researcher took this stance so as to reveal the recruitment strategies that were used in all parts of the country during the liberation war.
3. B. Cole, *The Elite*, p. 492.
4. Report of the Secretary for Native Affairs and Chief Native Commissioner for the Year 1938, Attached Reports of the Director of Native Education, the Native Land Board, the Agriculturalist of the Native Department and the Director of Irrigation (on water supplies in Native Reserves), p. 14.
5. Third Report of the Select Committee on Education, 16 April 1969, p. 1.
6. Rhodesia Parliamentary Debates, Vol. 80, Second Session-Twelfth Parliament, 1 September 1970, p. 371.
7. Third Report of the Select Committee on Education, 16 April 1969, p. 2. In fact, the amount spent on European education was way above on the basis that the European population constituted an insignificant figure of the total population.
8. Rhodesia Parliamentary Debates, Vol. 80, Second Session-Twelfth Parliament, 1 September 1970, pp. 369–70.
9. *Ibid.*, p. 370. There were two divisions in the ministry, one for African education and the other for European education.
10. *Rhodesia Herald*, 24 June 1974, p. 5.
11. Rhodesia Parliamentary Debates, Vol. 97, First Session-Fourteenth Parliament, 19 September 1977, p. 15.
12. Parliament of Rhodesia Third Report of the Select Committee on Education, 16 April 1969, p. 1.
13. *Ibid.*, p. 6.
14. *Ibid.*
15. Rhodesia Parliamentary Debates, Vol. 97, First Session-Fourteenth Parliament, 19 September 1977, p. 14.
16. *Rhodesia Herald*, 1 October 1976.
17. Rhodesia Parliamentary Debates, Vol. 97, First Session-Fourteenth Parliament, 12 October 1977, p. 983.
18. B. Salt, *A Pride of Eagles*, p. 485.
19. *Ibid.*, p. 491. See also Godwin and Hancock (pp. 85–86) on the reaction of the government to the attack of Altena farm. The incident immediately led to Operation Hurricane in the northeast.
20. Rhodesia Parliamentary Debates, Vol. 93, Third Session-Thirteenth Parliament, 25 June 1976, p. 242.
21. Zimbabwe Press Statement 372/89/MS/CC/EMM.
22. Rhodesia Parliamentary Debates, Vol. 86, Fourth Session-Twelfth Parliament, 28 March 1974, pp. 463–64.
23. *Ibid.*, pp. 442–43.
24. Rhodesia Parliamentary Debates, Vol.

83, Third Session-Twelfth Parliament, 29 March 1973, pp. 1076–77.
25. Rhodesia Parliamentary Debates, Vol. 99, Second Session-Fourteenth Parliament, 21 February 1979, p. 2897.
26. I. Martinez, "The History of the Use of Bacteriological and Chemical Agents during Zimbabwe's Liberation War," p. 1161.
27. B. Cole, *The Elite*, p. 12.
28. B. Salt, *A Pride of Eagles*, p. 491.
29. P.R. Warhurst, "The History of Race Relations in Rhodesia," *Zambezia* 3, No. 1, December 1973, p. 18.
30. *Ibid*.
31. Rhodesia Parliamentary Debates, Vol. 83, Third Session-Twelfth Parliament, 21 November 1972, pp. 60–62.
32. Parliamentary Debates, House of Assembly, Second Session-Thirteenth Parliament, 25 June 1975, pp. 14–15.
33. *Ibid*., p. 21.
34. J. Sprack, *Rhodesia*, p. 30.
35. *Ibid*., p. 31.
36. D. Moyo, "From Rhodesia to Zimbabwe: Change without Change? Broadcasting Policy Reform and Political Control," in H. Melber, ed., *Media, Public Discourse and Political Contestation in Zimbabwe* (Uppsala: Nordiska Afrikainstitutet, 2004), p. 26.
37. Rhodesia Parliamentary Debates, Vol. 93, Third Session-Thirteenth Parliament, 2 July 1976, p. 543.
38. *Umtali Post*, 27 November 1977, p. 1.
39. Rhodesia Parliamentary Debates, Vol. 97, First Session-Fourteenth Parliament, 22 February 1978, p. 2235.
40. *Ibid*., p. 2239.
41. *Ibid*., p. 2244.
42. *Ibid*., p. 2245.
43. Rhodesia Parliamentary Debates, Vol. 97, First Session-Fourteenth Parliament, 19 September 1977, p. 13.
44. *Bantu Mirror*, 18 March 1961.
45. Rhodesia Parliamentary Debates, Vol. 99, 19 December 1978, p. 1778.
46. *Bantu Mirror*, 15 April 1961.
47. P.R. Warhurst, "The History of Race Relations in Rhodesia," p. 18.
48. *Ibid*., p. 19.
49. D. Mutanda, "The Local Media and Zimbabwe's Land Reform Program," *Journal of Sustainable Development in Africa* 14, No. 3 (2012): p. 266. See also Southern Rhodesia Legislative Assembly Second Report of the Select Committee on Resettlement of Natives, 16 August 1960, p. 49.
50. *Ibid*.

51. *Ibid*. See also Southern Rhodesia Sabi-Lundi Development Second Interim Report, June 1948, p. 5.
52. D. Mutanda, "The Local Media," p. 266. See also Rhodesia Parliament, Third Report of the Estimates Committee-The Mining Aspect of the Mining of Mines and Land, 16 January 1969, p. 4.
53. Rhodesia Parliamentary Debates, Vol. 75, Fifth Session-Eleventh Parliament, 10 October 1969, p. 1351.
54. K. Flower, *Serving Secretly*, p. 191.
55. Catholic Commission for Justice and Peace in Rhodesia, *The Man in the Middle: Torture, Resettlement and Eviction* (Harare: Strand Multiprint, 1999), pp. 5–6.
56. Rhodesia Parliamentary Debates, Vol. 97, First Session-Fourteenth Parliament, 28 September 1977, p. 243.
57. Rhodesia Parliamentary Debates, Vol. 99, Second Session-Fourteenth Parliament, 1 September 1978, pp. 998–9.
58. Rhodesia Parliamentary Debates, Vol. 93, Third Session-Thirteenth Parliament, 25 June 1976, pp. 240–1.
59. *Ibid*.
60. Rhodesia Parliamentary Debates, Vol. 99, Second Session-Fourteenth Parliament, 9 February 1979, p. 2533. Security Force Auxiliaries was a militia made up of local Africans to guard their own villages. Auxiliaries had divided allegiances, some belonging to Muzorewa, others to Sithole and others to ZANU. They were created to address manpower challenges facing the RSF.
61. Rhodesia Parliamentary Debates, Vol. 99, Second Session-Fourteenth Parliament, 30 August 1979, p. 731.
62. *The Zimbabwe People's Voice—Official Organ of the ZAPU*, June 25, 1977, p. 3.
63. *Ibid*., p. 4.
64. *Ibid*., p. 3.
65. *Rhodesia Herald*, 15 June 1974, p. 6. The evidence was obtained from a letter written to the *Rhodesia Herald* by Tichawona Zuikapera.
66. Interview with Jonah Jegede, 80 years, 9 April 2012, Zaka District.
67. Interview with Chipiwa Mutake (pseudonym), approx. 88 years, 7 April 2012, Zaka District.
68. Interview with Livison Makamu, 57 years, 25 June 2012, Chisuma Business Centre.
69. Interview with Themba Nyati, 69 years, 2 July 2012, Chisuma Business Centre.
70. D. Cowderoy and R.C. Nesbit, *War in the Air*, p. 69.

71. Anti-Apartheid Movement, *Fireforce Exposed*, p. 27.
72. Interview with Sophia Chinyerani, approx. 80 years, 8 April 2012, Zaka District.
73. Interview with Mufandigere, approx. 73 years, 6 April 2012, Zaka District.
74. Interview with Petros Jeketera, approx. 68 years, 6 April 2012, Zaka District. Musa was a guerrilla leader who was light in complexion and a distinguished soldier mostly sought after by the RSF. The boy killed was a son of Jamukoko and his complexion was like Musa, which possibly caused him to be killed.
75. Rhodesia Parliamentary Debates, Vol. 97, First Session-Fourteenth Parliament, 14 March 1978, p. 2235.
76. Anti-Apartheid Movement, *Fireforce Exposed*, p. 27.
77. Rhodesia Parliamentary Debates, Vol. 97, First Session-Fourteenth Parliament, 22 February 1978, p. 2234.
78. *Ibid.*, pp. 2234–35.
79. *Ibid.*, p. 2235.
80. Interview with Easygo Mamboininga, war veteran, 55 years, 5 February 2013, Harare.

Chapter 10

1. A.D. Davis, "Back to the Basics An Aviation Solution to Counterinsurgent Warfare," Air Wright Flyer Paper No. 23, Command and Staff College, Air University Press, Maxwell Air Force Base, Alabama, December 2005, p. 1. http://research.maxwell.af.mil (Accessed June 2012).
2. King's College London and Richard Spencer, "What does Turkey's involvement in air strikes mean for Kurds, ISIL, Syria and NATO?," *The Telegraph*, 29 July 2015. http://www.telegraph.co.uk/news/worldnews/europe/turkey/11769463/What-does-Turkeys-involvement-in-air-strikes-mean-for-Kurds-Isil-Syria-and-Nato.html (Accessed July 2015).
3. H. Pamuk and N. Tattersall, "Turkey launches heaviest air strikes yet on PKK, stoking Kurdish ire," Reuters, 29 July 2015. http://www.reuters.com/article/2015/07/29/us-mideast-crisis-turkey-idUSKCN0Q30OF20150729 (Accessed July 2015).
4. J. Miller, "Strategic Significance of Drone Operations for Warfare," 19 August 2013. http://www.e-ir.info/2013/08/19/strategic-significance-of-drone-operations-for-warfare/ (Accessed July 2015).
5. J. Serle, "Drone Warfare in Pakistan, Yemen and Somalia. Surge in CIA Strikes," *Global Research*, 8 May 2015. http://www.globalresearch.ca/drone-warfare-in-pakistan-yemen-and-somalia-surge-in-cia-strikes/5448065 (Accessed July 2015).
6. A.D. Davis, "Back to the Basics: An Aviation Solution to Counterinsurgent Warfare," p. 5.
7. J. Kiras, "Irregular Warfare," in D. Jordan, J. Kiras, D. Lonsdale, I. Speller, C. Tuck and C.D. Walton, *Understanding Modern Warfare* (Cambridge: Cambridge University Press, 2008), p. 232.
8. *Ibid.*, pp. 231–232.
9. P. Sturges, "Information in the national liberation struggle: developing a model," *Journal of Documentation* 60, No. 4 (2004): p. 433.
10. W. Laqueur, "The Origins of Guerrilla Doctrine," *Journal of Contemporary History* 10, No. 3, 1975, p. 363.
11. *Ibid.*, pp. 377–78.
12. *Ibid.*, p. 378.
13. P.D. Hoffman, "Seeking Shadows in the Sky: The Strategy of Air Guerrilla Warfare," Air University, Maxwell Air Force Base, Alabama, June 2000, pp. 20–21. www.au.af.mil/au/awc/awcgate/saas/hoffman (Accessed June 2012).
14. *Ibid.*, p. 33.
15. J. Cilliers, *Counter-Insurgency in Rhodesia*, p. 189.
16. M. Tse-tung, *On Guerrilla Warfare*, translated by Samuel B. Griffith III (Urbana: University of Illinois Press, 2000).
17. B.D. Cole and P.H.B. Godwin, "Advanced military technology and the PLA: Priorities and capabilities for the 21st century," in L.M. Wortzel, ed., *The Chinese Armed Forces in the 21st Century*, p. 160.
18. W. Laqueur, *Guerrilla: A Historical and Critical Study* (London: Weidenfeld and Nicolson, 1977), pp. vi–vii.
19. Guerrilla warfare advocates in the United States, Report by the Committee on Un-American activities, House of Representatives, Ninetieth Congress, Second Session, Washington, D.C., May 6, 1968, p. 4.
20. *Ibid.*, pp. 4–5. The Communists in Yugoslavia were also defeated.
21. Guerrilla warfare advocates, pp. 8–9.
22. G. Beck, "Offensive Air Power in Counter-Insurgency Operations: Putting Theory into Practice," Royal Australian Air Force, Air Power Development Centre, Working Paper 26, 2008, p. 5.
23. Hoffman, Taw, and Arnold, *Lessons*, p. 26.
24. F. Pretorius, "Napoleon Bonaparte," in T. Van Wijk and M.C. Van Zyl, eds., *Europe 1555–1848* (Pretoria: Academia, 1985), p. 388.

25. *Ibid.*
26. *Ibid.*, pp. 401–02.
27. C. Guevara, *Guerrilla Warfare* (New York: Monthly Review Press, 1961), p. 15.
28. M. Yardley, *Backing into the Limelight: A Biography of T.E. Lawrence* (London: Harrap, 1985), p. 108.
29. http://www.bbc.co.uk/history/historic_figures/lawrence_te.shtml (Accessed June 2015).
30. P.D. Hoffman, "Seeking," p. 29.
31. M. Klare and D. Volman, "America, China and the Scramble for Africa's Oil," in Ray Bush and Jeremy Keenan, eds., *North Africa: Power, Politics & Promise, Review of African Political Economy* 33, No. 108 (2006): p. 297.
32. A.R. Wilkinson, "Political violence, counter-insurgency and change in Rhodesia," p. 125.
33. *Ibid.*, p. 303.
34. B.D. Cole and P.H.B. Godwin, "Advanced military technology and the PLA," p. 201.
35. K.D. Huebert, "The Role of Air Power in Irregular Warfare for the 21st Century," Master's thesis, Naval Postgraduate School, Monterey, California, December 2009, p. 1. www.dtic.mil/dtic/tr/fulltext/u2/a514119 (Accessed June 2012).
36. D. Shunk, "Primer on Russian Afghan War, 1979–1989, Lessons learned," 2008, p. 3. http://dnipogo.org/wp-content/uploads/2009/01/primer_on_afghan_war.pdf (Accessed 9 December 2014).
37. *Ibid.*, p. 4.
38. P. Gelling, K. Kim and T. McGrath, "A comprehensive 54-step guide to how the U.S. ruined Iraq," *Global Post*, 13 June 2014. http://www.globalpost.com/dispatch/news/regions/middle-east/iraq/140611/how-us-helped-turn-iraq-into-al-qaeda-haven-53-steps-isis-isil-syria-bush-obama (Accessed October 2014).
39. NATO: International Security Assistance Force, Facts and Figures, 15 May 2012. www.nato.int/isaf/docu/epub/pdf/placemat.pdf (Accessed June 2012).
40. R. Archer, *Vietnam: The Habit of War* (London: Catholic Institute for International Relations, 1983), pp. 13–15.
41. J. Buttinger, *Vietnam: A Political History* (London: Andre Deutsch, 1969), p. 357.
42. *Ibid.*
43. *Ibid.*
44. Abigail Pfeiffer, "Air power in Vietnam: A Strategic Bombing Analysis." http://www.abigailpfeiffer.com/2011/09 (Accessed June 2011).
45. M.K. Hall, *Vietnam War*, 2nd ed. (Harlow: Pearson Education, 2008), p. 3.
46. A. Pfeiffer, "Air power in Vietnam: A Strategic Bombing Analysis," p. 27.
47. K.D. Huebert, "The Role of Air Power in Irregular Warfare for the 21st Century," p. 31. The strategy is known as air guerrilla warfare.
48. R. Archer, *Vietnam*, pp. 27–28.
49. *Ibid.*
50. Guerrilla warfare advocates in the United States, p. 4.
51. Guerilbow, "Air Power—Douhet's Theory and Afghanistan," 2010. http://guerrillawartactics.blogspot.com/2010/08/air-power-douhets-theory-and.html (Accessed June 2012).
52. K.D. Huebert, "The Role of Air Power in Irregular Warfare for the 21st Century," pp. 18–19.
53. MercyCorps, "Quick facts: What you need to know about the Syria crisis," 15 May 2015. http://www.mercycorps.org/articles/turkey-iraq-jordan-lebanon-syria/quick-facts-what-you-need-know-about-syria-crisis (Accessed May 2015).
54. B. Aras and S. Akarçeşme, "Turkey and the Arab Spring," *International Journal* 67, No. 1 (Winter 2011–12), Special issue: Charting the new Turkish foreign policy.
55. K. Mohja, *Then and Now: The Syrian Revolution to Date: A Young Nonviolent Resistance and the Ensuing Armed Struggle*: A Special Report from Friends for a Nonviolent World (St. Paul: Friends for a Nonviolent World, 2013).
56. *Ibid.*, p. 4.
57. G. Greenwald, "After Feigning Love for Egyptian Democracy, U.S. Back to Openly Supporting Tyranny," 10 February 2014. https://firstlook.org/theintercept/2014/10/02/feigned-american-support-egyptian-democracy-lasted-roughly-six-weeks/ (Accessed December 2014).
58. *Daily News*, "Egypt court dismisses charges against Mubarak," 30 November 2014, p. 6.
59. R., Hall, "The refugee from Homs who can hardly afford to feed his family," 16 March 2015, *Global Post*. http://www.globalpost.com/dispatch/news/regions/middle-east/syria/150316/four-years-four-lives-the-refugee-homs-struggling-fee (Accessed March 2015).
60. P. Kingsley and M. Chulov, "Mohamed Morsi ousted in Egypt's second revolution in two years," *The Guardian*, 4 July 2013. http://www.theguardian.com/world/2013/jul/03/-mohamed-morsi-egypt-second-revolution (Accessed December 2014).
61. *Ibid.*

62. Press TV, "Morsi's trial over espionage charges postponed to March 26," 25 March 2015. http://www.presstv.ir/Detail/2015/03/25/403368/Morsis-Qatar-espionage-trial-adjourned (Accessed April 2015).

63. *Daily News*, "Egypt court dismisses charges against Mubarak," p. 6.

64. *Ibid*.

65. E. Boxx, "Observations on the Air War in Syria," *Air & Space Power Journal*, 2013, p. 147.

66. E. Boxx and J. White, "Responding to Assad's Use of Air Power in Syria," The Washington Institute, 2012. http://www.washingtoninstitute.org/policy-analysis/view/responding-to-assads-use-of-air power-in-syria (Accessed December 2014).

67. The terms ISIL, ISIS and IS are interchangeably used by writers and commentators.

68. M. Hove and D. Mutanda, "The Syrian Conflict 2011 to the Present: Challenges and Prospects," *Journal of Asian and African Studies* (2014), published online on 5 December 2014, p. 8.

69. https://securityintelligence.com/funding-terrorists-the-rise-of-isis/ (Accessed August 2015).

70. C. McDonald-Gibson, "War with ISIS: U.S. hails 'significant impact' of bombing raids but Syria's President Assad is not so sure," *The Independent*, 3 December 2014. http://www.independent.co.uk/news/world/middle-east/war-with-isis-us-hails-significant-impact-of-bombing-raids-but-syrias-president-assad-is-not-so-sure-9901605.html (Accessed 8 December 2014).

71. *Ibid*. Assad was not included to be part of the coalition fighting against the Islamic State because the U.S.'s primary mission was to topple him, yet their actions partly helped to prop him up.

72. J. Lederman, "War with ISIS: U.S. investigating chemical weapons attacks against Kurds in Iraq," *The Independent*, 14 August 2015. http://www.independent.co.uk/news/world/middle-east/war-with-isis-us-investigating-chemical-weapons-attacks-against-kurds-in-iraq-10456619.html (Accessed August 2015).

73. Amnesty International, *Libya: The Forgotten Victims of NATO Strikes* (London: Amnesty International Publications, 2012), p. 5.

74. *Ibid*., p. 7.

75. G. Beck, "Offensive Air Power in Counter-Insurgency Operations: Putting Theory into Practice," pp. 1–2.

Conclusion

1. Mugabe said this when addressing the 5th day of the ZANU PF congress in Harare on 6 December 2014. He also said that opposition leader Morgan Tsvangirai had garnered 73 percent of the vote in the 2008 presidential poll.

Bibliography

Primary Sources

Archival Files (National Archives of Zimbabwe)

A312/695 Air Force Headquarters-Old stables 1931–1948.
F128/L135 Race affairs: Discrimination in military training.
F244/19/2/CAV: Accidents to aircraft reports.
RG 3/AIR 61 RhAF Flight Safety Bulletin, January 1979–June 1979.
S/AS72 Assegai: The Magazine of the Rhodesian Army 5, No. 1 (May 15, 1965).
S131/40 Medical Attention for Air Forces in Southern Rhodesia.
S1801 Rhodesia's war efforts.
S1948/1 Financial Statements Minister's Copy.
S1949/1/2 RATG General Correspondence.
S1949/2/1 Promotions: SRAF and RAAC, Airmen policy RAAC.
S1949/2/12 Letters of appreciation.
S1949/2/2 Amalgamation of air and defence.
S1949/2/3 Rhodesian Air Askari Corps: Employment of natives on skilled labour.
S1949/2/4 Supply of information for publication.
S1949/2/5 Court of Inquiry: Accident to Harvard 163 NR.
S1949/2/8 Aircraft-state owned Southern Rhodesian Government.
S1949/3/44 Provision of supplies from the Union
S1952 RATG Memoranda.
S1953/1 RATG Minutes: General 1940 Sep.–1945 Nov.
S1953/3 Munitions Production Board-Minutes of meetings.
S1959 Air Ministry and RATG Publications.
S1962/1 RATG Statistics.
S235/398 Labour.
S2785/18 CMF: Southern Rhodesia war book 1949 July 16–1950 November 6.
S2785/4 CMF/1 Possible RAF assistance to the SRAF 1949–1951.
S2786/1 Visit of Air Ministry Mission to Southern Rhodesia in May 1946.
S2919/1 RAAC Discharges 1939–45.
S2921/1–3 RAAC Record of service cards.
S3132 Agreement UK/Southern Rhodesia Government post war air training.
S3292/56/7/4 War Assets: Disposal of RATG Workshop Equipment to Messrs. Crowther and Perry, 1945–46.
S3292/56/9/1 War Expenditure general: 1939.
S3292/56/9/19 War expenditure: Government Stationery office: 1939.
S3302/28 Reinforcing Line: Finance 1942.
S3309/28 RATG: Transport Establishment and Control: 1942–44.
S3311/3 RATG Financial section standing instructions 1944–45.
S482/471/39 Southern Rhodesian Air Force.
S482/88/43 Emergency landing grounds.
S745/12 RATG Unit Orders.
S748 Postwar Air Training Scheme 1945.
S759/4 Southern Rhodesia Defence Scheme.
S801/1 RATG 1943–1953.
S802 Certificates.
S817 Orders 1947–1954.

Interviews

Chavhundura Benz (Mutero), war veteran, 55 years, 6 February 2013, Harare.
Chinovava, Dick (nom de guerre), war veteran, 66 years, 10 April 2012, Jerera Growth Point.
Chinyerani, Sophia, approx. 80 years, 8 April 2012, Zaka District.
Dhliwayo, Amon, 68 years, 1 July 2012, Chisuma Business Centre.
Dhliwayo, Peter, war veteran, 57 years, 1 July 2012, Chisuma Business Centre.

Jegede, Jonah, 80 years, 9 April 2012, Zaka District.
Jeketera, Petros, village head, approx. 68 years, 6 April 2012, Zaka District.
Kazambara, Kingstone (Lt. Col.), war veteran, 56 years, 14 February 2013, Harare.
Mai, Mataruse, 48 years, 10 September 2015, Harare.
Makamu, Livison, 57 years, 25 June 2012, Chisuma Business Centre.
Makomva, Margret, war veteran, 54 years, 5 February 2013, Harare.
Mamboininga, Easygo, war veteran, 55 years, 5 February 2013, Harare.
Maphosa, war veteran, approx. 56 years, 5 February 2013, Harare.
Mhizha, Peter, war veteran, approx. 50 years, 17 May 2012, Masvingo Urban.
Mtombeni, Titos, 55 years, 9 August 2012, Chisuma Business Centre.
Mufandigere, approx. 73 years, 6 April 2012, Zaka District.
Mutake, Chipiwa (pseudonym), approx. 88 years, 7 April 2012, Zaka District.
Mutsikapasi, Zimbabwe (pseudonym), war veteran, 72 years, 11 May 2012, Masvingo Urban.
Ndlovu, Callistus, interviewed by Mary Ndlovu on behalf of South African History Archive on 6 July 2011, Bulawayo.
Nyanga, Chrispen, war veteran, 57 years, 9 February 2013, Harare.
Nyati, Themba, 69 years, 2 July 2012, Chisuma Business Centre.
Zvenyika, Edmore, war veteran, 56 years, 8 February 2013, Harare.

Personal Communication

Makunike, Lovert, 21 years, 22 April 2012, Harare.

Official Publications, Parliamentary Debates and Reports

Advisory Commission on the Review of the Constitution of the Federation of Rhodesia and Nyasaland, Survey of Developments since 1953, London, 1959 (Report by Committee of Officials).
Annual Report Defence and Aviation 1932.
Annual Report Defence and Aviation 1933.
Annual Report Defence and Aviation 1934.
Annual Report of the Commander of the Military Forces for the year ended 31 December 1952.
Annual Reports of the Secretary for Defence, the Chief of General Staff and Chief of Air Staff, 1964.
Annual Reports of the Secretary for Defence, the Chief of General Staff and Chief of Air Staff, 1967.
Annual Reports of the Secretary for Defence, the Chief of General Staff and Chief of Air Staff, 1968.
Annual Reports of the Secretary for Defence, the Chief of General Staff and Chief of Air Staff, 1969.
Annual Reports of the Secretary for Defence, the Chief of General Staff and Chief of Air Staff, 1970.
Annual Reports of the Secretary of Defence, the Commander of the Army and the Commander of the Air Force for the year ended 31 December 1972.
Appendices I, II and III to the Report of the Apportionment Commission containing lists of assets and liabilities of the S. Rhodesian Government designated for transfer to the Federal Government.
Bateleur, the newspaper of the Air Force, Salisbury, April 1977.
Bateleur, The newspaper of the Air Force, Salisbury, April 1979.
Bateleur, The newspaper of the Air Force, Salisbury, December 1976.
Bateleur, The newspaper of the Air Force, Salisbury, December 1977.
Bateleur, The newspaper of the Air Force, Salisbury, January 1977.
Bateleur, The newspaper of the Air Force, Salisbury, November 1976.
Bateleur, The newspaper of the Air Force, Salisbury, October 1977.
Bateleur, The newspaper of the Air Force, Salisbury, September 1978.
Bush Telegraph, Vol. 1, No. 6, 7 December 1976.
Bush Telegraph, Vol. 1, No. 7, 24 December 1976.
Bush Telegraph, Vol. 2, No. 8, 24 April 1977.
Career Opportunities in the Rhodesian Air Force: Pilot Training Scheme.
Debates of the Federal Assembly, Vol. 2, First Session-First Parliament, 22 July 1954.
Debates of the Federal Assembly, Vol. 3, First Session-First Parliament, 18 August 1954.
Debates of the Federal Assembly, Vol. 5, Second Session-First Parliament, 28 February 1956.
Debates of the Federal Assembly, Vol. 5, Second Session-First Parliament, 21 March 1956.
Debates of the Federal Assembly, Vol. 6, Third Session-First Parliament, 31 July 1956.
Debates of the Federal Assembly, Vol. 6, Third Session-First Parliament, 1 August 1956.
Debates of the Federal Assembly, Vol. 8, Fourth Session-First Parliament, 29 July 1957.

Debates of the Federal Assembly, Vol. 8, Fourth Session-First Parliament, 1 August 1957.
Debates of the Federal Assembly, Vol. 9, Fifth Session-First Parliament, 21 July 1958.
Debates of the Federal Assembly, Vol. 10, First Session-Second Parliament, 21 July 1959.
Debates of the Federal Assembly, Vol. 10, First Session-Second Parliament, 9 April 1959.
Debates of the Federal Assembly, Vol. 10, First Session-Second Parliament, 14 April 1959.
Debates of the Federal Assembly, Vol. 10, First Session-Second Parliament, 29 June 1959.
Debates of the Federal Assembly, Vol. 10, First Session-Second Parliament, 2 July 1959.
Debates of the Federal Assembly, Vol. 10, First Session-Second Parliament, 20 July 1959.
Debates of the Federal Assembly, Vol. 11, First Session-Second Parliament, 19 November 1959.
Debates of the Federal Assembly, Vol. 12, Second Session-Second Parliament, 19 July 1960.
Debates of the Federal Assembly, Vol. 13, Second Session-Second Parliament, 26 July 1960.
Debates of the Federal Assembly, Vol. 14, Second Session-Second Parliament, 27 Feb. 1961.
Debates of the Federal Assembly, Vol. 15, Third Session-Second Parliament, 29 June 1961.
Debates of the Federal Assembly, Vol. 16, Third Session-Second Parliament, 4 September 1961.
Debates of the Federal Assembly, Vol. 16, Third Session-Second Parliament, 13 Sep. 1961.
Debates of the Federal Assembly, Vol. 16, Third Session-Second Parliament, 11 Sep. 1961.
Debates of the Federal Assembly, Vol. 17, Fourth Session-Second Parliament, 12 February 1962.
Debates of the Federal Assembly, Vol. 18, First Session-Third Parliament, 5 July 1962.
Debates of the Federal Assembly, Vol. 18, First Session-Third Parliament, 18 July 1962.
Estimates of Expenditure from Revenue Funds 1937–38.
Federation of Rhodesia and Nyasaland Economic Report, 1959.
Federation of Rhodesia and Nyasaland Economic Report, 1961.
Guerrilla warfare advocates in the United States, Report by the Committee on Un-American activities, House of Representatives, Ninetieth Congress, Second Session, Washington, D.C., May 6, 1968.
Ndege, May 1970.
Northern Rhodesia Legislative Council Debates, 3rd Session-3rd Council, 25 November 1930.
Northern Rhodesia Legislative Council Debates, 3rd Session-3rd Council, 18 November 1930.
Parliament of Rhodesia Third Report of the Select Committee on Education, 16 April 1969.
Report of the Commission on the siting of the capital of Southern Rhodesia, 1955.
Report of the Secretary for Law and Order for the Year Ended 31 December 1965.
Report of the Secretary for Law and Order for the Year Ended 31 December 1964.
Report of the Secretary for Law and Order for the Year Ended 31 December 1968.
Report of the Secretary for Native Affairs and Chief Native Commissioner for the year 1938, Attached Reports of the Director of Native Education, the Native Land Board, the Agriculturalist of the Native Department and the Director of Irrigation (on water supplies in Native Reserves).
Rhodesia Nyasaland Annual Report of the General Officer Commanding Central Africa Command for the Year Ending 31 December 1954.
Rhodesia-Nyasaland Royal Commission Report 1939, Presented to Parliament by Command of His Majesty, March 1939.
Rhodesia Nyasaland Second Supplementary Estimates of Expenditure for the year ending 30 June 1960.
Rhodesia Parliament, Third Report of the Estimates Committee-The Mining Aspect of the Mining of Mines and Land, 16 January 1969.
Rhodesia Parliamentary Debates, 1st Session-12th Parliament, Vol. 78, 6 April 1971.
Rhodesia Parliamentary Debates, 1st Session-12th Parliament, Vol. 77, 11 June 1970.
Rhodesia Parliamentary Debates, 3rd Session-12th Parliament, Vol. 82, 1 September 1972.
Rhodesia Parliamentary Debates, 3rd Session-13th Parliament, Vol. 94, 6 August 1976.
Rhodesia Parliamentary Debates, 3rd Session-13th Parliament, Vol. 94, 24 August 1976.
Rhodesia Parliamentary Debates, 5th Session-11th Parliament, Vol. 75, 27 August 1969.
Rhodesia Parliamentary Debates, The Senate, Vol. 7, Second Session-Thirteenth Parliament, 25 June 1975.
Rhodesia Parliamentary Debates, The Senate, Vol. 7, Second Session-Thirteenth Parliament, 22 August 1975.
Rhodesia Parliamentary Debates, Vol. 73, No. 17, 16 April 1969.
Rhodesia Parliamentary Debates, Vol. 75, Fifth

Session-Eleventh Parliament, 22 October 1969.
Rhodesia Parliamentary Debates, Vol. 75, Fifth Session-Eleventh Parliament, 10 October 1969.
Rhodesia Parliamentary Debates, Vol. 76, Fifth Session-Eleventh Parliament, 14 November 1969.
Rhodesia Parliamentary Debates, Vol. 77, 11 August 1970.
Rhodesia Parliamentary Debates, Vol. 77, First Session-Twelfth Parliament, 11 June 1970.
Rhodesia Parliamentary Debates, Vol. 80, Second Session-Twelfth Parliament, 1 September 1970.
Rhodesia Parliamentary Debates, Vol. 81, Third Session-Twelfth Parliament, 21 June 1972.
Rhodesia Parliamentary Debates, Vol. 81, Third Session-Twelfth Parliament, 2 June 1972.
Rhodesia Parliamentary Debates, Vol. 81, Third Session-Twelfth Parliament, 6 June 1972.
Rhodesia Parliamentary Debates, Vol. 81, Third Session-Twelfth Parliament, 8 June 1972.
Rhodesia Parliamentary Debates, Vol. 81, Third Session-Twelfth Parliament, 9 June 1972.
Rhodesia Parliamentary Debates, Vol. 81, Third Session-Twelfth Parliament, 16 June 1972.
Rhodesia Parliamentary Debates, Vol. 82, Third Session-Twelfth Parliament, 1 September 1972.
Rhodesia Parliamentary Debates, Vol. 83, Third Session-Twelfth Parliament, 21 Nov. 1972.
Rhodesia Parliamentary Debates, Vol. 83, Third Session-Twelfth Parliament, 29 March 1973.
Rhodesia Parliamentary Debates, Vol. 84, Fourth Session-Twelfth Parliament, 26 June 1973.
Rhodesia Parliamentary Debates, Vol. 84, Fourth Session-Twelfth Parliament, 25 July 1973.
Rhodesia Parliamentary Debates, Vol. 85, Fourth Session-Twelfth Parliament, 4 December 1973.
Rhodesia Parliamentary Debates, Vol. 86, Fourth Session-Twelfth Parliament, 28 March 1974.
Rhodesia Parliamentary Debates, House of Assembly, second session, 13th parliament, 25 June 1975.
Rhodesia Parliamentary Debates, Vol. 86, Fourth Session-Twelfth Parliament, 20 June 1974.
Rhodesia Parliamentary Debates, Vol. 93, Third Session-Thirteenth Parliament, 25 June 1976.
Rhodesia Parliamentary Debates, Vol. 93, Third Session-Thirteenth Parliament, 2 July 1976.
Rhodesia Parliamentary Debates, Vol. 93, Third Session-Thirteenth Parliament, 20 July 1976.
Rhodesia Parliamentary Debates, Vol. 94, Third Session-Thirteenth Parliament, 24 August 1976.
Rhodesia Parliamentary Debates, Vol. 94, Third Session-Thirteenth Parliament, 6 August 1976.
Rhodesia Parliamentary Debates, Vol. 97, First Session-Fourteenth Parliament, 21 Sep. 1977.
Rhodesia Parliamentary Debates, Vol. 97, First Session-Fourteenth Parliament, 5 October 1977.
Rhodesia Parliamentary Debates, Vol. 97, First Session-Fourteenth Parliament, 12 October 1977.
Rhodesia Parliamentary Debates, Vol. 97, First Session-Fourteenth Parliament, 14 March 1978.
Rhodesia Parliamentary Debates, Vol. 97, First Session-Fourteenth Parliament, 19 September 1977.
Rhodesia Parliamentary Debates, Vol. 97, First Session-Fourteenth Parliament, 28 September 1977.
Rhodesia Parliamentary Debates, Vol. 97, First Session-Fourteenth Parliament, 22 February 1978.
Rhodesia Parliamentary Debates, Vol. 99, 20 December 1978.
Rhodesia Parliamentary Debates, Vol. 99, Second Session-Fourteenth Parliament, 1 September 1978.
Rhodesia Parliamentary Debates, Vol. 99, Second Session-Fourteenth Parliament, 7 September 1978.
Rhodesia Parliamentary Debates, Vol. 99, Second Session-Fourteenth Parliament, 19 December 1978.
Rhodesia Parliamentary Debates, Vol. 99, Second Session-Fourteenth Parliament, 20 December 1978.
Rhodesia Parliamentary Debates, Vol. 99, Second Session-Fourteenth Parliament, 9 February 1979.
Rhodesia Parliamentary Debates, Vol. 99, Second Session-Fourteenth Parliament, 21 February 1979.
Rhodesia Parliamentary Debates, Vol. 99, Second Session-Fourteenth Parliament, 30 August 1979.
Southern Rhodesia Annual Report of the Commander Military Forces for the year ending 31 December 1953.
Southern Rhodesia Annual Report of the Commander of the Military Forces for the year ended 31 December 1949.

Southern Rhodesia Annual Report of the Commander of the Military Forces for the year ending 31 December 1950.
Southern Rhodesia Annual Report of the Commander of the Military Forces for the year ended 31 December 1951.
Southern Rhodesia Central African Statistical Office, Official year book of Southern Rhodesia, No. 4, 1952.
Southern Rhodesia Department of Supply Report for the year ended 31 December 1944.
Southern Rhodesia Legislative Assembly Debates, Vol. 21, Third Session, Fifth Parliament, 21 May 1941.
Southern Rhodesia Legislative Assembly Debates, Vol. 22, Fourth Session, Fifth Parliament, 27 April 1942.
Southern Rhodesia Legislative Assembly Debates, Vol. 5, 26 November 1926.
Southern Rhodesia Legislative Assembly Second Report of the Select Committee on Resettlement of Natives, 16 August 1960.
Southern Rhodesia Parliamentary Debates, Second Session-Fourteenth Parliament, Vol. 99, 19 December 1978.
Southern Rhodesia Report of the Surveyor General 1939.
Southern Rhodesia Report on Defence for the Year 1926.
Southern Rhodesia Report on Defence for the Year 1927.
Southern Rhodesia Report on Defence for the Year 1928.
Southern Rhodesia Report on Defence for the Year 1929.
Southern Rhodesia Report on Department of Defence 1948.
Southern Rhodesia Report on the Department of Defence 1947.
Southern Rhodesia Report on the Department of Defence for the years 1945 and 1946.
Southern Rhodesia Sabi-Lundi Development Second Interim Report June 1948.
Southern Rhodesia: The Economic Outlook 1946–1951, Salisbury.
Southern Rhodesian Department of Statistics, Statistical Year Book of Southern Rhodesia 1947.
Survey of Federal developments from 1953–1958.
The Walrus, Vol. 1, No. 20, January 1, 1945, Salisbury.
The Zimbabwe People's Voice—Official Organ of the ZAPU, 25 June 1977.
Third Report of the Select Committee on Education, 16 April 1969.
War Effort, Vol. 1, No. 1, June 14, 1940, Salisbury.

War Effort, Vol. 1, No. 2, July 1, 1940, Salisbury.
War Effort, Vol. 1, No. 2, July 5, 1940, Salisbury.
Zambia Parliamentary Debates, Fourth Session, Third National Assembly, 8 February 1977.
Zimbabwe Chimurenga, Official Organ of ZANU Office in Scandinavia, Stockholm, Vol. 1, No. 1, 14 August 1974.
Zimbabwe Rhodesia Parliamentary Debates, Vol. 101, First Session-Fifteenth Parliament, 29 November 1979.

Zimbabwe Press Statements

208/89/CB/SK/SG
372/89/MS/CC/EMM
384/80/SFS
507/83/SK/JM
589/80/SFS
75/83/AC
784/80/SFS

Secondary Sources

Newspapers

Bantu Mirror, 15 April 1961.
Bantu Mirror, 18 March 1961.
Daily News, 15 August 2012.
Daily News, 30 November 2014.
Daily News, 2 December 2014.
Herald, 19 December 1978.
Herald, 23 November 2011.
Herald, 7 July 2011.
Mail and Guardian, 19 December 2014.
Rhodesia Herald, 8 March 1940.
Rhodesia Herald, 18 May 1974.
Rhodesia Herald, 15 June 1974.
Rhodesia Herald, 24 June 1974.
Rhodesia Herald, 1 October 1976.
Rhodesia Herald, 30 November 1977.
Rhodesia Herald, 6 July 1978.
Standard, 24 February 2013.
Sunday Mail, 31 March 1974.
Sunday Mail, 26 May 1974.
Sunday Mail, 2 June 1974.
Sunday Mail, 23 June 1974.
Sunday Mail, 26 May–1 June 2013.
Sunday Mail, 18–24 November 2012.
Sydney Morning Herald, 1 June 1977.
Umtali Post, 7 October 1977.
Umtali Post, 27 November 1977.
Zimbabwe Independent, 6 September 2013.

Books

Abbott, P., and P. Botham. *Modern African Wars (1): Rhodesia 1965–80*. Oxford: Osprey Publishing, 1986.

Amnesty International. *Libya: The Forgotten Victims of NATO Strikes*. London: Amnesty International Publications, 2012.

Anti-Apartheid Movement. *Fireforce Exposed: The Rhodesian Security Forces and Their Role in Defending White Supremacy*. London, 1979.

Archer, R. *Vietnam: The Habit of War*. London: Catholic Institute for International Relations, 1983.

Armitage, M.J., et al. *Air Power in the Nuclear Age 1945-82: Theory and Practice*. London: Macmillan, 1983.

Astrow, A. *Zimbabwe: A Revolution that Lost its Way?* London: Zed Press, 1983.

Beverley, W. *A Pride of Eagles: The Story of Rhodesia's Air Force*. Salisbury: Graham, 1976.

Bhebe, N., and T.O. Ranger, eds. *Soldiers in Zimbabwe's Liberation War*, vol. 1. Harare: University of Zimbabwe Publications, 1995.

Brendon, J.A. *Britain and her Neighbours: The Twentieth Century*. London: Black and Sun, 1923.

Buttinger, J. *Vietnam: A Political History*. London: Andre Deutsch, 1969.

Carruth, G. *The Encyclopedia of American Facts and Dates*, 8th ed. New York: Harper and Row, 1987.

Catholic Commission for Justice and Peace in Rhodesia. *The Man in the Middle: Torture, Resettlement and Eviction*. Harare: Strand Multiprint, 1999.

Catholic Commission for Justice and Peace in Rhodesia and the Catholic Institute for International Affairs. *The Man in the Middle: Torture, Resettlement and Eviction and Civil War in Rhodesia*. CCJP Zimbabwe, 1975.

Chung, F. *Re-living the Second Chimurenga: Memories from Zimbabwe's Liberation Struggle*. Harare: Weaver Press, 2007.

Cilliers, J.K. *Counter-insurgency in Rhodesia*. Sydney: Croom Helm, 1985.

_____. *Counter-Insurgency in Rhodesia*. Oxon: Routledge, 2015.

Citino, R.M. *The Path to Blitzkrieg: Doctrine and Training in the German Army, 1920-1939*. Boulder, CO: Lynne Rienner, 1999.

Clayton, A. *Frontiersmen: Warfare in Africa since 1950*. London: University College Press, 1998.

Cole, B. *The Elite: The Story of the Special Air Service*. Transkei: Three Knights Publishing, 1984.

Cowderoy, D., and R.C. Nesbit. *War in the Air: Rhodesian Air Force 1935-1980*. Alberton: Galago, 1987.

Douhet, G., translated By Dino Ferrari. *The Command of the Air*. New York: Coward-McCann, 1942.

Ellert, H. *The Rhodesian Front War: Counter-Insurgency and Guerrilla Warfare 1962-1980*. Gweru: Mambo Press, 1989.

Encyclopedia Rhodesia. Salisbury: College Press, 1933.

Flower, K. *Serving Secretly: An Intelligence Chief on Record Rhodesia into Zimbabwe, 1964 to 1981*. London: Murray, 1987.

Fuller, J.F.C. *The Conduct of War 1789-1961: A Study of the Impact of the French, Industrial and Russian Revolutions on War and its Conduct*. London: Eyre and Spottiswoode, 1961.

Gibbs-Smith, C.H. *The Invention of the Aeroplane 1799-1909*. London: Faber and Faber, 1996.

Godwin, P. *Mukiwa: A White Boy in Africa*. London: Picador, 1996.

Godwin, P., and I. Hancock. *"Rhodesians Never Die": The Impact of War and Political Change on White Rhodesia, 1979-1980*. Harare: Baobab, 1995.

Guevara, C. *Guerrilla Warfare*. New York: Monthly Review Press, 1961.

Hall, M.K. *Vietnam War*, 2nd ed. Harlow: Pearson Education, 2008.

Hoffman, B., J.M. Taw, and D. Arnold. *Lessons for Contemporary Counterinsurgencies: The Rhodesian Experience*. Santa Monica: RAD, 1991.

Kelly, F.C. *The Wright Brothers*. London: George G. Harrap, 1994.

Kriger, N. *Guerrilla Veterans in Post-war Zimbabwe: Symbolic and Violent Politics, 1980-1987*. Cambridge: Cambridge University Press, 2003.

Kulkarni, T., and A. Sinha. "India's Credible Minimum Deterrence: A Decade Later." Nuclear Security Programme, IPCS Issue Brief 179, New Delhi, 2011.

Laqueur, W. *Guerrilla: A Historical and Critical Study*. London: Weidenfeld and Nicolson, 1977.

Martin, D., and P. Johnson. *The Chitepo Assassination*. Harare: Zimbabwe Publishing House, 1985.

Mavriks, P., ed. *History of World War II*. Marshal Cavendish Corporation, 2005.

Miller, R.G. *Billy Mitchell—Stormy Petrel of the Air*. Washington, D.C.: Office of Air Force History, 2004.

Mohja, K. *Then and Now: The Syrian Revolution to Date: A Young Nonviolent Resistance and the Ensuing Armed Struggle*. A Special Report from Friends for a Nonviolent World. St. Paul, MN: Friends for a Nonviolent World: 2013.

Moorcraft, P.L. *A Short Thousand Years: The*

End of Rhodesia's Rebellion. Salisbury: Galaxie Press, 1979.
Moorcraft, P.L., and P. McLaughlin. *Chimurenga!: The War in Rhodesia 1965–1980.* Marshaltown: Sygma/Collins Books, 1982.
Moore-King, B. *White Man: Black War.* Harare: Baobab Books, 1988.
Morris, J.B., ed. *Encyclopedia of American History*, 6th ed. New York: Harper and Row, 1982.
Nacciarone, U., S.J. *Accidental African Blessings: A Memoir.* Bloomington, IN: Xlibris, 2012.
Nkomo, J. *The Story of My Life.* Harare: Sapes Books, 1984.
Owen, C. *The Rhodesian African Rifles.* London: Leo Cooper Ltd., 1970.
Peter-Bowyer, P.J.H. *Winds of Destruction: The Autobiography of a Rhodesian Combat Pilot.* Johannesburg: 30° South, 2005.
Preston, M. *Ending Civil War: Rhodesia and Lebanon in Perspective.* New York: Tauris Academic Studies, 2004.
Ranger, T. *Writing Revolt: An Engagement with African Nationalism.* Harare: Weaver Press, 2013.
Salt, B. *A Pride of Eagles: A History of the Rhodesian Air Force.* Solihull: Helion, 2012.
Sibanda, E.M. *The Zimbabwe African People's Union 1961–1987: A Political History of Insurgency in Southern Rhodesia.* Trenton, NJ: Africa World Press, 2005.
Sithole, V. *My Life with an Unsung Hero.* Bloomington, IN: AuthorHouse, 2006.
Smith, I.D. *The Great Betrayal: The Memoirs of Ian Douglas Smith.* London: Blake Publishing Ltd., 1997.
Spaight, J.M. *The Battle of Britain.* London: Geoffrey Bles, 1941.
Sprack, J. *Rhodesia: South Africa's Sixth Province, An Analysis of the Links Between South Africa.* London: International Defence and Aid Fund, 1974.
Stapleton, T.J. *No Insignificant Past: The Rhodesia Native Regiment and the East African Campaign of the First World War.* Waterloo, Canada: Wilfrid Laurier University Press, 2006.
Stiff, P. *See You in November.* Alberton, South Africa: Galago Publishing, 1985.
Tangye, N, *Britain in the Air.* London: William Collins, 1944.
Thompson, D. *England in the 20th Century 1914–1963.* Middlesex: Penguin Books, 1965.
Trealor, H. ed. *Fighting forces of Zimbabwe Rhodesia*, No. 6. Rhodesia: Amalgamated Publications.
Tse-tung, M. *On Guerrilla Warfare*, translated by Samuel B. Griffith III. Urbana: University of Illinois Press, 2000.

Vladimir, S. *The Hot "Cold War": The USSR in Southern Africa.* London: Pluto Press, 2008. (Review by Lt. Col. (Prof.) Deon Visser, Department of Military History, Faculty of Military Science, Stellenbosch University.)
Walker, P.B. *The Early Aviation at Farnborough: The History of the Royal Aircraft Establishment.* London: McDonald, 1971.
Walzer, M. *Just and Unjust Wars: A Moral Argument with Historical Illustrations.* New York: Basic Books, 1977.
Weiss, R., and J.L. Parpart. *Sir Garfield Todd and the Making of Zimbabwe.* London: British Academic Press, 1999.
Whiting, K.R. *Soviet Air Power.* London: Westview Press, 1986.
Yardley, M. *Backing into the Limelight: A Biography of T. E. Lawrence.* London: Harrap, 1985.

Chapters in Edited Books

Biddle, T. "Learning in Real Time: The Development and Implementation of Air Power in the First World War." In S. Cox P. and Gray, eds., *Air Power History: Turning Points from Kitty Hawk to Kosovo.* London: Frank Cass, 2002.
Brickhill, J. "Daring to storm the heavens: The military strategy of ZAPU 1976 to 1979." In N. Bhebe and T.O. Ranger, eds., *Soldiers in Zimbabwe's Liberation War*, vol. 1. Harare: University of Zimbabwe Publications, 1995.
_____. "Making peace with the past: War victims and the work of the Mafela Trust." In N. Bhebe and T.O. Ranger, eds., *Soldiers in Zimbabwe's Liberation War*, vol. 1. Harare: University of Zimbabwe Publications, 1995.
Cole, B.D., and P.H.B. Godwin. "Advanced military technology and the PLA: Priorities and capabilities for the 21st century." In L.M. Wortzel, ed., *The Chinese Armed Forces in the 21st Century.* Strategic Studies Institute, U.S. Army War College, 1999.
Dabengwa, D. "ZIPRA in the Zimbabwe War of National Liberation." In N. Bhebe and T.O. Ranger, eds., *Soldiers in Zimbabwe's Liberation War*, vol. 1. Harare: University of Zimbabwe Publications, 1995.
Ellert, H. "The Rhodesian security and intelligence community 1960 to 1980: A brief overview of the structure and operational role of military, civilian and police security and intelligence organisation which served in Rhodesia government during the Zimbabwean liberation war." In N. Bhebe and T.O. Ranger, eds., *Soldiers in Zimbabwe's Liberation*

War, vol. 1. Harare: University of Zimbabwe Publications, 1995.
Evans, M. "The Wretched of the Empire: Politics, Ideology and Counterinsurgency in Rhodesia, 1965–80." In *Small Wars and Insurgencies*. London: Routledge, 2007.
Jordan, D. "Air and Space Warfare." In *Understanding Modern Warfare*. Cambridge: Cambridge University Press, 2008.
Kiras, J. "Irregular Warfare." In D. Jordan, J. Kiras, D. Lonsdale, I. Speller, C. Tuck, and C.D. Walton, *Understanding Modern Warfare*. Cambridge: Cambridge University Press, 2008.
Lyall, G. "Marshal of the Royal Air Force: The Viscount Trenchard." In M. Carver, ed., *The War Lords*. London: Weidenfeld and Nicolson, 1976.
MacIsaacs, D. "Voices from the Central Blue: The Air Power Theorists." In P. Paret, ed., *Makers of Modern Strategy: From Machiavelli to the Nuclear Age*. New Jersey: Princeton University Press, 1986.
Mandiza, I. "Civil-military relations in Malawi: A historical perspective." In R. Williams, G. Cawthra, and D. Abrahams, eds., *Ourselves to Know: Civil-Military Relations and Defence Transformation in Southern Africa*. Pretoria: Institute for Security Studies, July 1999.
Monick, S. "The Rhodesian Air Force: A history from inception to the bush war." In S.J. McIntosh, *Armed Forces*. Booysens, 1982.
Moyo, D. "From Rhodesia to Zimbabwe: Change without Change? Broadcasting Policy Reform and Political Control." In H. Melber, ed., *Media, Public Discourse and Political Contestation in Zimbabwe*. Uppsala: Nordiska Afrikainstitutet, 2004.
Mtisi, J., M. Nyakudya, and T. Barnes. "War in Rhodesia, 1965–1980." In B. Raftopoulos and A. Mlambo, eds., *Becoming Zimbabwe: A History from the Pre-colonial Period to 2008*. Harare: Weaver Press, 2009.
Ndlovu-Gatsheni, S. "Mapping Cultural and Colonial Encounters, 1880s–1930s." In B. Raftopoulos and A. Mlambo, eds., *Becoming Zimbabwe: A History from the Pre-colonial Period to 2008*. Harare: Weaver Press, 2009.
Pretorius, F. "Napoleon Bonaparte." In T. Van Wijk and M.C. Van Zyl, eds., *Europe 1555–1848*. Pretoria: Academia, 1985.
Robson, E. "The Armed Forces and the Art of War." In *The New Cambridge Modern History: The Old Regime*, vol. VII. Cambridge: Cambridge University Press, 1957.
Wilkinson, A.R. "Political violence, counter-insurgency and change in Rhodesia." In C.R. Hill and Warwick, eds., *Collected Papers 1*. University of York: Centre for Southern African Studies, 1974.
Wortzel, L.M. "U.S.-Chinese Military Relations in the 21st Century." In L.M. Wortzel, ed., *The Chinese Armed Forces in the 21st Century*. U.S. Army War College: Strategic Studies Institute, 1999.

Journal Articles

Alexander, J., and J. McGregor. "War Stories: Guerrilla Narratives of Zimbabwe's Liberation War." *History Workshop Journal*, Issue 57 (2004).
Aras, B., and S. Akarçeşme. "Turkey and the Arab spring." *International Journal* 67, No. 1 (Winter 2011–2012), Special issue: Charting the new Turkish foreign policy.
Beadle, H. "Sir Ernest Lucas Guest: A Tribute." *Rhodesiana*, No. 30 (June 1974).
Boxx, E. "Observations on the Air War in Syria." *Air & Space Power Journal* (2013).
Bruton, J.K. "Counter Insurgency in Rhodesia." *Military Review* 59, No. 3 (1979).
Chimuka, T.A. "Ethics among the Shona." *Zambezia* 28, No. 1 (2001).
Coster, K.R. "The Training of Rhodesian officers at the Royal Military Academy." *Scientia Militaria: South African Journal of Military Studies* 9, No. 3 (1979).
Doyle, P., and M. Bennett. "Military Geography: The Influence of Terrain in the Outcome of the Gallipoli Campaign, 1915." *The Geographical Journal* 165, No. 1 (1999).
Hove, M. "War legacy: A reflection on the effects of the Rhodesian Security Forces (RSF) in south eastern Zimbabwe during Zimbabwe's war of liberation 1976–1980." *Journal of African Studies and Development* 4, No. 8 (2012).
Hove, M., and D. Mutanda. "The Syrian Conflict 2011 to the Present: Challenges and Prospects." *Journal of Asian and African Studies* (2014), published online on December 5, 2014.
Howman, R. "Orlando Baragwanath: A Centenarian pioneer of Rhodesia." *Rhodesiana* 28 (1973).
Klare, M., and D. Volman. "America, China & the Scramble for Africa's Oil." In R. Bush, and J. Keenan, eds., *North Africa: Power, Politics & Promise, Review of African Political Economy* 33, No. 108 (2006).
Laqueur, W. "The Origins of Guerrilla Doctrine." *Journal of Contemporary History* 10, No. 3 (1975).
March, W. "Air Power, Doctrine and the Anglo-

American Approach. Different Shades of Blue: Interwar Air Power Doctrine Development, Part 1." *The Canadian Air Force Journal* 2, No. 1, 2009.

Martinez, I. "The History of the Use of Bacteriological and Chemical Agents during Zimbabwe's Liberation War of 1965–80 by Rhodesian Forces." *Third World Quarterly* 23, No. 6 (2002).

McAdam, J. "The Flying Mapmakers: Some Notes on Early Development of Air Survey in Central and Southern Africa." *Rhodesiana*, No. 30 (June 1974).

———. "Pat Judson: First Rhodesian Born Airman." *Rhodesiana*, No. 16 (July 1967).

McLaughlin, P. "The Thin White Line: Rhodesia's Armed Forces since the Second World War." Essay Review, *Zambezia* 6, No. 2 (1978).

Meredith, C. "The Rhodesian Air Training Group 1940–45." *Rhodesiana*, No. 28 (1973).

Mlambo, A.S. "Civil Aviation in Colonial Zimbabwe." *Zambezia* 19, No. 2 (1992).

Mubako, S. "The Quest for Unity in the Zimbabwe Liberation Movement." *Issue: A Journal of Opinion* 5, No. 1 (1975).

Mutanda, D. "The Local Media and Zimbabwe's Land Reform Program." *Journal of Sustainable Development in Africa* 14, No. 3 (2012).

O'Keeffe, Lanigan S.M. "Southern Rhodesia's War Effort." *Journal of the Royal African Society* 39, No. 156 (1940).

Pope, A.U. "The Importance of Morale." *The Journal of Educational Sociology* 15, No. 4 (1941).

Sturges, P. "Information in the national liberation struggle: developing a model." *Journal of Documentation* 60, No. 4 (2004).

Ulio, J.A. "Military morale." *American Journal of Sociology* 47, No. 3 (1941).

Warhurst, P.R. "The History of Race Relations in Rhodesia." *Zambezia* 3, No. 1 (December 1973).

Unpublished Theses

Gilson, S.E. "A Study on Contrasts Similarities and Differences between Development of Airpower and Space Power." Air Command and Staff College, Air University, Alabama, 1998.

Huebert, K.D. "The Role of Air Power in Irregular Warfare for the 21st Century." Master's thesis, Naval Postgraduate School, Monterey, California, 2009.

Moyo, T. "Airborne Operations in the Mozambican Campaign 1982–1992: An analysis of the Zimbabwe Defence Forces Campaign Strategy." Master's dissertation, University of Zimbabwe, November 2007.

Musakuro, T. "The military role of FRELIMO in the liberation war of Zimbabwe from 1968 to 1980." Bachelor of arts honors dissertation, University of Zimbabwe, Harare, 2008.

Norton, J.M. "The French-Algerian war and FM 3-24, Counterinsurgency: A Comparison." Master of military art and science thesis, University of Maryland, 1992.

Powell, M.L. "Army Co-Operation Command and Tactical Air Power Development in Britain, 1940–1943: The Role of Army Co-operation Command in Army Air Support." Ph.D. dissertation, University of Birmingham, 2013.

Rupiya, M. "The Development of the Southern Rhodesia Armed Forces from the 1926 Defence Act to the Dissolution of the Federation in 1963." Ph.D. dissertation, University of Zimbabwe, Harare, 2000.

Policy Papers

Beck, G. "Offensive Air Power in Counter-Insurgency Operations: Putting Theory into Practice." Royal Australian Air Force, Air Power Development Centre, Working Paper 26, 2008.

Bräuner, O., M. Bromley, and M. Duchâtel. "Western arms exports to China." Solna: Stockholm International Peace Research Institute Policy Paper 43, 2015.

Flight International, Service Aviation: Air Force, Naval and Army Flying News, 4 June 1964.

Harmon, C.C. "Are we beasts?": Churchill and the moral question of World War II "Area Bombing." The Newport Papers, Newport Paper #1, Naval War College, Newport, 1991.

Mueller, K.P. "Air Power." Project Air Force, Rand Corporation.

Internet Sources

AFP. "Israeli strike on Syrian town kills 5 pro-regime forces: monitor." http://news.yahoo.com/israeli-strike-syrian-town-kills-five-pro-regime-100637132.html (Accessed July 2015).

Allvin, D.W. "Air power Strategy in the Interwar Years: Not Ready for Prime Time." www.dtic.mil/cgi-bin/GetTRDoc?AD=ADA441608 (Accessed April 2012).

Boxx, E., and J. White. "Responding to Assad's Use of Air power in Syria." The Washington Institute, 2012. http://www.washingtoninstitute.org/policy-analysis/view/

responding-to-assads-use-of-air-power-in-syria (Accessed December 2014).

Brodie, B. "The Heritage of Douhet". U.S. Air Force Project Rand Research Memorandum, 1952. www.rand.org/pubs/research_memoranda/2009/RM1013.pdf (Accessed March 2012).

Chordia, A.K. "Effect of Weather and Terrain on Airlift Operations." www.aerospaceindia.org/.../Winter%202011/Chapter%203.pdf. http://rhodesian.tripod.com/rrd.html (Accessed February 2013).

Conway-Lanz, S. "The Ethics of Bombing Civilians after World War II: The Persistence of Norms against Targeting Civilians in the Korean War." Online Encyclopedia of Mass Violence. http://www.massviolence.org/The-Ethics-of-Bombing-Civilians (Accessed August 2015).

Davis, A.D. "Back to the Basics: An Aviation Solution to Counterinsurgent Warfare." Air Wright Flyer Paper No. 23, Command and Staff College, Air University Press, Maxwell Air Force Base, Alabama, December 2005. http://research.maxwell.af.mil (Accessed June 2012).

Gelling, P., K. Kim, and T. McGrath. "A comprehensive 54-step guide to how the U.S. ruined Iraq." *Global Post*, 13 June 2014. http://www.globalpost.com/dispatch/news/regions/middle-east/iraq/140611/how-us-helped-turn-iraq-into-al-qaeda-haven-53-steps-isis-syria-bush-obama (Accessed October 2014).

Greenwald, G. "After Feigning Love for Egyptian Democracy, U.S. Back to Openly Supporting Tyranny." 10 February 2014. https://firstlook.org/theintercept/2014/10/02/feigned-american-support-egyptian-democracy-lasted-roughly-six-weeks/ (Accessed December 2014).

Guerilbow. "Air Power—Douhet's Theory and Afghanistan," 2010. http://guerrillawartactics.blogspot.com/2010/08/air-power-douhets-theory-and.html (Accessed June 2012).

Hall, R. "The refugee from Homs who can hardly afford to feed his family." 16 March 2015, *Global Post*, http://www.globalpost.com/dispatch/news/regions/middle-east/syria/150316/four-ears-four-lives-the-refugee-homs-struggling-fee (Accessed May 2015).

Hoffman, P.D. "Seeking Shadows in the Sky: The Strategy of Air Guerrilla Warfare." Air University, Maxwell Air Force Base, Alabama, June 2000, www.au.af.mil/au/awc/awcgate/saas/hoffman (Accessed June 2012).

Holman, B. "The bomber will always get through." http://airminded.org/2007/11/10/the-bomber-will-always-get-through/ (Accessed December 2014).

http://familysurvivalprotocol.com/tag/puerto-rico/page/11/ (Accessed October 2013).

http://info.uwe.ac.uk/news/UWENews/news.aspx?id=917 (Accessed September 2015).

http://nehandaradio.com/2015/10/12/when-we-revise-everything/ (Accessed November 2015).

http://news.google.com/newspapers?nid=1301&dat=19770601&id=oqApAAAAIBAJ&sjid=fOYDAAAAIBAJ&pg=1052,28491 (Accessed October 2013).

http://www.au.af.mil/au/awc/awcgate/au/faber.htm (Accessed December 2011).

http://www.bbc.co.uk/history/historic_figures/lawrence_te.shtml (Accessed June 2015).

http://www.compassionatejustice.com/projects/zimbabwe.html (Accessed November 2015).

http://www.herald.co.zw/vp-mujuru-stole-my-picture-war-veteran/ (Accessed November 2015).

http://www.history.com/this-day-in-history/tiananmen-square-massacre-takes-place.

http://www.historynet.com/william-billy-mitchell-an-air-power-visionary.htm (Accessed September 2015).

http://www.ipmsstockholm.org/magazine/2006/09/stuff_eng_photo_rhodesian_af.htm (Accessed November 2012).

http://www.radfanhunters.co.uk/mec.htm (Accessed November 2012).

http://www.raf.mod.uk/role/air_power.cfm (Accessed April 2012).

http://www.rhodesianforces.org/Aircraft Incidents.htm (Accessed April 2012).

http://www.rhodesianforces.org/AntiTerrorist Ops.htm (Accessed December 2012).

http://www.rhodesianforces.org/No2Squadron.htm (Accessed August 2012).

http://www.rhodesianforces.org/No3Squadron.htm (Accessed November 2012).

http://www.rhodesianforces.org/No4Squadron.htm (Accessed August 2012).

http://www.rhodesianforces.org/No6Sqn.htm (Accessed August 2012).

http://www.rhodesianforces.org/Operation Uric.htm (Accessed February 2013).

http://www.rhodesianforces.org/Rhodesian Air ForceHistory.htm (Accessed November 2012).

http://www.scramble.nl/zw.htm (Accessed November 2012).

http://www.thosemagnificentmen.co.uk/rheims/ (Accessed July 2015).

http://www.viscountdown.com/ (Accessed December 2012).

http://www.war-memorial.net/Maji-Maji-revolt-3.12 (Accessed November 2015).

http://www.wilsoncenter.org/publication/robert-mugabe-and-todor-zhivkov (Accessed November 2013).

http://www.zapu.org/index.php/2012-10-30-08-02-05/news-and-info/latest-zapu-news/item/74-mkushi-camp-survivors-tour-ZPRA-camp (Accessed December 2012).

http://www.zbc.co.zw/index.php?option=com_content&view=article&id=624:zim-celebrates-44th-anniversary-of-chinhoyi-battle&catid=41:top-stories&Itemid=86 (Accessed December 2011).

http://www.zbc.co.zw/news-categories/top-stories/4459-survivors-recall-chimoio-massacre.html (Accessed April 2012).

https://securityintelligence.com/funding-terrorists-the-rise-of-isis/ (Accessed August 2015).

Hungwe, B. "Zimbabwe's Emmerson Mnangagwa—Mugabe's heir apparent." BBC News, 11 December 2014. http://www.bbc.com/news/world-africa-30421768 (Accessed September 2015).

Institute for Security Studies. "External operations." www.iss.co.za/pubs/Books/rhodesia/s101-120.pdf (Accessed December 2012).

The Joint Air Power Competence Centre. "Air Power in Countering Irregular Warfare," June 2008. www.japcc.de (Accessed June 2012).

Jones, J.R. "William 'Billy' Mitchell's Air power." Air power Research Institute, Maxwell Air Force Base, Alabama, 1997, http://www.au.af.mil/au/awc/awcgate/mitchell/front.pdf (Accessed December 2014).

King's College London and R. Spencer. "What does Turkey's involvement in air strikes mean for Kurds, Isil, Syria and Nato?" *The Telegraph*, 29 July 2015. http://www.telegraph.co.uk/news/worldnews/europe/turkey/11769463/What-does-Turkeys-involvement-in-air-strikes-mean-for-Kurds-Isil-Syria-and-Nato.html (Accessed July 2015).

Kingsley, P., and M. Chulov. "Mohamed Morsi ousted in Egypt's second revolution in two years," *The Guardian*, 4 July 2013. http://www.theguardian.com/world/2013/jul/03/mohamed-morsi-egypt-second-revolution (Accessed December 2014).

Lederman, J. "War with ISIS: U.S. investigating chemical weapons attacks against Kurds in Iraq." *The Independent*, 14 August 2015. http://www.independent.co.uk/news/world/middle-east/war-with-isis-us-investigating-chemical-weapons-attacks-against-kurds-in-iraq-10456619.html (Accessed August 2015).

McDonald-Gibson, C. "War with ISIS: U.S. hails 'significant impact' of bombing raids but Syria's President Assad is not so sure." *The Independent*, 3 December 2014. http://www.independent.co.uk/news/world/middle-east/war-with-isis-us-hails-significant-impact-of-bombing-raids-but-syrias-president-assad-is-not-so-sure-9901605.html (Accessed December 2014).

McGrath, T. "Drone footage reveals what little now remains of Gaza," 2008. http://timeli.info/item/2462834/Salon_Politics/Drone_footage_reveals_what_little_remains_of_Gaza_right_now_Salon_com (Accessed September 2014).

MercyCorps. "Quick facts: What you need to know about the Syria crisis," 15 May 2015. http://www.mercycorps.org/articles/turkey-iraq-jordan-lebanon-syria/quick-facts-what-you-need-know-about-syria-crisis (Accessed May 2015).

Miller, J. "Strategic Significance of Drone Operations for Warfare," 19 August 2013. http://www.e-ir.info/2013/08/19/strategic-significance-of-drone-operations-for-warfare/ (Accessed July 2015).

Mulvenon, "Chinese and Mutually Assured Destruction: Is China Getting Mad?" se2.isn.ch/serviceengine/Files/ESDP/94831/ichaptersection_singledocument/F105BC88-8A1F-45E8-B... (Accessed March 2012).

NATO: International Security Assistance Force, Facts and Figures, 15 May 2012. www.nato.int/isaf/docu/epub/pdf/placemat.pdf (Accessed June 2012).

Pamuk, H., and N. Tattersall. "Turkey launches heaviest air strikes yet on PKK, stoking Kurdish ire," Reuters, 29 July 2015. http://www.reuters.com/article/2015/07/29/us-mideast-crisis-turkey-idUSKCN0Q30OF20150729 (Accessed July 2015).

Pettis, S. "The Role of Air power in the Rhodesian Bush War, 1965–1980." http://www.airpower.maxwell.af.mil/airchronicles/cc/pettis.html (Accessed May 2012).

Pfeiffer, A. "Air power in Vietnam: A Strategic Bombing Analysis." http://www.abigailpfeiffer.com/2011/09 (Accessed June 2011).

Press TV. "Morsi's trial over espionage charges postponed to March 26," 25 March 2015. http://www.presstv.ir/Detail/2015/03/25/403368/Morsis-Qatar-espionage-trial-adjourned (Accessed April 2015).

Rasmussen, N.F. "For years, military has tested the waters on the bay," 2005. http://articles.baltimoresun.com/2005-03-12/features/0503120090_1_billy-mitchell-battleship-chesapeake-bay (Accessed December 2014).

Renz, B. "Airpower in the 21st Century," 2014. http://nottspolitics.org/2014/03/24/airpower-in-the-21st-century/ (Accessed September 2015).

Salisbury, P. "Yemen has turned from a local conflict into a regional Cold War," Global Post, 26 March 2015. http://www.globalpost.com/article/6502603/2015/03/26/yemen-has-turned-local-conflict-regional-cold-war (Accessed March 2015).

Schwartz, N.A. "Air power in Counterinsurgency and Stability Operations." *Prism* 2, No. 2, NDU Press, http://www.ndu.edu/press/air power-in-counterinsurgency-stability-operations (Accessed April 2012).

Serle, J. "Drone Warfare in Pakistan, Yemen and Somalia. Surge in CIA Strikes." Global Research, 8 May 2015. http://www.globalresearch.ca/drone-warfare-in-pakistan-yemen-and-somalia-surge-in-cia-strikes/5448065 (Accessed July 2015).

Shunk, D. "Primer on Russian Afghan War, 1979–1989, Lessons learned," 2008. http://dnipogo.org/wp-content/uploads/2009/01/primer_on_afghan_war.pdf (Accessed December 2014.)

Thomson, M. "Did UK warn Mugabe and Nkomo about assassination attempts?" 1 August 2011. http://www.bbc.co.uk/news/world-africa-14311834 (Accessed January 2013). www.air-britain.com/zambia.pdf (Accessed August 2015).

Index

aerial photography 40, 51, 76, 81, 88–9, 99, 103, 116, 165
Air Force of Zimbabwe 21, 80, 118, 188
air search 1, 76, 89, 97, 184, 191
Aviation Act of (1929) 50, 146

biological and chemical weapons 29

Caldicott, John Moore (Minister of Defence, Minister of Economic Affairs) 81, 82, 85, 129
casualty evacuation/casevac 1, 7, 41, 88, 95–8, 184, 191
Chikumbi (Freedom Camp), bombing of 103, 104, 106, 110
Chimoio/Operation Dingo, bombing of 5, 99, 100–1, 103, 104, 106, 109, 110, 115, 119, 144, 149
China, role in liberation war 23, 25, 147, 153, 177
Chinhoyi/Sinoia 20, 21, 168
Chitepo, Herbert 22, 23–4, 26, 27, 28, 101, 148, 177
civil aviation, effects on development of military aviation 6, 47, 50–5, 69, 76, 84, 122, 129, 130, 146, 155, 189
civilian bombing 6, 8, 31, 35, 40–5, 43, 102, 113–15, 153, 158, 165–169, 175, 176, 181–3, 190
Combined operations/Joint Operations Command (JOC) 6, 26, 106, 108, 111, 127, 128, 130, 131, 141, 191
Cordon sanitaire 133, 134

Dabengwa, Dumiso 20, 144, 145, 154
Defence Act(s) 48–9, 64, 69, 82, 91, 132, 146

Empire Air Training Scheme (EATS) 47, 53, 54, 58, 59, 61, 62, 65, 66, 67, 73, 105

Federation of Rhodesia and Nyasaland 7, 17–9, 71–2, 77–87, 91, 93–4, 96, 122, 129, 130, 139, 146, 150–1, 187
Fireforce 1, 25, 89, 102, 104, 106–9, 122, 127–8, 142, 188
Flower, Ken 28, 128, 138, 147, 151
Fort Victoria fuel storage tanks, burning of 130
frontline states 7, 23, 24, 25, 28, 32, 96, 99, 104, 120, 123, 125–7, 142, 188, 189

guerrilla challenges 1, 96, 101, 102, 104–6, 108, 109, 111, 149, 158, 169
guerrilla counterstrategies 112–121
guerrilla infiltration 1, 21, 26, 29, 95, 96, 104, 109–10, 126, 131, 151–2
guerrilla strategy 1, 5, 7–8, 24, 29–30, 104, 105–6, 115, 122, 124, 158, 170–77, 179, 182, 191
Guest, Honourable Sir Ernest (Rhodesia's first Minister of Air) 57, 64, 79, 154

Harris, "Bomber" Arthur 6, 44, 54, 84
Hawkins, Roger (Air Vice-Marshal, Minister of Defence, Minister of Combined Operations) 106, 129, 131, 133, 141
hot pursuit 1, 25, 98–9, 110, 188; *see also* RhAF cross-border operations
Huggins, Godfrey (Rhodesia Prime Minister [1933–1953] and first Prime Minister of the Federation of Rhodesia and Nyasaland [1953–1956]) 54, 59, 64, 73, 87, 154, 162

Islamic State of Iraq and Levant (ISIL)/Islamic State 171, 181, 182, 183, 185, 191

Lardner-Burke, William D. 20, 117, 119, 123, 125, 126, 133, 140
Liberation Committee: OAU 24, 125
Luso training center 100, 149, 151, 153

Index

Mapai (FRELIMO base) 102, 104, 136
McLaren, Michael John (Air Marshal, Commander Air Force [1973–1977], Deputy Commander of Combined Operations until 1980) 107, 126, 128, 129, 130
Meredith, Charles (Minister of Air, Air Officer Commanding the RATG) 54, 58, 59, 60, 62, 63, 66, 68, 72, 73, 79, 154
Mkushi Training Camp attack 103, 104, 106, 109, 110
Mudzingadzi Camp 102, 104, 106, 115, 118
Mugabe, Robert 20, 21, 22, 23, 24, 28, 29, 146, 149, 152, 164, 188
Mulungushi training center 100, 104, 110, 153, 173
Muzenda, Simon V. 22, 24
Muzorewa, Abel 29, 133

National War Fund 61
Nhari rebellion 25, 26, 27, 148
Nkomo, Joshua 102, 103, 124, 144, 145, 146, 147, 148, 149, 150, 152, 154, 167
Nyadzonia raid 98, 99, 101, 110, 113, 118, 149

protected villages/keeps 133, 160–2, 174

reconnaissance 1, 7, 31, 36, 39–40, 41, 58, 76, 81, 83, 88–9, 94, 97–8, 103, 112–13, 116, 121 137, 178, 184, 187, 189, 191
RhAF cross-border operations 98–9, 102–4, 106, 110, 143; see also hot pursuit
Rhodesia Air Askari Corps (RAAC) 64–6, 68, 154
Rhodesia Air Training group (RATG) 7, 47, 50, 51, 53, 55, 56, 57, 58, 59, 60, 61, 62. 63, 65–9, 71, 72, 73, 74, 75, 92, 93, 96, 186
Royal Rhodesian Air Force (RRAF) 21, 60, 78–85, 87–9, 92–4, 98, 130, 137, 139, 150, 187

Salisbury fuel storage tanks: burning of 155
Sikombela declaration 23
Sithole, Ndabaningi 22, 24, 29, 148, 156
Smith, Ian 29, 100, 137, 151, 177, 186

South Africa/Pretoria: assistance to Rhodesia and Imperial defence 50, 59, 60, 67, 79, 102, 105, 106, 125, 128, 132, 133, 136, 142, 144, 153–7, 177
Southern Rhodesia Auxiliary Air Force (SRAAF) 76
Southern Rhodesia Tobacco Industry Aeroplane and Munitions Fund 61
Southern Rhodesia Women's Auxiliary Service 72
Southern Rhodesia Women's Military and Air Service 76
Southern Rhodesian Air Force (SRAF) 41, 54, 58–9, 64, 71–3, 76–9, 82, 86–8, 91, 135
Southern Rhodesian Defence Forces (SRDF) 48, 53
Soviet Union: role in liberation war 24, 25, 103, 145, 147, 153, 154, 176, 177

tactical deployment 96, 184, 191
tactical mobility 1, 96–7, 177; see also troop transportation
terror missions: by the RhAF 97, 102
Tongogara, Josiah 23, 24, 26, 27, 28
Total National Strategy Document/1 (TNSD/1) 154
troop transportation 7, 39, 62, 86, 89, 95–7, 110, 189, 191; see also tactical mobility

Unilateral Declaration of Independence (UDI) 17, 19, 137

Viscount: downing of 102–3, 110, 144, 149, 153

Walls, Peter 26, 103, 108, 123, 124, 125, 131, 138, 155, 189, 191
Wilson, Archibald O.G. (air marshal) 108, 126, 130, 132, 133, 141, 155

"X" factor 139

Zero Hour Plan 143–57
Zimbabwe People's Army (ZIPA) 23, 25, 28, 149

www.ingramcontent.com/pod-product-compliance
Lightning Source LLC
Chambersburg PA
CBHW032050300426
44116CB00007B/671